Eyes of Faith

Eyes of Faith

A STUDY IN THE BIBLICAL POINT OF VIEW

Paul Sevier Minear

Norris Professor of New Testament Interpretation
Andover Newton Theological School

PHILADELPHIA
THE WESTMINSTER PRESS

The American Standard Edition of the Revised Bible quoted in this publication is copyright, 1929, by The International Council of Religious Education and is used by permission.

To Gladys

ACKNOWLEDGMENTS

I AM grateful for permissions to quote from the various books cited in the text, and to make frequent use of the American Standard Edition of the Revised Bible (copyright, 1929, by The International Council of Religious Education). Citations from the latter have been made with some liberty, particularly in the adoption of various equivalents for the term Jehovah. In chapters 4, 5, and 6, I have drawn upon essays previously published in *Religion in Life, The Journal of Religious Thought,* and *The Journal of Religion,* respectively. To the editors of these periodicals I express thanks.

Many people have contributed to the continuing discussion of which this book is one tangible result. Though it is not possible to name them here, I wish to speak of particular obligation to three: J. Leslie Dunstan, General Secretary of the Hawaiian Board of Missions; Richard Kroner, of Union Theological Seminary; Nels F. S. Ferré, of Andover Newton Theological School. None of these is aware of the extent to which he has aided me in apprehending the deeper relevance of Biblical tradition, an apprehension which I have been quite unable to transfer to the written page. Above all, I am grateful to my wife for her critical discernment and constant encouragement.

PAUL S. MINEAR.

Newton Center, Massachusetts,
Feb. 17, 1946.

EYES OF FAITH
A Study in the Biblical Point of View

INTRODUCTION

This Life's dim windows of the Soul
Distorts the Heavens from Pole to Pole
And leads you to Believe a Lie
When you see with, not thro' the Eye.
— William Blake, *Complete Poetry*, p. 614. Random House, 1941.

THIS is a book about perspectives, those " dim windows " through which man receives and gives the primal impressions of life. In a painting, perspective may be dissociated — at least for the sake of analysis — from the objects depicted. One does not need to be an artist to distinguish some of the elements which combine to shape this perspective. It includes background and foreground, and their intricate and intimate interaction which conveys the actualities of depth and dimension. It involves the interplay of light and shadow, contrasts in colors which communicate the selectivity of vision. It incorporates a single configuration of line and pattern, which one eye discerns among the many patterns which each setting affords. And these are unified by a single center: the point at which the artist stands. Unless the onlooker stands at that center he does not see the painting as the artist sees it. If there is to be communication, the onlooker need not share the painter's views but he must share the painter's *point of viewing*. He need not agree with his *standpoint,* but he must *stand* at the same *point.*

This analogy is of course too simple to cover adequately the complexities of man's history and his relation to the Eternal. It omits what Gerard Manley Hopkins called " inscape," and envisages man as an onlooker only. Yet it may suggest the object of this book, that of coming to terms with the Biblical perspective. We assume that there is a recoverable unity in the outer and inner dimensions of Biblical experience. This assumption will be challenged by some as untenable, but that issue can be resolved only by testing the results to see if they do represent a *uni*verse of vision. We assume also that this unity can be grasped only by outlining the perspective in its wholeness. This necessitates a concentration upon the frame of reference, rather than upon the details which find their significance within that frame. Our desire is not to

I

construct a Biblical theology, but to provide a preface for such theology by charting its context of presuppositions, those axiomatic attitudes and convictions that lie so deep that they are taken for granted. Our desire is not to make converts to one or another school of modern thought, but to remove some of the obstacles that frustrate men in many schools from understanding the witness of prophet and apostle.

These purposes are far too extensive and difficult to be fulfilled by any book or by any author. They are so ambitious as to be extremely embarrassing. Yet perhaps the audacity of aim is mitigated by a frank confession that the study is not so much for the reader's edification as for the writer's. Propelled by the push of tangled circumstances and the pull of intangible attraction into the study and teaching of the New Testament, I have been increasingly impressed by what could be briefly stated as: (1) the strangeness of the Biblical perspective; (2) the unity of this perspective throughout the Biblical period; (3) the futility of trying to understand any segment of thought detached from its hidden context; (4) the germinal power and universal relevance that emerges whenever that context is uncovered and appropriated; (5) the unsuspected value of the more objectionable patterns of thought in locating distinctive dimensions.

I may say that each of these convictions has been forced upon me against my own inclination; when I started the study of the New Testament I had almost the opposite expectations. Over and over again, I have been chagrined to have my convictions reversed. When I have been most certain that I understood Isaiah or Jesus, because a particular teaching seemed to agree with my fund of opinions, I have in fact been farthest from understanding them. Over and over again, confidence that a particular strand in Biblical thought was outmoded has been negated. Gradually I have been taught that any interpretation of an apostle is unsound unless it springs from a personal (and necessarily subjective) comprehension of the apostle's point of standing within his own history. And finally the suspicion dawned that perhaps the strange history within which the apostle stood *is* the true history within which I too stand. This suspicion has prompted so many intimations of the true dimensions of my own existence that I am impelled for my own sake to try to think through the various ramifications of the Biblical perspective.

This task is an impossible one, and will remain so. The basic Biblical affirmations defy explanation. The prophet expounds them by taking them for granted. He insists that " the fear of the Lord is the beginning of wisdom," that only he who hears and obeys the Word of the Lord will understand it. The Bible calls for witnesses, not for teachers. It is written from faith to faith; not from objective knowledge to faith, or from faith to objective knowledge. It demands subjective appropriation, not dispassionate evaluation. It assumes from its interpreters not a hectic shuttling back and forth between two alien worlds, but a sharp " Here I stand." The Bible does not present a system of theology; a *systematic* preface is therefore *not* a preface to *it*. The task is thus made impossible by the very character of the Biblical point of view.

Add to this the fact that the tools available to the modern scholar are not adapted to the task. There is a fundamental disparity between the forms of communication expected in our academic world and those used in the Bible, an irreducible opposition between a scholarly thesis and an apostle's witness. To transmit ideas in orderly fashion seems today to require prosaic statements, adapted to the requirements of a classroom lecture or public debate. No writer in the Bible tries to do what is here attempted: the objective analysis and communication of the frame of reference. Neither Jesus nor Paul assumed that, prior to the call to repentance, they must define for scholars the precise nature of the Kingdom of God. For them a parable served to define man's existence in relation to God. As for us, we first try to reduce the meaning of a parable to a nonparabolic proposition. This focuses our attention upon our relation to the interpreter and his interpretation of the parable rather than upon our relation to God as illuminated by the parable. Such a book as this confuses the question of the prophet's authority by raising the question of the modern writer's historical methods and his conclusions.

Objective study also confuses the situation by transposing problems of life into problems of thought, by abstracting conceptual ideas from their origin in personal living. Biblical writers wrestled with the immediate issues which were crucial for their own suffering and destiny; they were not philosophers bandying about their own pet notions for the sake of students. Our task does not lie in the direction of imitating the fund of concepts that they held; rather, it lies in the direction of so seeing ourselves in relation to their God that a kind of inner life may ensue that will be productive of their perspective. The sharing of perspectives calls for sympathetic imagination rather than synthetic cogitation.

There is inevitable irony, therefore, in seeking to fulfill by an academic treatise the purpose as stated. To succeed in defining the indefinable is to prove oneself guilty of *lèse-majesté* or of consummate befuddlement — or of both. The author of such an attempt would be wise to pray for failure rather than success; and this is no idle double talk. Although the problem be thus insoluble, it cannot be ignored. Well aware of the difficulties, we shall seek to describe the angle of vision at the " innermost center " of Biblical experience, to re-create the view seen from that point of standing, to depict the horizons of history within which men of the Bible found their duty and destiny.

If the author of such a study faces peculiar difficulties, the reader also finds stubborn obstacles between himself and the goal. Fully to apprehend the immediate, personal outlook of Ezekiel or Peter is no easy task. There is the initial difficulty which we all sense in seeking to share the inner perspective of our next-door neighbor, to look through his eyes at his past and his future. There is the further difficulty that in reading the Bible we are dealing with men whom we cannot meet over the back-yard fence. They are not in a position to answer our probing questions, to communicate by subtle nuances of tone, emphasis, and gesture their basic attitudes toward life. Twenty centuries, after all, do constitute a considerable chasm to be bridged. Since then, as John Mason Brown so aptly remarks, " a good many bridges have gone under the water." We can listen to very few people, so remote in time, without a baffling sense of separation.

Comprehension is also inhibited by lack of close cultural affinities. Not many Oriental books are intelligible to Occidentals. Spiritual distance is increased by a thousand factors: race, language, political institutions, economic techniques, social stratification, ideological tradition. Considering all these factors, one is not surprised at a lack of rapport with Abraham.

But there are obstacles to a meeting of minds that are greater even than these. A perfect translation into current idiom would contribute to intelligent reading, but it would by no means make the reader feel at home in the world of Jeremiah. Thorough study of social customs in Bible lands would clarify the imagery of many passages, but it would not convey the more subtle nuances of meaning. When one has dispelled all the external and accidental factors that mark the foreignness of the Biblical world, he becomes more impressed than ever with the internal and intrinsic otherness of the patterns of imagination. Here is a history that is different from all other histories.[1] Here are men who remain to our time strangers and enigmas.[2] Here are forms and moods of apprehension which always look " untenable, and even a little ridiculous, . . . placed within the framework of European prose." [3] With progress in understanding the Bible comes an increasing recognition of the fact that there is

" a profound discontinuity between the Bible and any other book not dependent upon it, between the mind of the Bible and any ' natural ' mind, between the soul of the Hebrews and the soul of the others." [4]

It is this inner and intrinsic otherness of the prophetic point of view which arouses the greatest listener-resistance. To leap this hurdle, the reader must become aware of this resistance in himself. Its core is at times located in the unconscious worship of modernity, and in the corresponding assumption that any ancient point of view is invalidated by defects of the primitive mind, whether these defects be attributed to credulity, superstition, fear, subservience to priestly authority, or childish views of nature and history. It is tragically easy (and it simplifies the problem) to assume that the world of Biblical thought is of interest only to antiquarians, with their peculiar " squirrel instinct."

Or the core of resistance to a personal rapport with the prophets may lie in the nest of emotional and intellectual antipathies where minds snuggle down in comfort. We react negatively, if not violently, to all talk about foreknowledge and election, to claims of absolute divine sovereignty, to thoughts of pre-existence and postexistence, to the stories of miracles and wonders, to ideas of a wrathful Deity who punishes men in dire calamities, to predictions concerning history's end, to the grandiose dreams of special destiny on the part of impotent Jewish tribes. And wherever in the Bible we meet such attitudes (which is on almost every page), a barrier is immediately raised between our mind and the

[1] Cf. K. Barth, *The Word of God and the Word of Man*, trans. by D. Horton, Ch. 2. 1936.
[2] Cf. A. Schweitzer, *The Quest of the Historical Jesus*, trans. by W. Montgomery, p. 397. 1926.
[3] A. Guillaume, *Prophecy and Divination*, p. 227. Harper & Brothers, 1939.
[4] J. Haroutunian, in *Religion in Life*, Vol. XII, p. 382. 1943.

author's. What we think we understand, we don't like; it is only natural that we don't waste energy in seeking to understand more.

Situated even deeper than these citadels of resistance are those centers of rebellion which were active in the Biblical period itself, whenever the word of God was proclaimed by men claiming to be his messengers. Inherent in that word was scathing condemnation of sin, assertion of final authority, and demand for total obedience. In the presence of such a word men become uneasy. They sense an emptiness in present preoccupations, an insecurity about present hopes, an uncertainty about present wisdom, a vulnerability of soul. Little wonder that men do not like to meet the eyes of Isaiah or Hosea, not to mention Jesus or Paul!

We set out upon this book, then, as a joint venture of author and reader. Let us be quite aware of the peculiar obstacles which each must surmount; or at least let us know *why* we cannot surmount them. If we begin with a mutual confession of ignorance and inadequacy, well and good, for honesty and self-awareness are necessary for any advance. If we begin with a mutual eagerness to hear what the Biblical writers say, and to look through their eyes so far as that is possible, so much the better. If we can together stretch to the utmost our powers of imagination and empathy, better still. And if, perchance, our conversation should eventuate in improved ability to hear God speak to us through the Bible itself, the effort spent in writing and reading will not be wasted.

One further word about the method of approach to the problem and the plan of procedure. It is exceedingly difficult to reconstruct in speculative terms situations in which men of the Bible participated in personal terms. It would be quite misleading to codify their thought under logical captions provided by a modern theological system. Yet an orderly procedure is necessary. We have chosen to move from the perspective center to the circumference, following various radii of thought and mood. *In the first part,* we deal with the single angle of vision. Within the turbulence of their days, these men detected the activity of God directed toward themselves, and this activity precipitated a situation which they described in such terms as visitation, vocation, decision, rebellion, salvation. We shall inquire what such terms signified to them.

In the second part, we describe the character of the event in the foreground on which they focused their vision. God addresses them in an event which discloses his purpose, and this event becomes the occasion for faith and unbelief. Seen through the eyes of faith, it refracts the light of God's demand and promise; to eyes of unbelief it bears a contrary meaning. The revelatory event thus becomes the focal point of ever recurrent controversies between Biblical and non-Biblical perspectives.

Because the God who speaks in the immediate situation is the God who is Lord of all history, man finds his range of vision widened to span far horizons. From that angle of vision which has been determined by the event in the foreground, man is enabled to see both the beginning and the end of a dynamic divine purpose. *The third part* of the book deals with these horizons of history. These boundaries of the field of vision are themselves defined by the inauguration of covenants, through which God holds out distinctive promises to his chosen people. These promises, however, seem evermore to be denied by the course of history. Fidelity to the promise plunges man into the storm center of conflict between God and the world, between faith and despair. Consideration of horizons must therefore culminate in consideration of these contradictions, and the suffering that they occasion. The conflict seems to invalidate the horizons, and with them the perspective as a whole.

In the first century of our era, men of faith experienced this conflict and suffering at their maximum potency, in the coming and rejection of Jesus. But at that very point, according to the disciples, God triumphed over all his enemies by manifesting in Jesus as Messiah the fulfillment of his promise and the gift of his salvation. This event (in the foreground) revolutionized the perspective of the faithful, creating a new point of standing and new horizons. Their vision was subjected to drastic revision. *The concluding section* calls attention to the character and implications of this revision.

TO BE KNOWN by God in time makes life so acutely strenuous. Wherever He is, there every half hour is of tremendous importance. But to live in that manner is not endurable for sixty years; it is scarcely possible to endure even for three years the severe study required for the professional examinations which is however not nearly so strenuous as such a half hour.

— S. Kierkegaard, *Concluding Unscientific Postscript,* trans. by D. F. Swenson, p. 402. Princeton University Press, 1941.

1

GOD $VISITS$ MAN

I HAVE surely visited you " (Ex. 3:16). God visits man! God speaks and man responds. God acts and man becomes aware of the true ground of his existence. Because he confronts God-in-relation-to-himself, he sees himself as man-in-relation-to-God. Radii stemming from this center penetrate every cranny of created life. From this point of reference all Biblical testimony proceeds; within the circumference established by this center all testimony derives its significance. This is the event that produces a new angle of vision on the part of man, and new eyes. This is the moment of present experience where past and future fuse into a single dynamic whole.

Each visit is a point where two persons meet. It is that meeting of two persons that creates the strange perspective in the Bible, that makes those who share it strangers and sojourners. For the Biblical man finds in these visits an ultimate frame of reference for all his thinking, feeling, and willing. If one deletes from the Bible all references to God's visits and their implications, nothing is left. If he tears these threads from the tapestry of thought, the fabric unravels into meaningless bits of multicolored snippets. There remains no Biblical faith; there remains no Bible.[1]

> " O Lord, thou hast searched me, and known me. . . .
> Thou searchest out my path and my lying down,
> And art acquainted with all my ways. . . .
> Thou hast beset me behind and before,
> And laid thy hand upon me.
> Such knowledge is too wonderful for me;
> It is high, I cannot attain unto it.
> Whither shall I go from thy Spirit?
> Or whither shall I flee from thy presence? . . .

[1] Cf. E. Brunner, *The Divine-Human Encounter*, trans. by A. W. Loos, pp. 66 f. 1943.

If I say, Surely the darkness shall cover me,
And the light about me shall be night;
Even the darkness hideth not from thee,
But the night shineth as the day. . . .
Thine eyes did see mine unformed substance;
And in thy book they were all written,
Even the days that were ordained for me,
When as yet there was none of them. . . .
Search me, O God, and know my heart:
Try me, and know my thoughts;
And see if there be any wicked way in me,
And lead me in the way everlasting "
(Ps. 139).

In this psalm is expressed a point of view sharply in contrast to the usual attitudes that we adopt in the rough-and-tumble of daily life. Yet there is one situation in which this strangeness is at times dissipated: that rare moment of genuine worship when man stands naked before God, when he sees his whole life judged by him, and when his voice is heard above the tumult of preoccupations and self-interests. Then and there, if at all, can the appropriateness of the psalmist's perspective be sensed. For this reason the message of the Bible seems more easily grasped in the chapel than in the classroom. For this same reason the reader of the succeeding chapters should seek to correlate the material within the context of the intimate history that stems from his own meetings with God.

But even when the Bible is heard in worship, the strangeness of outlook does not evaporate. For our luminous moments of visitation are sporadic; they give but fleeting glimpses of an order of reality that is only obliquely related to most of our concerns. In the Bible, as typified by the above psalm, God's visits do not commonly originate in regular worship services; nor are they limited to such periodic occasions. They are not isolated from secular affairs, nor restricted to the category of " religious experiences." These visits draw within their orbit all the experiences of life. But the same can hardly be said of us. The very naturalness of the psalms in worship services exaggerates their incongruity in describing our consciousness as a whole. A close reading of this psalm may indicate reasons for this remark. It is natural for us to " place " and " date " our encounters with God *within* the course of our life; the psalmist sees the whole course of his life encompassed within the knowledge and purpose of God. It is natural for us to view God's visits as taking place within the framework of a supposedly autonomous history; the psalmist does just the opposite. For us, life and history may be punctuated by these strategic moments of dialogue with God; for the psalmist, all places, all days, the entire past and the entire future, are sentences incorporated within the authorship of God. Small wonder, then, that the psalmist confesses:

> "Such knowledge is too wonderful for me;
> It is high, I cannot attain unto it."

Because the visit takes place between the invisible God and the soul of man, no metaphor can describe exactly what happens. The Biblical narratives, however, leave no doubt as to the reality of the visit, its dynamic impact upon man, and its all-inclusive significance. Each visit is an event; narration is therefore the only adequate witness to its import. The meeting of God and man is not a relation that exists in and for itself, something timeless, static, or constant, which may be objectivized and reduced to formula. Each specific visit bears its own peculiar, personal stamp which can be preserved only in story form.[2]

Think for a moment of the frequency and dramatic intensity with which these meetings are narrated in the Bible: Adam in the Garden, Noah preparing for the Deluge, Abraham's interviews with the messengers, Joseph guided in the midst of temptations, Moses on Horeb, Amos among his Tekoan herds, Isaiah in the Temple, Jeremiah in the ruined Jerusalem . . . The list would be as long as the dramatis personae, because what qualified a man for this cast was an interview with God, prompted by God's intrusion into man's consciousness. The meaning of each role, of each critical choice, springs from the encounter.

To describe all the consequences of God's visits is utterly impossible. To outline the frame of reference within which those consequences are to be interpreted is more nearly within the range of the possible. That is the object of this book. The purposes of the present chapter are simpler: to underscore the central importance of God's visits; to suggest five immediate repercussions in man's situation in terms of the angle of vision thus created — a new awareness of himself; of his efforts to escape from this intruder; of the futility of these efforts; of the togetherness-and-tension in the encounter; and of the authority of the God who addresses him.

[2] Cf. E. Brunner, *op. cit.*, pp. 47 f.

SELF-AWARENESS

God's address crystallizes a new and peculiar kind of self-consciousness. He speaks to man directly and personally: "Come now, and let
us reason together," or, "Where are you hiding?" By speaking directly
he ceases to be a third party or an object *about* which man speaks and
becomes a Person *to* whom man must reply.[3] He recounts the story of
the past in terms of his own acts: "I took . . . [I] led . . . I gave
. . . I sent . . . I plagued . . . I brought . . . I destroyed . . . I delivered" (Josh., ch. 24). He claims a similar authority over the future:
"I will make thee a great name . . . I will appoint [thee] a place . . .
I will cause thee to rest . . . I will establish his kingdom" (II Sam.,
ch. 7). He claims to be the ever-present Companion of man's way: "I
have been with thee whithersoever thou wentest" (II Sam. 7:9).

The upshot of such a dialogue is a keen awareness on the part of the
listener that he *is known,* and this awareness conditions all areas of consciousness.

"The existence of a parent conditions that of his child, and the child's existence that of the parent, even when each is temporarily absent from the other
and neither thinking of him nor specifically acting toward him. While the
parent lives, the child's life-context is different from that of the same child
become an orphan, . . . not merely or even primarily by reason of the parent's detailed behavior but by reason of the existence of a living person whose
very being what he is helps to define the being of the child." [4]

The child who has lost his parents cannot know what family means
except by being a spectator of the families of other children. And a poor
substitute that is. Only children having parents can know family life
from within, because there *they are known.*

For, to a child, it is more important to be known than to know. The
ground of his confidence depends less upon how much he knows about
his family than upon the inner awareness that he is known by his family. The psalmist's testimony, "O Lord, thou hast searched me, and
known me" (Ps. 139:1), articulates such awareness, an awareness which
rises to a climax in the Christian consciousness of being "foreknown,"
and in the expectation, "Then shall I know fully even as also I was
fully known" (I Cor. 13:12). To hear God's address, "You only have

[3] Cf. S. Kierkegaard, *op. cit.,* pp. 61, 62.
[4] R. L. Calhoun, in the *Journal of Religion,* 1942, XXII, p. 128.

I known," is the seal of election, vocation, and promise. Edna St. Vincent Millay writes, "Man has never been the same since God died." To this one may add, Man is never the same again after the living God speaks to him.

Thus to be known by God is the precondition of authentic self-consciousness. Prior to this meeting there is, of course, an already formed self-consciousness; but true self-consciousness emerges within the context of the meeting when man is forced to respond to God's address. To be sure, a man may become aware of his individuality through meeting other men, but only a visit from God can precipitate awareness of his existence in its relation to God. And because he is the vessel molded by the divine potter, it is not for him an open option to initiate, choose, or control God's coming. By appearing before man, God creates the only ground on which he may understand his existence, i.e., as creature of God. Genuine impressions of reality can never be emancipated from this primal encounter with Another.[5]

Herein the Biblical testimony contradicts our usual assumptions. It is customary for us to assume that man inherits or arrives at a common awareness of selfhood by a natural if not inevitable process. Men of the Bible, on the contrary, assume that there are many types of self-consciousness, and that all are distorted and deceptive except such awareness as is created within the context of God's speaking and man's hearing. The self finds itself in being found by God.

In this encounter a relationship is precipitated from which all other relations are derived. Our thought usually moves in a single direction: from the known relations with men and nature to the unknown relations with God. We seldom experience the relation to God as primary and the relation to our brothers as derived. The latter seems to us far more intimate and inescapable than the former. Yet the opposite direction prevails in the Bible. It is by knowing God that men come to know themselves, their brothers, their enemies. No relationship to other men can be as real, as certain, as primary, as this. No friendship and no enmity among men can rival for intensity or ultimacy the dialogue with God. It is through God's demands that obligations to fathers and brothers are seen to be binding (Eph. 5:22 to 6:9). The cliché of preachers, to the effect that Jesus chose the term " Father " for God because of the

[5] Cf. M. Buber, *I and Thou*, trans. by R. G. Smith, pp. 3–34. 1937. H. F. L. Cocks, *By Faith Alone*, pp. 176–182. 1943.

noble traits of Joseph, throws more light on the speaker's assumptions than it does on Jesus' parent. It is only faith stemming from a meeting with God that leads man to say,

> "When my father and my mother forsake me,
> Then the Lord will take me up"
>
> (Ps. 27:10).

The primacy of this I-Thou relation in determining all other relations is the more amazing when one considers its comparative intangibility. After all, a child has very tangible evidence (sometimes all too tangible!) of the existence of his human parent. But the evidence of the power of a heavenly Father belongs to another dimension. Man's relation to an idol is far more tangible: an idol can be seen and felt; it is an immediately recognizable objective certainty. God remains hidden; he makes forever impossible any certainty grounded on external appearance.[6]

Orientation of life within this context of communication plunges man into an intensely dramatic participation in history. Every situation is pregnant with ultimate possibility; every moment is made explosive by the presence of infinite power. When God the Subject speaks, the reverberations in human existence cannot be silenced. He is not a problem to be solved; he creates problems through his nearness, his threats, his insistent demands, his irresistible intention. It is not so much that men raise questions about him, but that he raises questions of men. He speaks, he acts, he calls, he leads, he judges, he knows. In each situation man is confronted not with his own inner life, his thoughts and emotions; he is wholly concerned with what God has done, is doing, is about to do. A Biblical writer does not give advice on how a man may so understand and treat himself as to banish unrest and collect his senses in solitary contemplation; he points to God's passionate and powerful dealings with himself and with the chosen people; he calls upon man to respond in ways appropriate to the object of such dealings.

EFFORTS TO ESCAPE

One of the first reactions of man to God's voice is the sense of awe, fear, dread, and the impulse to run. In fact, the Bible might aptly be described as the drama of man's efforts to flee from God.

[6] Cf. S. Kierkegaard, *op. cit.*, pp. 178 ff.

> "Whither shall I go from thy Spirit?
> Or whither shall I flee from thy presence?"
>   (Ps. 139:7).

In a sermon on this psalm, Paul Tillich has described how we hate the Companion who is always present, how we resent the Knowing One from whom no secret is hid, how we try to escape from Him who is always interfering with our plans. Job laments that God will not let him alone long enough to swallow his spittle (Job 7:19).

> "Man wishes to flee from God. . . . Men of all kinds, prophets and reformers, saints and atheists . . . have had the same experience. . . . A man who never has tried to escape God never has experienced God, namely, that God who is really God." [7]

All such roads of escape lead to idolatry, for one of the basic urges of idolatry is man's desire to initiate his own relationship to God and thereby to control God. In choosing their own gods, men choose gods from whose searching it *is* possible to escape. They can have dealings with such gods on man's own terms, arranging their conversations at convenient times and places. But such conversations remain self-generated and one-directional. A god from whom one can successfully flee is proved by that very success to be an idol. "God is inescapable. He is God only because he is inescapable, and that alone is God which is inescapable." [8]

> "If I ascend up into heaven, thou art there:
> If I make my bed in Sheol, behold, thou art there.
> If I take the wings of the morning,
> And dwell in the uttermost parts of the sea;
> Even there shall thy hand lead me,
> And thy right hand shall hold me"
>   (Ps. 139:8 ff.).

One inveterate form of escape, a hidden expression of idolatry, is man's effort to leave the arena and become a spectator, to reverse the roles, to become the investigator of God's claims. Man is a runner who, in the midst of his race, tries to photograph himself in transit. He is a wrestler with God who tries to increase his power over his opponent by an objective knowledge of that opponent. But such an effort is doomed by his very status as creature.

[7] P. Tillich, in *The Protestant,* Feb.-March, 1943, p. 43.
[8] *Ibid.*

> " Canst thou by searching find out God?
> Canst thou find out the Almighty unto perfection?
> It is high as heaven; what canst thou do?
> Deeper than Sheol; what canst thou know?
> The measure thereof is longer than the earth,
> And broader than the sea "
>   (Job 11:7–9; cf. also 12:13 f.; 26:14; 28:20–28).

Particularly is knowledge of this sort denied to man on those questions most decisive in determining his destiny. He cannot assure himself prosperity or number his days; neither can he guarantee a posterity nor cleanse himself from secret sins, nor measure the power of God. " God is great, and we know him not " (Job 36:26). Yet, in spite of the utter impossibility of his undertaking, man seeks to extend his objective knowledge over realms beyond his ken. He repeatedly craves the apple that is supposed to confer a divine knowledge of good and evil. He rebels against his destined status and seeks freedom and control over his own future by such knowledge as belongs to God alone. This pride is inseparable from idolatry. Man worships idols precisely because of his ability to see them, to know them, to have power over them. But he can never observe the activity of God in the same way in which he can reflect upon the beauty and power of his idol.

" There is no fierier pride in the world than that of the intellectual. Though hungry and shelterless, he is sure that God did not place him on life's stage, but invited him to sit in the royal box. The consciousness that he does not belong to the mimes who play the play but among the objective observers fills him with an intoxication of superiority which makes even a life of utter want endurable." [9]

Or, as Tertullian pointed out:

" This is the substance of secular wisdom that it rashly undertakes to explain the nature and dispensation of God. . . . Heretics and philosophers deal with similar material, and their arguments are largely the same." [10]

THE FUTILITY OF ESCAPE

But God, when he visits man, impresses him with the impossibility of escaping. For though he flee to the gallery, man finds that even that last place of escape is held by God. Here God pursues him relentlessly,

[9] F. Werfel, *The Song of Bernadette*, p. 336. The Viking Press, 1942.

[10] *On Prescription Against Heretics, 7,* as quoted by C. N. Cochrane in *Christianity and Classical Culture,* p. 223. Oxford University Press, 1940.

raising again his importunate query, " Where are you hiding? " It is as if in the theater, where I am hugely enjoying an aesthetic view of life, God interrupts the show with a stentorian announcement: " Is John Smith in the house? " And I am John Smith. And the interruption continues: " Report immediately . . . for a task intended for you alone."

Similarly, the first impact of divine visitation in the Bible destroys man's speculative detachment and forces him into the arena, whether he wishes or not. Here he discovers that " the fear of the Lord is the beginning of wisdom." Here he learns from other creatures how to accept his true status. He is shaken out of his preoccupation with ontological arguments or with psychological introspection. His monologue becomes dialogue; his inner life loses its self-contained peace by an invasion from without. His own question, What do I know? is supplanted by the prophet's, " What doth the Lord require of thee? "

It is from the arena that prophets and apostles speak. Each of them has tried to find an escape route, but has come to the blank wall of Job: " He shutteth up a man, and there can be no opening " (Job 12:14). Henceforth man speaks as a wrestler with God. The prophet resents God's intrusion, and yet his resentment is overborne. The psalmist struggles with immediate danger, convinced that the outcome of his conversation with God is a matter of life or death. The historian tells his story in an emergency to mobilize the memory of the community for the crucial choice. These writers do not analyze their situation as objective sociologists, probing causes and anticipating results of their action before they act. With the odds against them, they are confronted by the Determiner of destiny and hear him say, " I have a controversy with my people." Their situation is not that of airmen triumphantly speeding over the sea in a four-motored plane; rather, they are airmen who find themselves drifting in the open sea on a life raft. Existential concern expels speculative detachment.

Trying to escape in still other directions, man finds every exit blocked. For example, man is prone to preserve mementoes of God's former visits in cultus and law, to idolize these, to substitute legal observance and cultic sacrifice for " knowledge of God." He is also inclined to speak of God in the third person, albeit with apparent reverence, and thus to remove himself from the magnetic field of divine compulsions. Man can forget God in the very act of speaking of him. But every act of indifference or disobedience flouts the real basis of man's existence as man. Regardless of the ways in which man may deny the contemporaneity of the I-Thou relation, such a denial is adultery of the worst sort.

Such adultery tempts God to disown his people and to destroy his covenant with them. Yet he never does. He continues to determine their destiny. Whatever men may do, he is still the Alpha and Omega of their lives, and it is this persistence of God's purpose, rather than the consistence of their loyalty, that witnesses to the ultimacy of their relation to him. When they remove their hearts from God, though their lips continue to honor him, his word becomes a sealed book. The commandment becomes a dead word which they embalm and not the living source and energy of their actions. Safe in their conventional respect for inherited wisdom, they turn that wisdom into folly (Isa. 29:9 ff.). In effect their works are done "in the dark"; in effect they say: "Who seeth us? and who knoweth us?" But to them comes a living word:

> "Ye turn things upside down! Shall the potter be esteemed as clay; that the thing made should say of him that made it, He made me not; or the thing formed say of him that formed it, He hath no understanding?" (Isa. 29:16).

And through this very imprecation God acts to turn his people back again to the living center. He visits them anew with the protest of their forgotten postulate.

Man perennially attempts to construct still another type of defense. He builds walls designed to confine the invading Sovereignty within one sphere of his thought or behavior. He consents to God's authority in the area where that seems desirable, but at the same time tries to maintain his autonomy in other areas. But God does not respect these man-made fences. Man's total existence is known by him. When he speaks, he claims total sovereignty. When he acts, he commands a total response on the part of man's thought, feeling, and will. He shapes man's prenatal and post-mortem history. There is no time or place in which he may not intervene, revealing the hidden purpose and power that permeate every time and place. No compartment of life may evade such totalitarian rule.

In self-defense men try to erect a wall between the sacred and the secular. But the God of the Bible demolishes it. The very term "religion" appears rarely in the Bible, for there is no experience which as such can be defined as religious, and no experience which lies outside the circle of the divine radius. When God speaks, he declares war on all other gods; when he makes a covenant, he makes it broad enough to cover every detail in the life of the covenant community. He does not establish one religion among others, but brings all religions under judgment. He does not call man to endorse a religion, but to view all life religiously, i.e., in its relation to God.

Men try to draw a sharp line between flesh and spirit, between physical and spiritual reality. But the Biblical God is the Creator of man, both body and spirit. In every personal encounter, he forces man to participate as a unit; he does not draw the line between spirit and flesh, and deal with one in isolation. This helps to explain the inveterate anthropomorphic conceptions of God, and the impossibility of conceiving a redemption that does not include the body.

God also destroys the customary discrimination between private and public life, between events of significance to the individual and those with great social impact. The measure of importance is not the influence upon the lives of millions, but the inner connection with God's central intention. Every event is social, for it takes place within the web of personal relations and involves, in however small a compass, issues of ultimate concern. And, on the other hand, no event is social in the sense that the immediate personal dealing of God with man becomes measured by the quantity of social consequences.

This totalitarian character of Biblical thinking explains the lack of conscious involvement in problems which have troubled philosophers of all centuries, as, for example, the relation of the particular and the universal, of the real and the ideal, of time and the timeless, of fact and value. Biblical thinking avoids or transcends these antinomies, not because of dullness of wit or intentional stubbornness, but because of its perspective center. God's visit to man in a specific event links the background of the absolute to the foreground of the relative in such a way that neither can be abstracted from the other without destroying the reality of the event. From a single point of standing, man views the whole horizon; in the angle of vision is comprehended the Biblical ontology, not in abstract generalizations, but in a concrete particular story that includes the being and becoming of both God and man.

This same totalitarian compass of each event likewise explains the absence of distinctions usually found in ethical theory. Man's cultic obligations are not disjoined from his moral obligations; the mixing of such duties in Leviticus, for example, has long given offense to systematic moralists. To be sure, the prophets often protest against the emphasis on animal sacrifices and ceremonial ablutions, but rarely is such protest directed against all sacrifice as such. Rather, it is occasioned by the deep-rooted tendency to create in practice a double standard that exempts social obligations from the sphere of divine obedience. The prophets are fighting against a false separation of sacred from secular, against any reduction in the territory under divine rule. It has often been observed that in neither Testament can ethics and religion be separated. One finds an *ethical religion* and a *religious ethic* precisely because every aspect of life is seen from a single center, and every aspect is therefore potentially religious and no aspect is *per se* religious.

Such a position seems to many moralists to open the road to a historical pantheism, within which the boundary between moral good and evil is obliterated. The prophet did not find this to be the result. Ultimately he ascribed both good fortune and ill fortune to God. God is the Lord of all life and all history. Yet, when he visits man with his claim to sovereignty over all man's deeds, that very claim reveals current rebellion and stubborn efforts on man's part to preserve his autonomy in certain areas. God is a " man of war " engaged in combat against every agent of disloyalty, and this conflict is implicit in his every visit.

TOGETHERNESS-AND-TENSION

The relation between God and man which this visit precipitates may be characterized as one of " togetherness-and-tension." Heaven is near to earth as an invisible realm of power and glory which irradiates all creation, touching earth at every point. God's activity underlies creation at every moment in such a way that heaven and earth cannot be separated; they form in their belonging-togetherness the entirety of God's creation (Luke 10:21; Acts 4:24; 17:24; Rev. 10:6). Both heaven and earth belong to God (Matt. 5:34, 35). Though God's relationship to heaven is different from that to earth, this does not mean that there are *two* localities, from *one* of which God is excluded. To be sure, Jewish-Christian thought was so concrete in its imagery that spatial categories could no more be eliminated from references to heaven than anthropomorphic terms could be avoided in speaking of God. But neither time nor space categories are fully applicable to heaven. It is the invisible background of every visible foreground, the home of God's sovereignty and the source from which his power invades the earth; it is the point of issue for the intentions, energies, and loyalties which impel men to action, the hidden and mysterious womb of time and events. To say that John's baptism was from heaven was to say that this particular historical phenomenon derived authority and significance from a divine origin. Because God speaks from heaven, and because his word returns to him there, heaven is the origin and home and end of all historical reality. No phantom oasis in the sky this; rather, its actuality is far more real and enduring than the tangible and ephemeral objects of sense. Every encounter with God assumes this togetherness of heaven and earth.

But it also makes man aware of the sharp otherness of the heavenly. God is no inner-worldly spirit into whose life one can become so fully absorbed that the meeting becomes a monologue rather than dialogue. In God's visits with man, man is made acutely conscious of tension. Man is not God; nor is God man. " My thoughts are not your thoughts, neither are your ways my ways, saith the Lord " (Isa. 55:8). It would therefore be presumptuous to cultivate or profess any union with God which would erase this otherness. When God meets man, earth is not mixed with heaven, but heaven convicts earth of its rejection of Him whose will is done in heaven. The High, Holy, and Mighty One confronts men with demands for sole mastery, demands that are terribly near in their urgency for the very reason that they stem from and point to his otherness.

However acute this tension becomes, it does not lead the men of the Bible to view their Adversary as an other-worldly god. When God is so understood, an intervention can be treated as external, occasional, and nonhistorical. Such an intervention then contradicts and overturns the regular relation of God to his world; it comes as a sporadic incursion from Mars which has little relationship to the whole panorama of history, communicating no meaning that is intrinsic to man's life as a whole.

" God was from the beginning transcendent in that He was different from man, but He was by no means transcendent in that He was remote from men." [11]

[11] N. H. Snaith, *The Distinctive Ideas of the Old Testament*, p. 47. The Epworth Press, 1944.

Because Biblical faith springs from God's visitation, it is not receptive to the philosophical antinomy of transcendence-immanence. God is neither inner-worldly nor other-worldly but over-worldly.[12] But even such a statement is meaningless when separated from the meeting within which man becomes conscious both of himself and of this particular over-world, God.

"The Biblical revelation . . . deals with the relation of God to men and of men to God. It contains no doctrine of God as He is in Himself, none of man as he is in himself. It always speaks of God as the God who approaches man and of man as the man who comes from God."[13]

THE GOD WHO SPEAKS

Within the situation created by God's visit, the prophet and apostle could not do other than exclaim, "The Lord thy God is *one* Lord." For this reason, monotheism is a corollary of the exclusive claim of Jahveh, rather than a conceptual hypothesis resulting from man's effort to gain a unitary view of his world. It is important, therefore, to distinguish Biblical monotheism from philosophical monism.

In what sense is monotheism basic to Biblical faith? If it is, when did it appear? How is it to be distinguished from polytheism and henotheism? Is the whole Bible consistent in holding to this fundamental axiom? Much academic blood has been spilt over such questions, and much of it has been spilt in vain. It has been a futile fight partly because the Western mind insists on forcing the Semitic imagination into the strait jacket of its own conceptual logic. Alfred Guillaume describes the Semitic outlook thus:

"There is no necessary contradiction between gross superstition and monotheism. . . . No Semite is afraid of a logical contradiction."[14]

The fight has been futile partly because the modern philosopher poses the question in a form alien to the outlook of prophets and apostles. The philosopher makes the problem one of thought, rather than of action; he views the problem speculatively in I-It terms rather than

---

[12] E. Stauffer, in G. Kittel, *Theologisches Wörterbuch zum Neuen Testament*. Vol. III, pp. 116–120.

[13] E. Brunner, *The Divine-Human Encounter*, trans. by A. W. Loos, pp. 46, 47. The Westminster Press, 1943. Cf. also J. Hempel, *Gott und Mensch im Alten Testament*, pp. 1–3. 1936.

[14] *Prophecy and Divination*, p. 92, note 5. Harper & Brothers, 1939.

existentially in I-Thou terms. To him, monotheism is to be defined as "the doctrine of, or belief in, the existence of but one God." Either a man is a monotheist or he is not. And whether he is or not can be determined by objective standards. Man may hold the doctrine of the existence of one God without involving the character of his own personal relationship to that God. Phrased thus, the question of when the Israelites arrived at monotheism, whether Moses or Amos were monotheists, becomes virtually unanswerable. Moreover, the answer is unimportant to the student, except to satisfy historical curiosity — unless he feels that the authority of the Biblical accounts depends upon their conformity to orthodox doctrine. And if the question becomes a matter of doctrinal orthodoxy, one may remark that the devil is perhaps the best monotheist.

Existentially, monotheism cannot even be defined, and no Biblical writer essays such a definition. At the most there is a witness to a meeting, a description of God's visit, to which a specific man (or community) responds in faith that for him (or them) there is only one *Lord*. He alone is our Creator and Redeemer. He and he alone has the right to determine our duty and demand our loyalty; our destiny lies in his hands alone. Others may have their gods, but in reality they are idols. To us only one power is sovereign — the God of Abraham and Isaac and Jacob.

But the encounter wherein God convinces man of his Kingdom and power also convicts man of the sin of serving other gods. He who says, "I am the Lord thy God," also says, "Thou shalt have no other gods before me." And he says the latter because his people in practice are serving other gods. In saying, "No man can serve two masters" (existential monotheism), he also says, "you now are serving two masters" (existential polytheism).[15] The sole sovereignty of God is realized *only* by stern struggle with other gods, with all the forces that oppose his will. This is to say that, to the Biblical writers themselves, monotheism begins, not as a stage of metaphysical speculation, not as a final step in the development out of polytheism, not as the merging of all gods into one (as in Hinduism), but when one God becomes the decisive reality for a particular man and thereby calls for the dethronement of all his other gods.

This helps to explain why early Christians found in the *total obedience* of Jesus a supreme and final manifestation of God, a manifestation

[15] Cf. S. Kierkegaard, *Judge for Yourselves,* trans. by W. Lowrie, pp. 162–170. 1941.

which by its very nature transcended history, judged history, and re-deemed history; it points to the reason why, in dying with him to the world, they themselves experienced true knowledge of God and true power from God. And this message of the oneness of God intensified their struggle against false gods. To them, the conflict with heathen gods had entered its final stage. Everywhere their testimony is ambivalent: there are no such gods *for us,* yet there are many demonic powers which have tyrannized over men and now have attacked us most viciously. This ambivalence that inheres in the struggle between God and upstart deities will disappear only when all others have been subdued by Christ and brought within the sovereignty of God.

Christian belief does not consist in saying, " There is one God." The devil knows that! Christians respond to the true God by faith in his deeds, trust in his power, hope in his promise, and passionate abandonment of self to do his will. Only within the context of such a passionate vocation does the knowledge of the one Lord live. And this knowledge necessitates rather than eliminates the struggle with the devil and all his works.[16] Only in unconditional obedience, spurred by infinite passion, infinite resignation, infinite enthusiasm (Kierkegaard) is such " monotheism " wholly manifested in human existence, as, for example, in Jesus.

The philosopher, who seeks to solve the question of monotheism in objective, impersonal, I-It fashion, may claim that polytheism is found throughout the Bible. On the other hand, the Biblical writer would perhaps recognize such a philosopher, confident of the rational unity of his system, as a prime example of idolatry. Belief in angels and demons is an example of the two approaches. The rationalist may view such belief as necessarily in contradiction to monotheism. But the Biblical writer accepts such belief without the slightest awareness of contradiction. From his angle of vision angels are messengers of God to fulfill his will. In their relations with men, their sole importance lies in their work of mediation. They have no historical or community life of their own. Their existence never touches the aloneness of God. Likewise the Jew was receptive to demonology, to Persian eschatology with its warfare between God and Satan. This dualism remained consistent with monotheism, because it is the true God who proves his sovereignty by

[16] Cf. E. Stauffer, *op. cit.,* Vol. III, pp. 95–107.

precipitating the struggle with Satan. In the beginning and in the end God is all in all.[17]

Likewise the objective conceptualist is inclined to label the Christian attitudes toward Jesus as an infringement upon pure monotheism. Speculatively understood, a high Christology may perhaps be confused with worship of a second God. But the apostles are not aware of that danger. In Jesus the Christ, the God who is one Lord confronts, convicts, and saves men. However " high " may be the Christology in the New Testament, Jesus Christ remains the Servant of God who came to establish God's sole Lordship. And he accomplishes that task only as the Son of God, and only by bringing to nought the works of the devil.

Men of the Bible, therefore, anticipated the full manifestation of " monotheism " only in the future; its perfect realization awaits the time when God takes his great power and reigns alone. This consummation will be marked by renewal and perfecting of the covenant. " Ye shall be my people, and I will be your God " (Ezek. 36:28). " Ye shall know that I am the Lord " (Ezek. 20:44). " They shall teach no more every man his neighbor, and every man his brother, saying, Know the Lord; for they shall all know me " (Jer. 31:34; cf. 3:16 f.). With the perfection of this knowledge will come the perfection of man's nature; he will become what he is: a son of God. Both the knowledge of self as creature and the knowledge of God as Creator will then be uncontaminated by the worship of false idols. And throughout the Bible, this future is pictured in terms of a final visitation of God, an eventful meeting of persons, a new coming down of the heavenly to the earthly.

" The Hebrew does not say that Jehovah is, or that Jehovah exists, but that He does. Properly speaking, the Hebrew verb Hayah does not mean ' to be ' so much as ' to come to be.' Hebrew has no real verb of ' being,' but one of ' becoming.' The verb is active and not static." [18]

Both the present meeting, which promises that future revelation, and that future meeting, which brings to consummation the present hope, confront man with a Person who is hidden from human eyes. However clear and sharp the experience of a prophet or apostle, he cannot describe what " eye saw not, and ear heard not." God visits man as the

[17] For further exposition of this point, see Chapter 4.
[18] N. H. Snaith, *The Distinctive Ideas of the Old Testament*, p. 48. The Epworth Press, 1944.

Holy One who is incomparable and unfathomable. The meeting place of heaven and earth is the point where the mystery of God's action is seen with greatest intensity.[19]

"His existence transcends all conceptions, it transcends all realms of ideas, things, and beings. He is before and beyond the world we know or ever will know. This world is in Him, He is not in this world. The doctrine of God as Creator means just this." [20]

To behold him, to meet him, to hear his voice, is to be made aware of his majesty and glory. To be confronted by him is to be humbled in awe, fear, and contrition.

What has been said about the relation of God and man may clarify the purposes outlined in the introduction. We do not mean to defend the thesis of a unity of views on the part of all Biblical writers, but to maintain that they had a common point of viewing. We do not seek to reduce all Biblical theology to a minimum of agreement, an attenuated residuum which none of the writers of the Testaments would feel adequate. There is little to be gained by the attempt to define the genius of Jewish and early Christian religion by selecting dominant psychological traits or sociological phenomena, by finding and describing the typical Jew or the representative Christian. Why blind ourselves to the relativity of each writer in his own particular situation, to the variations in God's messages at different times and places, to the contradictions to be found in concrete formulations of law and cultus? We have tried to locate the living center, the creative seed from which thinking and acting proceeded. We have tried to describe some of the distinctive attitudes that radiate from this single point. To say that specific encounters with God constitute the source of their thinking is not to claim for all Biblical writers a common high level of achievement. They were aware of deviations from it, but *it was precisely this center which made them aware of such deviations.* When God visited them, he exerted a centripetal force, the strength of which was measured by the centrifugal attractions which were overcome. The pull toward the center can therefore be detected even in writings which approach the periphery of the circle. It would hardly signify loyalty to the prophets, who fought ramp-

[19] Cf. W. Stählin, *The Mystery of God,* trans. by R. B. Hoyle, pp. 15–23. 1937.
[20] R. Kroner, *How Do We Know God?* p. 34. Harper & Brothers, 1943.

ant idolatry so vigorously, to claim that they or other Jews of their day achieved a high level of obedience to God. But neither would it be loyalty to them to ignore their witness to a peculiar covenant obligation, through which the God of the covenant was constantly seeking them, revealing his power in the very futility of their rebellion. The unity which we sense in the Bible derives from this strange quest of God for a strange people, and his refusal to let them go.

It is this quest which produced the responses outlined in this chapter. Six other consequences will be distinguished in the following chapters, each of which must be considered unique and essential: the sense of election, of decision, of conflict, of community, of time, and of destiny. In the appraisal of each type of awareness, its derivation must be traced to the initial context in personal communication.

2

GOD CHOOSES MAN

WHEN God visits the men of the Bible he says, " I have chosen thee." When the risen Christ calls his disciples under the yoke of the Kingdom, he says, " Ye did not choose me, but I chose you." Our analysis of the primacy of the I-Thou encounter thus leads to the consideration of *the primacy of God's purpose* in that encounter. The visit of God with man is motivated by a specific intention; the investigation of the character of this purpose is therefore necessary to any understanding of the Biblical point of view.

The word " I have chosen thee " suggests at once that the initiative begins and remains with God. " There is none that can deliver out of my hand: I will work, and who can hinder it? " (see Isa. 43:10–13; 41:21–24). The divine I addresses the human Thou as One who claims to be and who wills to become the sole center of human allegiance. In his purpose as Creator rests the ultimate ground of human existence. In his activity as Judge lies the ultimate outcome of human striving. He is the source of energy, not the end product of thought; he provides " the locus of commitment, not a problem for debate." When he calls, we are not impelled to rigorous analysis of a previous happening by investigating its causes, by separating each cause from the others and by linking them all into a single sequence that extends from the first beginning to the last ending. Rather, we face the call to act now in the line of a single, ultimate purpose which works in a hidden way through all the dynamic energies of life.

The objective tracing of a purpose upstream to its ultimate source remains impossible for man. What man can by introspection follow the crosscurrents of purposes back to their real beginning? They emerge from the secret places of the soul where the strands of desire are already plaited together. What man can by external observation of the life of groups distill from the amalgam of present behavior the original drives which determine that life? Men's purposes point to impenetrable mystery; the springs of action lie in an invisible realm of influences that shape man's will. The initial formation and ultimate validation of God's purpose are revealed only when he addresses man. " Sovereignty, by its very nature, resembles the Nile; it conceals its source." [1]

The word " I have chosen thee " implies not only God's initiative but also his authority. He speaks as One who has the sole right over those who are chosen. " I am God, and there is none else " (Isa. 46:9). His demand is absolute because of his exclusive right, and this right stems from his power as Creator.

"Look unto the rock whence ye were hewn, and to the hole of the pit whence ye were digged. Look unto Abraham your father, and unto Sarah that bare you; for when he was but one I called him, and I blessed him, and made him many " (Isa. 51:1, 2).

This insistent recognition of the unconditional sovereignty of God pervades Biblical thinking, from first to last. In his covenant with Israel, he makes men the recipients of a deliberate, uncaused, undeserved, selective love.

" God is always the superior; man is always the inferior. God always is in control. . . . He conforms to no norm apart from Him Himself. . . . There is no necessity laid upon Him from outside. He decides what is to be and what is not to be." [2]

The apparent arbitrariness of the love in which he calls man is not equivalent to inconstancy and fickleness. The typical witness of faith runs: " Of thy faithfulness there is no end."

Consequently, the consciousness of being chosen does not lead man to concentrate upon that single, isolated antecedent event. The initial call is continuous with an inclusive design. He who " took me out of my mother's bowels " (Ps. 71:6) is also he who " didst make me trust when I was upon my mother's breasts," (Ps. 22:9). He who speaks to me now in this moment of crisis is he who sustains all my life:

" With thee is the fountain of life:
In thy light shall we see light "
(Ps. 36:9).

[1] De Maistre.
[2] N. H. Snaith, *The Distinctive Ideas of the Old Testament,* pp. 139, 140. The Epworth Press, 1944.

Hence, consciousness of special vocation is inseparable from an awareness that his purpose pervades all creation.

> " These wait all upon thee,
> That thou mayest give them their food in due season.
> Thou givest unto them, they gather;
> Thou openest thy hand, they are satisfied with good.
> Thou hidest thy face, they are troubled;
> Thou takest away their breath, they die
>   (Ps. 104:27).

Human purposes are fickle and frail, but God's purpose continues forever (Isa. 40:8).

FOREKNOWLEDGE

The experience of being selected leads men also to assume the priority of divine intention. " Before I formed thee in the belly I knew thee." The stronger the sense of vocation, the stronger is the conviction of such foreknowledge. It comes to a clear articulation in the story of Samuel, in the prayers of the psalmists, and in the witness of Isaiah and Jeremiah. It underlies the stories of the patriarchs. It is presupposed by Israel's faith in the ancestral covenants, wherein, through guidance of Abraham and Moses, God was calling the race and nation into existence. Equally intense is the consciousness of foreknowledge among the Christians. The apostle realizes that he had been called from his mother's womb; the humble believer comes to know himself as one who has always been known. The bond of fellowship among all members of the Way is this common participation in a calling which reveals both foreordination and foreknowledge (Rom. 8:29, 30). The stories about John the Baptizer and Jesus, telling of births in accordance with divine purpose, belong in this milieu.

But such foreknowledge never becomes in the Bible a dogma separable from the passion of faith, a known equation in a cosmic algebra which men may reduce to formula. When faith withers, consciousness of God's prevenience also evaporates. There is no evidence for this prevenience outside the context of divine-human encounter. The scoffer says: " He cannot see "; " our ways are hidden from his eyes "; " he shall not see our latter end." Only the faithful know that Sheol and Abaddon are open before God, that his purpose encompasses our going out and our coming in, that our life remains in his hand.

Seen from the vantage point of faith, this foreknowledge is not a dogma but an inference, not an analysis of cause and effect but a description of contemporaneous experience. When God speaks, " I have chosen thee," he does not invite man to explore at will the intricacies of the divine mind. He does not endow the elect with omniscience. In fact, he makes it even less possible for them to define the nature of divine foreknowledge than for a philosopher or historian to do so.[3] His call makes men of the Bible less confident of their inquisitorial powers, thus preventing them from developing systems of doctrinal affirmations. They do not speak of foreknowledge as if it means a completed blueprint of all subsequent events; nor do they identify it with the first cause in some remote point of time, an antecedent restraint dictated in the original act of creating the world. God's knowledge is not an exhaustive encyclopedic knowledge of the facts about a person's history, nor the sum of propositions entertained by a divine mind. The recipients of the call do not feel confronted by an impersonal mechanistic determinism, a necessity that eliminates all chance and all freedom. They do not, as did the Greek tragedians, tend to identify Providence and Fate, for the prophets have to deal directly with a living Person and to respond to him as a present Lord.

"Fate is a relation to spirit as something external, it is a relation between a spirit and another which is not spirit, and with which nevertheless it has to stand in a spiritual relationship."[4]

God's foreknowledge is not one factor within history, but a continuum within which events take place, and from which each present moment derives its momentum. The experience of being known in the present moment makes man's life a single unit by manifesting the meaning of his past and future. That same experience reveals that the lives of all creatures are comprehended within the activity of God. And it is thus that man comes to recognize that all history is included within the movement of the one sovereign Will. God's foreknowledge is coextensive with the purpose underlying his creative activity, with his ordaining of times and seasons. The element of priority in such knowledge is therefore not to be defined in temporal terms but in terms of personal

---

[3] Cf. R. Kroner, *The Primacy of Faith*, pp. 1, 2. 1943.

[4] S. Kierkegaard, *Concept of Dread*, trans. by W. Lowrie, pp. 86, 87. Princeton University Press, 1944.

volition. Even in those terms, of course, it cannot be defined but remains a mystery. As the psalmist confesses, " Such knowledge is too wonderful for me."

But although man cannot grasp the nature of the divine mind, he can grasp God's commands, when God speaks. This disclosure gives him an understanding of his immediate role in the drama of creation. The new sense of selfhood which stems from this understanding of his true destiny is often so overwhelming as to revolutionize man's orientation. He describes the change in striking language, such as " a new creation," " a new birth." He has been given a new name, a name which for the first time truly represents his position in the divine drama (e.g., Jacob becomes Israel and Saul becomes Paul), and which therefore expresses the real person, whose history is now actually constituted by the relationship to God. " I have given thee a name," becomes thus practically synonymous with, " I have chosen thee." This commission is no afterthought, no casual occurrence, no stroke of fate; it is recognized by man as an essential expression of God's inclusive purpose.[5]

This consciousness of foreknowledge is the natural presupposition of predictive prophecy. It is not surprising, therefore, that in the Bible one finds many cases of men foretelling the future. In calling men, God reveals to them a message concerning the future. At first sight this predictive element may seem identical with that in other religions. Many cults provide means by which men may tap God's store of information about coming events. The consultation of omens and the guidance of soothsayers are supposed to diminish the hazards of human ventures. And one must freely admit that such practices are present in the Bible. Viewing such phenomena objectively, it is hard to distinguish Biblical practice from secular and pagan superstitions that seek to extend man's knowledge over the future and his control of it. Appreciation of the existential perspectives of the Bible, however, calls attention to salient contrasts in this area.

For example, in the Bible ability to discern the signs of the times is everywhere a result of God's election and not of man's search. It posits the experience of being chosen and is unthinkable outside that experience. Only when the prophet is called, only when the nation is viewed as an instrument of divine purpose, is any understanding of the future

[5] Cf. F. J. A. Hort, *First Epistle of Peter,* comment on ch. 1:1, 2. 1898.

communicated. Moreover, this experience does not yield a recondite body of instructions to be sold to the highest bidder; tomorrow's secrets are not offered on the market to chance comers. Man, the subject, does not penetrate the maze of divine mind, but man, the object, becomes the instrument of a divine purpose in ways surprising and usually distasteful to the recipient. It is the inner compulsion of a call to share in this purpose that prompts prophecy. The primary imperative is not to read tomorrow's newspaper today, but to obey an insistent taskmaster. Prophets are led to see the direction of God's acting from within the vortex of personal struggle with him. On them is laid the painful but inescapable vocation of proclaiming the " word of the Lord," of witnessing to a divine will on which the future depends. They shout to their fellows about the coming doom and dawn because they cannot restrain the fire in their bones.

Another point of distinction in Biblical prophecy is the awareness of God's sovereignty over time. Other gods foreknow the future from within the temporal process, their powers being due to only a partial freedom from the temporal limitations that permeate man's knowledge. Jahveh knows the future because he creates the various times. Every time is the instrument of his purpose, and because he has power to fulfill this purpose, his word determines the future. Foreknowledge is intrinsic to the purpose which creates. It is not some special superhuman access to the scroll of fate, but the natural concomitant of continuing purposive creation. It does not, therefore, assume the existence in heaven of a detailed chronology which records in advance all events in exact order. This would make both God and man the victims of an impersonal, deadly time clock. To say, " The time is at hand," does not mean that a certain day with its prearranged load of woe is due on the thirteenth of January. Rather, it stresses the assurance that a strategic moment in the maturing of personal intentional activity has even now arrived.

The priority of the divine purpose remains a mystery which defies precise definition, but perhaps enough has been said to undermine three usual misconceptions. Foreknowledge does not mean that the biography of every man and nation is written in advance; it is not the arbitrary power of a deistic God to intervene sporadically in the realm of natural law whenever and however he sees fit; it is not an omnipresent law or reason which pervades all nature, an impersonal fate to which all men must bow in bitter acceptance.[6]

So far in this chapter we have discussed the experience of being known, and four inferences from that experience: the primacy, authority, continuity, and priority of God's purpose. Perhaps it is easier for the modern mind to grasp these four than to comprehend a fifth inference: the *particularity* of that purpose. When God says, " I have chosen thee," it is a particular *you* who is singled out and set over against all others. That God has a general intention for all mankind, for the ultimate outcome of all history, is a platitude that quickly becomes a pointless cliché. That God has a special intention for *me now* is far more incredible. That a particular man, inconspicuous and short-lived, should be chosen for an assignment which no other can fill is something hardly to be taken as an innocuous abstraction, at least by that single figure. And from such convictions the prophet and the apostle were unable to free themselves. Nor was this call limited to the so-called leaders. Awareness of it is reflected in Old Testament histories, in the psalms, in the apocalypses, and to a less intense degree in the legal and wisdom literature. In the New Testament it is presupposed as central to the experience of rebirth of every Christian. The Holy Spirit singles him out, moving him to respond in faith to the preaching of the word, and giving him a particular function the Body of Christ.

What has been suggested concerning the elect individual is true also of the elect community. Throughout the Bible, the community traces its origin to the sovereign purpose of God, expressed in his choice of a peculiar people to be his inheritance, to serve him, to manifest his glory. The Old Testament tells of the marvelous events through which this call was mediated: the deliverance from Egypt, the crossing of the Red Sea, the giving of the Law, the conquest of Canaan. They had had no name; he gave to them a name. They had had no destiny; he gave to them a promise. They had not chosen him; he had chosen them. They were obliged to worship him, not because he was God of all men, but because he was the God who had made them his people; not because he

<hr>

[6] Cf. C. N. Cochrane, *op. cit.,* pp. 238 f.

was Creator of the heavens and the earth, but because he was the God of
Abraham, Isaac, and Jacob; not because he gave all nature life, but because he " smote Egypt." W. J. Phythian-Adams is justified in claiming
as he does that " there is no parallel to this in the literature of any other
nation." [7]

Just as the Old Testament recounts the election of a nation to witness
to his glory, the New Testament narrates the sequel in which God freely
chooses and brings into being a new community, the Church. And members of this new organism persist in calling it by the name of its fore-
runner: Israel. This remains the basic social category. It is not perhaps
surprising that this term should be adopted in the early days of the
Church, for Jesus and his followers were Jews, worshiping the God of
Israel, awaiting the consolation of their nation. But it is surprising that
this identification was maintained after the separation of Church from
synagogue, after the two groups broke into bitter rivalry. Even Gentile
Christians were so insistent upon the solidarity with Israel that able
leaders like Marcion were unable to cut the ties. The tenacity with which
aliens clung to this despised and offensive name is an index of its intrinsic importance to them as the name by which they were known to
God.

But all the while Christians so stubbornly affirmed continuity with
the covenant community of Israel, they affirmed a radical discontinuity
with that community. There was a link that both united and separated
the two parts of the chain. This link was not forged by a new set of
doctrines, a novel form of religious experience, or by a peculiar con-
catenation of cultural influences. It was created by the impact of unique,
unrepeatable events which had taken place in their midst. These multiple events — the ministry, death, resurrection of Jesus, the pouring out
of the Spirit, the adoption of sons — represented a single divine act,
comparable to the epoch-making events of the Exodus which had constituted the nation Israel. Apart from this act the existence of the Church
is inconceivable. From this objective work of God stems the realism of
the Christian Gospel, comparable to the realism of the Jewish tradition.
In both cases, the sole basis of community is the revealed purpose of
God. To the Jews God had spoken: " My people, my chosen, the peo-

---

[7] *The Call of Israel*, pp. 12 ff. Oxford University Press, 1934. For this, and the para-
graphs immediately following, cf. P. S. Minear, in *Journal of Religious Thought*, Vol. I,
1944, pp. 78 f.

ple which I formed for myself, that they might set forth my praise"
(Isa. 43:20, 21). To the Christians he speaks:

"Ye are an elect race, a royal priesthood, a holy nation, a people for God's
own possession, that ye may show forth the excellencies of him who called you
out of darkness into his marvellous light: who in time past were no people,
but now are the people of God" (I Peter 2:9).

The impartial observer of history has always been inclined to challenge this particularity of election as an unjustified rationalization of
self-interest and self-righteousness. That the King of the universe should
commission an obscure shepherd to manifest his hidden purpose, or
that an impotent tribe of slave laborers should be singled out to be the
light of all the nations, seems to be a fantastic case of megalomania or
a superiority complex. Is not the Biblical view of election arbitrary, artificial, and contrary to historical facts? In the arena of historical conflict,
do not individuals and groups achieve their destiny by manifestation
of superior power, wisdom, culture, or social organization? Are not the
bearers of culture those institutions that dominate a whole epoch or
continent? To attribute unique status to an obscure Semitic tribe in
exile or to the poor Christian community at Corinth seems to absolutize
their visions of grandeur. The more impotent their status, the more stupendous became the vocation which their God assigned, and the more
preposterous in the eyes of their neighbors.[8]

Yet, in some ways, the recipients of election in the Bible are more intensely aware of the absurdity of their "call" than are these neighbors.
To be singled out by the Lord of history magnifies their own sense of
unworthiness and insufficiency. They had not been chosen, they knew,
because of merit of racial or national identity, or because of wisdom,
power, or virtue. To be called is to be baffled over the reasons for that
call; those reasons remain hidden in the depths of God's will. To hear
the word, " I have chosen thee," confronts man with the most astounding possibility, arouses the keenest sense of dread, and provokes the most
decisive occasion for rebellion.

The line which divides such election from the rationalization of group
interest is the line between the worship of God and the worship of
idols. When people choose a god to support their own interests they
choose an idol. He obliges them by accepting their standard of historical

---

[8] Cf. Origen, *Against Celsus*, 4:23.

greatness, whether it be the " white man's burden " or the " American Century." He assures them of their superior power and righteousness, offering a maximum of security and a minimum of sacrifice. The idol is unable, however, to take the initiative in choosing a people. He is unable to take a people without a name and to give to them a name. He is unable to create, to redeem, to destroy. Only the true God has such power. To be sure, the history of the covenant community is filled with examples of men using their election as a private possession that enhances their egoistic ambitions and confirms their self-importance. But over and over again, a fresh call from Jahveh condemns this adultery. He appears as a judge with power to destroy any elect person who considers himself " elite," any nation that assures itself of his favor. Consciousness of election bears within itself the knowledge that God exerts full freedom to alter the boundaries of the elect community, that he can expel insiders and draw in outsiders without being arbitrary or faithless. It is this aspect of Biblical experience which sharply separates Jewish-Christian particularism from that of other racial or national groups.

THE DIRECTION OF PURPOSE

The particularism of the divine purpose is further intensified in the fact that when God calls a man, or a nation, he sends him on a special mission, to do a specific thing. From the herdsmen of Tekoa, he selects one unknown figure and impels him to go to Beth-el with a message of doom relative to that single historical occasion (Amos 7:14–17). He appears to Isaiah in the Temple and, finding him responsive, gives him a sharply defined commission. And each such specific command is invested with an absolute authority which man cannot evade. The importance of a command is not to be measured *relatively* in human terms by anticipated results, but *absolutely* by its Author's power. And every command that God gives is absolutely important. Whatever the immediate situation may be, when God calls a man, the relative is invested with the authority of the absolute. Man becomes absolutely related to the relative, because through the relative he is absolutely related to the absolute.[9] This does not mean that God's demands force every man into the stage of public life as an influential figure, making dramatic

[9] Cf. S. Kierkegaard, *Concluding Unscientific Postscript,* trans. by D. F. Swenson, pp. 352–374. 1941.

entrances while the audience waits breathlessly for his word. Frequently, the hardest command of all is to accept one's sufferings, to endure in quiet patience, to give thanks, and to glorify God. Yet this demand is no whit less urgent than the order to confront kings with defiance of their imperial policies.

Each specific command is directly related to God's ultimate purpose for the whole of creation. He is not indulging in idle sport or in impulsive action. Every call fits into his design. He works in mysterious ways, but ultimately the single thrust animating his works will be manifest, his glory will shine through all creation. It is illuminating to trace Ezekiel's conception of this underlying purpose. The most frequently recurring motif is this: " And ye shall know that I am Jahveh " (Ezek. 6:7). God wants to be recognized as the Determiner of destiny (ch. 5:17), as one who fulfills his word in power (chs. 6:10; 7:9; 12:25), as one who is able to reverse all human expectations (ch. 17:24). He wants to demonstrate the inability of other gods to fulfill their claims (ch. 6:13) and the futility of Israel in achieving its own goals (chs. 20:7; 32:15). He seeks to sanctify Israel (chs. 20:12; 37:28), to purify, forgive, deliver, and renew his people (chs. 20:44; 34:27; 36:22–38). Yet he works these marvels, not for their sake (ch. 36:22, 32) but for his own glory. In the final outcome, all nations will join Israel in the new order where God will be all in all (Isa. 19:19–25; 25:1–8). The end of each purpose, in however small a compass it may be expressed, thus lies beyond the limits of human imagination in the mysteries of God's glory. The beginning and end of each call are encompassed in the same invisible design.

THE SCOPE OF PURPOSE

Confrontation with this divine purpose thus links the immediate moment both forward and backward to the beginning and the end of creation; it also links one's special vocation to the destiny of all men and nations. Although God chooses particular men and groups for special tasks, his activity is by no means limited to these men. He achieves his purposes through people who are blind to his will. He makes the wrath of men to praise him. The fate of all nations is in his hand as dust in the balances. To each he allots a peculiar inheritance and a separate *kairos* (Deut. 2:5, 9). He even assigns to them their various objects of worship. He stirs up civil war in Egypt and sets a tyrant on the throne. He blinds their wise men and carries on the fight with their idols until, through the process of smiting and healing, Egypt will come to worship him (Isa., ch. 19). He uses pagan nations as tools to punish or free Israel, and uses Israel as a sign to the nations. Prophets foretell disasters threatening neighboring nations as well as those awaiting Israel (Amos, ch. 1; Isa., chs. 14 to 24; Micah, chs. 1; 5). All such activities are directed toward the Omega of his redemptive promise.

Implicit in such a perspective is confidence that God's purpose is active in both good and evil events. Neither good nor evil may befall a person or a nation outside the range of his control. " Shall evil befall a city, and Jahveh hath not done it " (Amos 3:6)? If people hear, it is because he has opened their ears; if they are deaf, it is because he has closed them. To claim that he will do neither good nor evil is blasphemy (Zeph. 1:12). His actions may seem unjust, his motive may be hidden from men, the results may confound expectations; but ultimately his deeds are harmonious with his word. His creation will be brought to an understanding of his will and men will give him the glory that belongs to him alone.

> " I know that thou canst do all things,
> And that no purpose of thine can be restrained "
> (Job 42:2).

How thoroughgoing is the confidence of his election! How wide-ranging are the ramifications when he utters his voice: " I have chosen thee."

These implications reach through the whole history of nature as well as of man. The invincibility of his " word " to the elect generates the faith that he is Lord of nature. A corollary of his power to say, " Thou art my people," is his right to rule over all creation. And only the disclosure of his reality to men can give them confidence that it is he, the God of Abraham and Isaac and Jacob, who created the ends of the earth. For them it is he who launches storms, blasts or blesses crops, looses " the fateful lightning " and the plagues of locusts. And his control of earthquakes and hurricanes is everywhere correlated to the one historical purpose, the manifestation of his glory. The salvation which he promises is not contingent upon the accidents of weather, not dependent upon natural forces, not subordinate to space-time limitations.

" The heavens shall vanish away like smoke, and the earth shall wax old like a garment; and they that dwell therein shall die in like manner: but my salvation shall be for ever " (Isa. 51:6).

Thus the mystery of election interpenetrates the history of all creation. But its reality is witnessed, not by abstract doctrines, but by attitudes that are produced by the impact of God's purpose in his visitations. As we have seen, the experience of the primacy of that purpose lies behind the formulation of doctrines of foreknowledge and predestination. But we have not distinguished between single and double predestination, between irresistible and indefective grace, between supralapsarianism and infralapsarianism. Nor are we interested in wrestling with those questions, for they lie outside the immediate sphere of prophetic concern.[10] This is partly because it is difficult to establish them as typical of the entire Bible, and partly because they belong, not to the realm of basic existential assumptions, but to speculative theological discussion on the part of those conducting post-mortems. Election always creates problems. But on the part of the man called, the problem is whether he will respond in faith to the responsibility thrust upon him, whether he will obey the stringent demand. On the part of the neutral bystander, the problem is one of thought, to be decided by rational analysis. The latter appears only at the boundary between the Biblical and alien perspectives. The chapter following this carries farther the exposition of these two problems.

[10] Cf. H. F. L. Cocks, *By Faith Alone*, pp. 189–192. 1943.

3

GOD SAYS, "CHOOSE"

HISTORY, in the Bible, is the story of successive divine visitations. Its mystery is the mystery of continuing divine election, wherein God discloses his purposes. Each visit and each call is oriented toward a particular end. He confronts man in the valley of decision with an uncompromising word: " Choose you this day whom ye will serve." To the Biblical mind it is impossible not to serve some god, for every decision is related in terms of origin and end to some power which transcends the immediate actor. A godless folk is inconceivable (Micah 2:11; 4:5).

" If a man does not love the *Lord* with all his mind he does not thereby become a pure reason with no loves; he simply loves something else with all his heart, soul, strength, and mind. One's loves are always deeper than his reason; and reason is always in the *employment* of some love." [1]

When God speaks he commands the total allegiance of man and the total rejection of every competing sovereignty.

This presence of responsibility reaches its maximum at the point where the consciousness of election approaches its zenith, i.e., in the personal call of prophet and apostle. Here the tension of wills becomes articulate in a sharp either-or of decision. But the lawgiver, like the prophet, reads the human situation in these same terms.

" Behold, I set before you this day a blessing and a curse: the blessing, if ye shall hearken unto the commandments . . . ; and the curse, if ye shall not hearken. . . . I have set before thee this day life and good, and death and evil " (Deut. 11:26–28; 30:15).

The orientation of both prophet and lawgiver is expressed likewise by the historical narrator: " How long go ye limping between the two

[1] Paul Ramsey, *Christianity and Society,* Vol. VIII, 1943, p. 31.

sides? if Jahveh be God, follow him; but if Baal, then follow him " (I Kings 18:21).

Beginning at this point where man is confronted with the necessity of choice, we shall proceed in this chapter to analyze the character of the divine demand and the components of human response. First in order is consideration of the immediate and total character of the demand, and the promise by which that demand is supported. Then must come an investigation of the web of influences from which man's decision emerges, and the interim situation in which it appears. Finally we must deal with the inner connections between divine power and human will.

OBEDIENCE — PRESENT AND TOTAL

Prophet, lawgiver, and historian agree in sensing the utter seriousness of the issue facing man. On its resolution hangs man's ultimate destiny. No matter how localized the immediate situation may be, there lie within it both final demand and ultimate consequence. The either-or of decision includes the either-or of destiny. A specific act of obedience is required, with no exceptions, reservations, or qualifications permitted. Only in such an act is the divine purpose realized. The Biblical ethic is an ethic of *obedience*.

Within this situation, every decision takes the form of a response to what God has done and is doing. When two persons meet, two wills begin to interpenetrate. There is a distinction between active and passive: I do something and something is done to me. " There is no act which does not imply at the same time a being acted upon. Every action is the overcoming of some opposition." [2] Whether the answer be yes or no, it is an answer to a question raised by another. When the question is asked by Jahveh, then the consciousness is inescapable that any answer is a response to him.

" Work out your own salvation with fear and trembling; for it is God who worketh in you both to will and to work, for his good pleasure " (Phil. 2:12, 13).

The Biblical ethic is an ethic of faithful *response to God's demand*.

Although every act thus registers a response to prior activity on God's

[2] K. Heim, *God Transcendent*, trans. by E. P. Dickie, p. 163. Charles Scribner's Sons, 1936. J. Hempel, *Gott und Mensch im Alten Testament*, pp. 274–298. 1936.

part, the compulsion to choose is always conceived in immediate, contemporaneous terms.

> "What is man, that thou
> Shouldest magnify him,
> And that thou shouldest set thy mind upon him,
> And that thou shouldest visit him *every morning,*
> And try him *every moment?*"
>
> (Job 7:17, 18).

Now alone is the time for repentance. Now I stand at the crossroads and must take a step down one path or another. Even though the historian tells of marvelous events in the past, it is only because he believes the present situation to be crucial. The concentration on the serious business of living *now* provides the basic motivation for retrospect. The question, What has God done? has relevance only because the same God is insistently demanding loyalty today. The plea of the historian is this:

> "Let us search and try our ways, and turn again to Jahveh" (Lam. 3:40; cf. Neh., ch. 9; Josh., ch. 24; I Kings 18:21).

The importance of immediate concerns also furnishes the motivation for scanning the future horizon. What God is about to do has direct bearing upon today's decision.

The consciousness of responsibility thus bears within itself a unique consciousness of time. Because man stands now at the crossroads, the present has a different dimension from that of either the past or the future.

> "The present is not merely just another point on the infinite line of temporal points following one another. It is a normative point, a point which in a definite way does not belong to this line at all, because it is the turning point between the past and the future. The present decrees the future; it is the immediate actuality of life, the only time in which man really acts." [3]

The ways in which man tries to mitigate the crucial character of immediate decision are legion. He may try to live in the past, cashing in on his heritage, glorying in aesthetic eulogies of his forebears. Or he may try to live in the future and to daydream about coming triumphs, to speculate about the time in which he will look back at the present moment

---

[3] R. Kroner, *How Do We Know God?* p. 111. Harper & Brothers, 1943.

and measure the consequences of his action. But God opposes these refusals to live in the present. He calls man to run the race now set before him. He does not give man leisure even to meditate upon the importance of the decision now thrust upon him; even that is a step in evasion. Nor does God offer man opportunity for analyzing the possible results of his action; that would be a postponement and in itself a negative response to God's call. The Biblical ethic remains throughout an *ethic of present decision*.

The demand of God in the present moment is not hedged about with qualifications concerning the limited response which the conditions of life make possible; it is always clear, uncompromising, absolute, as a call to total obedience. The power of God makes his purpose realizable; when man yields his heart to that purpose, God's power undergirds his own weakness in accomplishing the desired end. Thus the disjunction between good and evil is sharpest, not in the past or the future, but in this present choice.

When God encounters man, man becomes aware both of his own purpose and of God's intent at their juncture in this single situation. The resultant action records the interplay of these purposes in the form of an event. " Choose you this day " calls for action and not meditation. Obedience is too concrete to be reduced to a qualitative attribute. Man does not obey by learning the *art* or developing the *habit* of obedience. Obedience to God cannot be absorbed into a stable character pattern so that each subsequent decision becomes easier and more assured. It cannot be organized into an ethical system as one level of value in a hierarchy of values. However many times repeated, it does not become a fixed personality trait. Every present moment presents a new occasion for disobedience as well as a new need for divine help. When one objectifies obedience as a virtue to be cultivated, his choices become determined by his relation *to that virtue* rather than by relation to God. And obedience to one's own virtue is far removed from obedience to God. When transferred from the area of contemporaneous demand to the area of character development, obedience may easily be turned into its opposite.

For example, one may relate himself to his love rather than to the person loved. " He is, as we say, in love with love, or in love with himself as a lover or as loved, more than he is in love with his beloved." [4] But

---

[4] Paul Ramsey, *Christianity and Society,* Vol. VIII, 1943, p. 33.

the divine commandment to love unmasks concealed self-centeredness of this sort.

The other basic teachings of Jesus likewise resist the tendency to be reduced to progressive increments of virtue, which a man may possess and cultivate. The demand for repentance, forgiveness, sacrifice, or trust is not to be confused with the need for the gradual development of character. When repentance, for example, becomes identified with the spirit of humility, an object to be nurtured by those who seek the good life, it becomes an acquired humility in which one takes pride, a merit which distinguishes one man from another man. Conscious self-improvement via a humble spirit logically diminishes the sense of need for repentance before God. Repentance turns into its own opposite; the *virtue* of humility inhibits the *act* of true repentance, when the latter is known to be required now by the divine will.[5]

" Humility, it has been said, is pride turned wrong side out, and worn that way in order to attract more attention. Whether it be through works of individual moral perfection, or through worship, or through social action that we hope to serve God, one of our selves climbs up on the shoulders of the other self and reaches out a hand to congratulate him." [6]

This approach may throw light on the question of ethical perfectionism in the Bible. This question revolves around the precise definition of perfection and the distinction between God's command and man's fulfillment at the moment of meeting. The command for perfection is unequivocal: " Be perfect, as your heavenly Father is perfect." If perfection means that in this moment of decision it is possible to act in complete accord with God's purpose, that in this choice I can obey God rather than men, that my heart can be inclined to serve him in absolute repentance and trust — if it means this, then the whole Bible assumes its possibility — yes, its very necessity.

But this command always finds man in the situation of disobedience. Often that disobedience takes the form of false confidence in former achievement, in the assumption of a satisfied and settled relation of virtue vis-à-vis God. The demand is for perfect obedience, but no man can claim perfection. Man does not have a " nature " susceptible to preserving such an achievement; his life is a history composed of encounters with

---

[5] Cf. P. S. Minear, " The Relevance of the Message of Jesus," in *Journal of Bible and Religion,* Vol. X, 1942, p. 92.

[6] Paul Ramsey, *Christianity and Society,* Vol. VIII, 1943, pp. 33, 34.

God, in each of which man is made acutely conscious of rebellion and frustration. God's speaking presupposes incomplete obedience; but his speaking at the same time assumes the possibility of complete obedience, now, in this *event*. As Kierkegaard declares, man *is* both good and evil, but the moment of decision confronts him with the impossibility of *becoming* both good and evil.[7] And the possibility of *becoming* good produces a sense of dread, because perfect obedience requires perfect repentance in this immediate act of decision. This orientation provides the clue to understanding the paradoxical relationship of the sin and sinlessness of Jesus, and the New Testament witness that Jesus *becomes* perfectly obedient in the act of perfect renunciation, i.e., in the death of the cross. The Biblical ethic is thus characterized by the imperative *to act in complete obedience*.

Nor can man shift the burden of this dilemma to other shoulders. It is he himself who must choose good or evil, life or death, whether to worship God or Baal, whether to seek God's glory or his own. God addresses him directly, pointing his finger at his disobedience. Man's inveterate tendency to turn God's finger toward someone else boomerangs into the demand for his own repentance. To consider first the mote in a brother's eye is an evasion that God does not tolerate. Duty is not defined in general terms for other men's guidance, but in concrete terms for the hearer. " Judge not, that *ye* be not judged." The parable that seeks to answer the general question, " Who is my neighbor? " shifts from a definition of neighbor to a specific demand to become a neighbor (Luke 10:29 ff.). The claims of my neighbor on me are inescapable only because they are derived from God's claims on me. The call for repentance, forgiveness, trust, sacrifice, or love is strictly nontransferable. This serves to suggest why the heteronomous character of the Biblical ethic produces a sharper sense of personal responsibility than does the autonomous character of the Hellenistic ethic, where virtue is considered its own reward. The ever-present imperative of a living God creates a sense of compulsion greater than the four cardinal virtues of Platonic and Stoic teachings.

[7] S. Kierkegaard, *Concluding Unscientific Postscript,* trans. by D. F. Swenson, p. 376. 1941.

PROMISE AND REWARD

The centering of emphasis upon man's immediate responsibility before God is matched by a distinctive and dynamic accent upon self-regarding sanctions for human behavior. Throughout the Bible, God's imperatives are supported by promises of rewards and threats of punishment, both applied to the recipient of the word as the actor in the situation. The sanction even of altruism is usually stated in terms of the return to the one who gives rather than the advantage to the one who receives. This characteristic is most strikingly evident in the teaching of Jesus on the rewards of love and service, an observation which is both surprising and offensive to many modern interpreters, but one which can be extensively documented.[8]

But whether or not one agrees with this emphasis of Jesus, or whether one considers it an unfortunate inheritance from his predecessors, one must believe that at this point Jesus stands within the perspective common to the Bible as a whole. *The Biblical ethic is an ethic of reward.* Every choice which man makes carries with it an ineluctable recompense for that man himself, which heightens immeasurably his personal responsibility.

In understanding this ethic of reward, it is of course necessary to understand its context — the paradoxical situation of a man before God. As Jesus exemplifies perfect obedience only by perfect repentance, so also he exemplifies the realization that before God one saves his life by losing it. The promise of reward is a corollary to the demand of complete obedience. It is no accident, therefore, that the Prophet of Nazareth, in whose consciousness the divine demand reaches its maximum, is the Prophet in whose teaching appears the maximum appeal to save one's life, and that this same Prophet proclaims that the reward is wholly eschatological — a hope that involves losing one's life in this age. His own final act of obedience was thus an act of hope and confidence in God's promise.

The ethic of reward is thus intrinsically an *eschatological* ethic. The exhortations in the Torah are oriented toward the promises revealed to

[8] Cf. H. J. Cadbury, *The Peril of Modernizing Jesus,* p. 101. 1937; P. S. Minear, *And Great Shall Be Your Reward,* pp. 43–50. 1941.

the patriarchs and to Moses; the catechetical instructions of early Christians are oriented toward the imminent judgment and the Kingdom of God. The promise is the ground of the law, whether it be assurance of return from Exile or the proclamation of the returning Messiah, and whether the law be the Decalogue or the Sermon on the Mount. One must act now in such a way as to inherit the promise. In almsgiving one lays up treasure in heaven. Amos' prophecy, " Seek ye me, and ye shall live," reflects the same assumptions as Jesus' plea, " Seek ye first his kingdom; . . . and all these things shall be added unto you." In their continuing dialogue, God and man become most aware of each other at the point of converging and diverging wills. The purpose of each is intrinsically future-regarding and future-creating. In his act, man registers the hope by which he lives. If that hope coincides with God's, then he is blessed; if not, the future will but disclose the vanity of present effort.

> " A man's heart deviseth his way;
> But Jahveh directeth his steps "
> (Prov. 16:9).

The *presentness* of this future is what makes present decision so decisive. The intensity of this *present future* is expressed eschatologically in terms of its nearness. A distant future, which articulates a sense of futurity disjoined from the present, tends to diminish the eternal consequences of the present step. In the Bible, consciousness of the future is never expressed in terms of that " far-off divine event, to which the whole creation moves," but is always articulated in proclamation of that imminent divine judgment in which the vanity or fruitfulness of this present act is disclosed. Similarly, it is not primarily a vision of the ultimate end of the " *whole creation* " in general, but the certainty of the immediate end of *this particular creature* (individual or group) that generates the serious urgency of man's present act. Always eschatological, the Biblical ethic is an ethic of an imminent *eschaton*.

To sum up the ubiquitous aspects of the Biblical ethic: When God visits and chooses man, he communicates a demand for decision. Man apprehends his responsibility in terms of ultimate seriousness. He must respond in immediate, absolute obedience; nor can he transfer to others the task laid upon himself. The demand is supported by promises of reward in the future, an imminent future linked directly to the present hope.

THE GENEALOGY OF ACTION

This description of the human situation, however, is more simple
and clear than is usually the case for the man who finds himself involved in a complex historical situation. God's purpose is not easily recognized, and, if recognized, is not readily achieved. Likewise, man's
purpose is hidden in a maze of conflicting motives and contradictory
actions. In the case of both divine and human wills, the very manifestation of purpose reveals a hiatus between actuality and possibility, an
interim between the present realization and the imminent *eschaton*. In
gaining man's obedience, God faces the problem of dealing with secret
desires and secret sins. And in seeking God's end, man faces the problem
of understanding the present as an interim in the realization of the
divine purpose. To grasp the complexity of this situation calls for deeper
analysis of the character of purpose itself.

An invisible will becomes visible through two channels: word and
deed. In the Bible each of these has a significance which seems strange
to outsiders. A word is more than a word; it is a bearer of power, a projection of the authority and purpose of him who speaks. Once uttered,
it produces an effect that cannot be canceled. Jacob blesses the wrong
son and cannot revoke his blessing (Gen., ch. 27). Covenant vows are
sacred, even when undertaken by accident or deception; alliances by
treaty with another nation are tantamount to worshiping the god of
that nation (Isa. 19:23). An oath is binding: to swear " as God lives " and
then to break the vow is equivalent to denying God's existence and
power. The dread of broken oaths, of shattered covenants, is symptomatic
of the authority inherent in a word, as the objective index to a man's
purpose. He *is,* in fact, his purpose. His word manifests his direction
and destiny as they express themselves in the present.

But deed is a more accurate index than word. Jesus' complaint, " Why
call ye me, Lord, Lord, and do not the things which I say? " is the complaint of God throughout the Old Testament.

" They bend their tongue, as it were their bow, for falsehood. . . . Their
tongue is a deadly arrow . . . : one speaketh peaceably to his neighbor with
his mouth, but in his heart he layeth wait for him " (Jer. 9:3–8).

This explains the constant insistence upon integrity, the coincidence of
word and deed. The Hebrew word for " hear " is also the word for

"obey." The truth is not something thought or spoken, but something done. The way man walks is sure evidence of what he really says.

"For all the peoples walk every one in the name of his god; and we will walk in the name of Jahveh for ever and ever" (Micah 4:5).

Lying deeper than word and deed is man's heart, the home of his desires, where his ultimate trust is determined. "Where . . . [man's] treasure is, there will . . . [his] heart be." And the removing of one's heart from God is the source of rebellion (Isa. 29:13). The inclination of a man's heart is determined by that power in which he trusts, and the outcome of all his labor depends on that inclination. To lean upon one's own understanding, to make one's own strength or virtue the object of confidence, assures the futility of all action.

"He shall be like the heath in the desert, and shall not see when good cometh, but shall inhabit the parched places in the wilderness, a salt land and not inhabited" (see Jer. 17:5 f.).

No king is saved by the size of his army (Ps. 33:16 f.). Power belongs to God, who alone can establish a man's goings (Ps. 37:23; 62:11).

THE INTERIM SITUATION

Present existence is thus always marked by tragic contradictions in man's purposive activity: the contradiction between word and deed, and the deeper contradiction between man's heart and his true destiny. Both contradictions produce the frustration of hopes. Both aggravate the alienation between the two wills, so that knowledge of God's design becomes locked in a sealed book (Isa. 29:11). All hope for a realignment of wills stems from God's penetration into the secrets of man's desires (Isa. 29:15, 16) and from a fresh invasion of man's consciousness which fashions his heart anew according to God's creative intention. Only the fresh impact of his purpose can recall a man to his appointed time (Jer. 8:7) and his immediate vocation. "Open thou my lips; and my mouth shall show forth thy praise." The fatal contradictions in present existence can be resolved only by a repetition of God's creative act. And herein lies the confidence in the future held by the man of faith.

The demand of God always finds man in this interim of alienation, but this interim is challenged by the promise of imminent doom and dawn. Consciousness of alienation of heart parallels in intensity consciousness of God's purpose; consciousness of imminent judgment is inseparable from confidence in imminent renewal of heart. In the future visitation which now presses upon this present, God will reveal his purpose and thus restore harmony between man's word and deed, and between man's heart and God's. Only with the perfecting of such integrity does God establish man's " goings " so that in all the vicissitudes of history he " shall not be moved." " I will give them a heart to know me, that I am Jahveh " (Jer. 24:7).

But God's purpose, like man's, is hidden from external gaze. Like man's, it is manifested in word and deed. Each of these is therefore invested with immeasurable significance. His word is charged with his authority and power; by it he creates; by it he exerts sovereignty. When he speaks to the prophets, his word does not return to him void (Isa. 55: 11). When he swears by himself, that oath is absolutely certain of fulfillment. But he does not need to swear, because, unlike man's, his promise never fails. In him there is perfect co-ordination of knowledge, speech, desire, and action.

"I am God, and there is none like me; declaring the end from the beginning, and from ancient times things that are not yet done; saying, My counsel shall stand, and I will do all my pleasure. . . . I have purposed, I will also do it " (Isa. 46:9–11; also I Kings 8:15 f.; I Chron. 16:14 f.; Neh. 9:8).

Such integrity of word and deed is the very substance of his righteousness, faithfulness, and truth. Lack of such integrity is characteristic of idols. Idols are illusory realities, deceptive in their promises because they lack power to fulfill them. Only the true God speaks and fulfills his promise.

Yet, in the effecting of God's intention, at least from man's standpoint, there is often a hiatus between his word and his deed. The tragic character of present existence stems from this deferment; the present is always an interim between creative word and redemptive deed. The hope for the future lies in the termination of this interim.

"I am Jahveh; I will speak, and the word that I shall speak shall be performed; it shall be no more deferred: for in your days, O rebellious house, will I speak the word, and will perform it " (Ezek. 12:25).

In this sense, the ethic of the whole Bible is an ethic for the present interim, the interim between God's word and his deed.

And it is important to note that there is an inner, intimate correspondence between this interim in God's activity and the interim in man's personal destiny separating his present status from that end for which he is created. In the existential consciousness, these two interims fuse into one. And always this interim is short; always its brevity is proportionate to the intensity of awareness of God's revealed word. "For a *small* moment have I forsaken thee; but with great mercies will I gather thee " (Isa. 54:7). Isaiah, Jeremiah, Jesus, and Paul agree with the witness of Ezekiel: " The days are at hand, and the fulfilment of every vision." This explains why prophets mix up the present and future tenses in their prophecies in a way that baffles modern commentators. The prophetic *fore*telling is a *forth*telling, and vice versa. And this alternation is perfectly intelligible in the present existential moment and perfectly bewildering in our reflective efforts to comprehend the past. (Compare the current discussions of Isa., chs. 43; 44; Ezek., ch. 12; and also the teachings of Jesus, Paul, and John concerning the present-future Kingdom.)

Reinhold Niebuhr has attempted to describe this interim character of Biblical thought by making the distinction between " in principle " and " in fact." In the following excerpt what is said of history after Christ may be applied to the parenthetical character of present existence throughout the Bible:

> "In thus conceiving history after Christ as an interim between the disclosure of its true meaning and the fulfillment of that meaning, between the revelation of divine sovereignty and the full establishment of that sovereignty, a continued element of inner contradiction in history is accepted as its perennial characteristic. Sin is overcome *in principle* but not *in fact*." [9]

Although this problem is discussed more fully below, we may here suggest two reservations: (1) The Biblical distinction between *promise* and *fulfillment* is preferable to the distinction between *principle* and *fact*. *Promise* is more congenial to the existential viewpoint than *principle;* it is more personal, concrete, direct. God's word is an act, wherein he releases power; it is a fact which *now* actually defines and determines human destiny; his word is now in the process of returning to

[9] *Nature and Destiny of Man,* Vol. II, p. 49. (The italics are mine.) Charles Scribner's Sons, 1943.

him — not void, but filled with his judgment and glory. It now represents the overcoming of sin in fact (Isa. 44:21–23). (2) Since this interim category for viewing history is found in the Old Testament, the effect of the new word-deed in Christ must be so defined as to bring out the distinctively new promise and new fulfillment. Perhaps a step in this direction would be to define the new revelation not alone by the statement, " Love must continue to be suffering love rather than triumphant love," [10] but also, in a dialectic fashion, by the statement that suffering love is now manifested as triumphant love, as the very event in which God's power produces joy and peace. Thus the cross is seen as the true fulfillment of the two-sided prophetic hope: (1) a final removal of the contradiction between God's promise and its fulfillment; (2) a final removal of the contradiction between man's heart (expressed in word-deed) and God's creative will. In dying with Christ, one is raised to new life with him. The cross can thus be viewed as a power-laden word-act which, ever repeated, resolves the tensions of the present without destroying the hope for the time when all the kingdoms of the earth will become the Kingdom of our Lord.

This apparent digression is simply an illustration of the point that man's decision stems from the interrelationship of the present and the future, from the mingling of divine and human purposes in togetherness-and-tension. The inclination of man's heart leads him to rebellion, thus deferring the consummation of the Creator's purpose; and the only salvation from rebellion and its consequent frustration lies in the revelation and fulfillment of God's promise.

ELECTION AND FREEDOM

The observations concerning the interdependence of man's obedience and God's promise, an interdependence in which the primacy of the divine power enhances man's sense of responsibility, raises the age-old problem of the precise relation between God's part and man's in every event. In secular and speculative thought, the problem is that of the apparent logical incompatibility of divine election and human freedom. How can an action be at the same moment an expression both of God's power and of human responsibility? The treatment in Chapter 2 underscored the sovereignty of God's purpose in determining the course

[10] *Ibid.*

of history; the emphasis in this chapter has been placed upon the inescapable obligation of each creature. Must we posit the autonomy of man's will if this responsibility is to be real?

The presence of the problem cannot be denied. The apparent contradiction is present in every book of the Bible, is axiomatic in all Biblical thinking, and becomes most sharply articulated in the experience of prophets and apostles. The men who were most obsessed by the priority and power of God's activity were most seriously absorbed in the dilemmas of human responsibility. "He that heareth, let him hear; and he that forbeareth, let him forbear" (Ezek. 3:27). But it is God who opens his ears or closes them to the message of life. The single act of *hearing* represents the interpenetration of the wills of God and man.

The Biblical histories are filled with events which are interpreted in terms of both divine foreknowledge and human responsibility. Rehoboam consciously chooses to repress his people by unrestrained violence; his choice is attributed both to evil counselors and to God's desire to fulfill his word (I Kings 12:15). Ahab is enticed into a disastrous foreign war both by the advice of false prophets and by God's design, for God persuades the lying spirit to mislead these false prophets (I Kings, ch. 22). Solomon establishes his regime by a ruthless purge of rival claimants and by the help of God. His wisdom, power, riches, honor are at once a divine gift and his own achievement (I Kings, ch. 2). When Shishak chooses to support Jeroboam for obvious political reasons, it is in response to God's leading. God places a good impulse in Artaxerxes' heart toward the Jews, creates political favor for Ezra, stimulates public opinion in favor of releasing the exiled Jews, and gives to successive Persian rulers a benevolent attitude toward them (Ezra 7:27 f.; 9:8–13). So, also, he puts it into the heart of Nehemiah to return to Jerusalem, inclines the king to grant him leave of absence, and stirs up the hearts of the repatriates to rebuild the wall (Neh. 2:8, 12, 18; 7:5). The wall is built by both their labor and God's support (Neh. 6:16). A still more pointed example is the common early Christian assumption that in the death of Jesus the sin of his opponents, the wiles of the devil, the specific intention of God, and the responsible obedience of Jesus himself were all at work.[11]

The omnipresence in the Bible of this problem of election and freedom cannot be contested; the most striking fact, however, is not its

[11] Cf. K. Heim, *op. cit.*, pp. 31–33.

ubiquity but the lack of viewing its presence *as a problem*. Why were Biblical writers not disturbed by what seems to modern readers a glaring contradiction? Why did they assume so easily that when God meets man and addresses him, man becomes conscious of both election and freedom? Why did they sense no incongruity in speaking of the same event in terms both of God's action and of man's?

The very absence of objective discussion of the problem indicates the antitheses of the two perspectives, in only one of which does the problem arise. Such absence underscores the contradictory assumptions and approaches which separate the speculative and existential views of history. Standing at the perspective center of the divine-human encounter, Biblical writers assume that the essence of every situation lies in the interpenetration of personal purposes, that each event is the outcome of the confluence and conflict of wills, that man the *actor* is an actor precisely because he must *respond* to the various purposes which are acting upon him. He assumes that man the *spectator* will never understand any event, will never see the hand of God in it.

> " Blind unbelief is sure to err,
> And scan his work in vain;
> God is his own interpreter,
> And he will make it plain." [12]

Perhaps it may advance the understanding of the Biblical attitude if we suggest three factors involved in this problem, which indicate why the spectator and the actor stand in different worlds, speak a different language, and are unable to convince each other. The first of these three is the contrast between cause-effect and purpose-end orientations. The spectator seeks to understand an event by cutting away the separate causes, recovering and weighing the impact of each cause in isolation from the others. On the other hand, in response to God's visit, the actor must come to a decision by choosing ends. Made aware of a sovereign will, he must shape his purpose by taking sides among competing wills. He must respond to a Person, and not to a web of impersonal causes. To analyze the causes requires postponement of response, requires objective isolation of various forces, requires careful balancing of the relative degree of good and evil. To respond to a will requires the sharing of purpose, requires definite answer now, either of opposition or of surrender.

[12] William Cowper.

God's command inhibits man from viewing his history as a chain of causes and effects by catapulting him into a drama of doubt and faith, rebellion and resignation. Consciousness of God's sovereignty produces rather than prevents the consciousness of responsibility.[13]

A second observation lies in the difference in the point from which the *past* is viewed. In his effort to separate the divine from the human components in a single event, the spectator reflects upon that event as *past*. To separate God's action from man's action presupposes a complete and artificial disjunction between the human and the divine. To the actor, life is an activity of subjects in the present. Here the past is present not so much in the sense of causes determining results as in the sense of the history of persons defining the present situation in terms of guilt and memory. The past is real only as it is included in this living present, shaping the context of decision but not modifying the necessity of responsible choice.[14] But the attempt to analyze that past in speculative terms is bound to reduce to an abstraction the concrete meaning which it originally had to the men involved. "The past always is mediated; it is no longer life, but only the *image* of former life."[15] In the past, man's freedom is no longer discernible because the *becoming* has been frozen into an unchanging *become*.

A third observation is that which E. Cailliet makes in discussing Pascal:

"Our salvation is of God. Let us work out our salvation. Being a student of the Bible, Pascal quite evidently recognized the cogency of these two affirmations, which seem contradictory *only when viewed at the level of nature.*"[16]

The speculative problem of election and freedom presupposes an estimate of nature different from that presupposed by the prophet speaking with authority. The prophet, when confronted by his call, becomes more aware of his history than of his nature. He may ask, "What is man, that thou art mindful of him? and the son of man, that thou visitest him?" But for an answer to this question he does not look in the direction of natural law. He does not seek to formulate a philosophical anthropology. He does not visualize the concrete situation by placing it

[13] Cf. R. E. Cushman, in *Journal of Religion*, Vol. XXV, 1945, pp. 197–212.
[14] Cf. K. Heim, *op. cit.*, p. 197 f.
[15] R. Kroner, *How Do We Know God?* p. 111. 1943; cf. also Heim, *op. cit.*, pp. 111–125.
[16] *Pascal, Genius in the Light of Scripture*, p. 77. (The italics are mine.) The Westminster Press, 1945.

within the orbit of nature. On the contrary, he views nature within the orbit of the situation vis-à-vis God in which he stands, and is led to see all creation as sharing the history of rebellion-and-return (Rom., chs. 1; 8). His understanding of immediate responsibility is not derived from his investigation of the impersonal laws governing nonhuman phenomena, although he may be prompted to contrast the behavior of men and birds at the point of obedience to God's will (Jer. 8:7). One should be wary of all generalizations, yet one might affirm of the prophetic view: " Nature does not have a nature; it has a history." And this history is the history of creation and rebellion. Before God, man represents this history; in the decision which confronts him he shares with all creation the responsibility of obedience. What Bultmann says of Jesus in this connection is applicable to his prophetic predecessors:

" In the concrete situation, that is, in this world, in this nature, man stands before God; there is no need of escaping beyond the present or outside of nature. Nowhere does Jesus say that nature is evil, that therefore one ought not to have this or ought not to do that. The will of the man who is disobedient is evil; it is for him to surrender, not to deny nature. Jesus . . . does not have the concept ' nature ' at all. . . . Rather, that which we call nature comes into consideration only so far as it characterizes that present condition of men which is determined by the necessity of decision. That is, nature as ' objective,' which can be observed separately from the action of men, does not come in question, except as it presents the manifold possibilities for human conduct. Hence not even God Himself can be considered under the category of nature." [17]

These three observations are offered, not in the effort to solve the insoluble riddle of election and freedom, but to describe the boundary between the Biblical and non-Biblical points of view. On this boundary these are signposts pointing to the center where the God who chooses forces men to choose.

The problem with which men of the Bible wrestle is not that of the logical incompatibility in causal analysis of predestination and freedom; rather it is the problem of contradiction of wills. It is not a result of the fact that man and God are separate causes in an objective sequence of events, but of the fact that " I and Thou " are now working at cross-purposes. As an individual, my problem in any situation is rightly to discern God's intention and obediently to respond to it, so that my destiny may

[17] *Jesus and the Word*, p. 102. Charles Scribner's Sons, 1934.

be assured through the coincidence of purpose and power. The word of God confronts me with the realization that my knowledge and obedience, on which destiny depends, are both jeopardized by the active presence of other-than-divine purposes which contend for my loyalty in the arena of decision.

It is thus that God's address drives from my consciousness the illusion that the choice lies between his power and my own autonomy, for he makes clear that the assertion of autonomy is simply the demonstration of my desire to serve another god's deceptive compulsions.

> "Since Adam, being free to choose,
> Chose to imagine he was free
> To choose his own necessity,
> Lost in his freedom, Man pursues
> The shadow of his images." [18]

Here, as elsewhere in the Bible, appears an irreducible mystery in personal relationships, for in his dealings with men God is wholly incomparable. His omnipotence is different from all human conceptions of power. Finite power can operate only by making its subjects dependent upon itself. One man, by the exercise of his power, can never make another wholly free.

"Omnipotence alone can take itself back while giving, and this relationship is nothing else but the independence of the recipient. God's omnipotence is therefore His goodness." [19]

The greatest good for man lies in serving the God who alone can make him fully free. Finite gods offer to make man free, but end by making him dependent upon finite power that is ultimately deceptive and futile.[20]

[18] W. H. Auden, "For the Time Being," in *Collected Poetry*, p. 420. Random House, 1945. Reprinted by permission.

[19] S. Kierkegaard, *Journals*, trans. by A. Dru, p. 180. Oxford University Press, 1938.

[20] This contrast between illusory and true freedom receives a clear analysis in H. F. L. Cocks, *By Faith Alone*, pp. 81–92. 1943.

4

MEN SEEK OTHER LOVERS

AS CONTINUING testimony to " his mighty acts," history is the autobiography of God, for he is the major actor who determines its beginning, course, and end. But history also discloses the operation of contrary purposes and powers.

" It is not only God's will that is to be found in history. There is another will to be found there, which is more opposed to the will of God than the brightest brightness is to the darkest darkness." [1]

Within the web of decision-making, man is involved in this dramatic conflict between personal forces that seek to attract his loyalty and dominate his destiny. Historical events exteriorize the course of spiritual struggle, wherein the rhythm of rebellion-and-return produces a symphonic counterpoint of tragic frustration and renewed hope. Man rebels, is carried into captivity, returns from exile, and starts anew to build the Temple. History begins with man's rebellion and ends only when that rebellion has been finally quelled; at every point it is marked by a denial of God's original design and a reassertion of his *eschaton*.

CONTEXT OF CONFLICT

Implicit in this perspective are four omnipresent assumptions: (1) It is impossible for man in every action not to serve some god. (2) Jahveh's claim on his elect is absolutely exclusive — " Thou shalt have no other gods before me." (3) The impact of this claim reveals the fact that man is now actually whoring " after the strange gods." (4) The encounter always precipitates a controversy between a jealous Husband and an

[1] G. Aulén, *Revelation*, ed. by J. Baillie and H. Martin, p. 288. The Macmillan Company, 1937.

adulterous wife, the purpose of which is reconciliation. In this chapter we will examine these axioms further and explore their implications. The starting point must be that same perspective center which has provided the angle of vision in the preceding chapters.

In immediate personal experience, men are always involved in events in which the primary constituents are intangible influences and forces. God's controversy with his creation, apprehended from within, can be described only in dramatic narratives in which the key actors are invisible. Apprehended from without, these narratives seem to partake of the characteristics of myth. To the Biblical writer, the story is the only way of communicating the truth; to the analyst, the story belongs in the realm of mythology.

" Christianity is entirely mythological, as indeed all religion is, and Christian myths express the deepest and most central realities of the spiritual world. It is high time to cease being ashamed of Christian mythology and trying to free it from myth. No system of theological or metaphysical concepts can destroy Christian mythology, and it is precisely this collection of myths which constitutes its greatest reality, for it becomes an abstraction as soon as it is freed from them. . . . It is only myths which can explain life." [2]

As Berdyaev finds the language of mythological struggle indigenous to personal spiritual experience, so also A. J. Toynbee finds it peculiarly adapted to the description of the rise and fall of civilizations. Surveying the twenty-one civilizations known to man, he finds in their rise and fall a rhythm to which the forms of mythological drama can alone do justice. And among the various myths which articulate the motifs of time's tapestry, the Biblical myth of a history-long conflict between God and Satan is defended as most adequate and most valid.[3]

Biblical myth, however, does not emerge from man's effort to reduce the entire *course* of history to the dimensions of a single formula; rather, it articulates man's effort to understand the *source* of history, the hidden springs of personal choices whence historical events originate. Man is caught in the cross fire of conflicting loyalties. God's command is bitterly contested, and man can discover no point in place or time whither he can flee from the battle. His immediate choice is at once an *outcome* of the prior alignment of forces, an *incident* in a larger battle, and an

    [2] N. Berdyaev, *Freedom and the Spirit*, pp. 24, 71–74. Charles Scribner's Sons, 1935. Cf. also *The Meaning of History*, pp. 51, 52. 1936.
    [3] A. J. Toynbee, *A Study of History*, Vol. I, pp. 271–288. 1934–1939.

event that determines his fate. The source of history — his own dealings with God — produces the course of history. Each separate battle, on however isolated a sector, discloses to the participant the age-long proportions of the war. The sense of the seriousness of his choice makes him view the whole drama with deadly earnestness. This mood of urgency pervades the Biblical myths, making them qualitatively different from most non-Biblical myths.

Another distinctive mark of Biblical myth is the omnipresent stubbornness of rebellion. The Bible is the story of perpetual revolt, a striking monument both to human intransigency and to divine persistence. No other national saga, the deposit of millennial history of an entire people, has ever been so rigorous in its criticism of the culture which produced it. Century after century, prophets apprehended a judgment more severe on Israel than on other folk. Israel suffers from a chronic malady, variously described as a stiff neck, a forehead of stone, stuffed-up ears, uncircumcised heart. Every generation backslides (though history is never pictured as one long decline); the recurring testimony is, " We have sinned with our fathers." No generation is encouraged to feel superior to preceding generations. The charge of Stephen, " Ye do always resist the Holy Spirit," can be duplicated a hundredfold in the Old Testament.

Nor is an individual ever freed from potential or actual involvement in rebellion. In none of the Old Testament legends is there a character who wholly pleases God by perfect obedience throughout his lifetime. Even the most revered figures of the past, such as Moses, David, Solomon, and Elijah, are subject to the same sins as ordinary men. " There is none that doeth good, no, not . . . one." " In thy sight no man living is righteous." " If thou, Jahveh, shouldest mark iniquities, . . . who could stand? " The aphorism of Jacques Todd is eminently true even of eulogistic legends in the Bible: " The biography of the saint never obliterates the autobiography of the sinner."

And it is precisely the men most conscious of God's election who become most conscious of deep-lying roots of sin. Thus the testimony, " Thou art he that took me out of the womb," is paralleled by the lament, " I was brought forth in iniquity; and in sin did my mother conceive me " (Ps. 51:5; cf. Ps. 53:3; 106:6; 130:3; 143:2). Neither cry envisages an analysis of natural causes; neither sets forth a doctrine of the " nature " of man; both describe the history of a man who is torn between contrary purposes. Regarding the typical Biblical man, Thomas Mann's phrase is quite apt: " He does not live aright who does not and cannot despair." At some points the witness of George Fox is also relevant:

" I found that there were two thirsts in me; the one after the creatures, to get help and strength there; and the other after the Lord, the Creator . . . I saw all the world could do me no good . . . for nothing gave me comfort but the Lord by his power . . . I saw the great love of God . . . I saw death, how it had passed upon all men, and oppressed the seed of God in man, and in me. . . . There seemed to be two pleading in me; questionings arose in my mind . . . I was tempted again to despair." [4]

FORMS OF REBELLION

Another characteristic of Biblical thinking is resolute resistance to the tendency to equate rebellion with a single personal or social vice. Biblical writers were not concerned with discovering, by the process of comparative analysis, the root cause of sin. They were not concerned with arranging all sins in carefully defined hierarchies. Any act may be an expression of disobedience; any road may lead away from God's purpose. Man is not aided in locating infection by standard tests; he does not measure the extent of sickness by external criteria. As Professor Snaith insists, sin is not transgression of law but personal revolt.[5] Sin is a specifically religious category everywhere related to the context of a particular creature's meeting with a particular God. No definition of sin *per se* apart from this context is possible. The very act of definition may be directed to reduce the existential tension of human choice. It may seek to replace qualitative purposes by quantitative causes, relaxing the character of each individual sin as a new " leap." [6] Rebellion, like repentance, is never simply a state, but an act in which I respond to an act of Another.

Though the nature of rebellion cannot be objectified in this manner, it is frequently described in the Bible in recurrent patterns — each of which reflects the primacy of unique personal relationships. Thus, where the primal bond is imaged as that of son and father, disloyalty is imaged in family terms:

[4] *Journal*, ed. by W. Armistead. Seventh edition, Vol. I, pp. 56–57. 1852.
[5] *The Distinctive Ideas of the Old Testament*, p. 62. 1944.
[6] Cf. S. Kierkegaard, *Concept of Dread*, trans. by W. Lowrie, pp. 27–32. 1944.

"I have nourished and brought up children, and they have rebelled against me. The ox knoweth his owner, and the ass his master's crib; but Israel doth not know, my people doth not consider" (Isa. 1:2 f.).

Frequent is the charge of broken marriage bonds:

"They say, If a man put away his wife, and she go from him, and become another man's, will he return unto her again? will not that land be greatly polluted? But thou hast played the harlot with many lovers" (Jer. 3:1).

Sometimes these metaphors get strangely mixed:

"Return, O backsliding children, saith Jahveh; for I am a husband unto you" (Jer. 3:14; cf. ch. 5:7).

Occasionally the people appear as confirmed thieves:

"As the thief is ashamed when he is found, so is the house of Israel ashamed; they, their kings, their princes, and their priests, and their prophets; who say to a stock, Thou art my father; and to a stone, Thou hast brought me forth. . . . According to the number of thy cities are thy gods, O Judah" (Jer. 2:26–28).

Even where a metaphor that seems impersonal is employed, the personal bond remains primary:

"My people have committed two evils: they have forsaken me, the fountain of living waters, and hewed them out cisterns, broken cisterns, that can hold no water" (Jer. 2:13).

The most oft-repeated descriptions of rebellion are apostasy, idolatry, adultery. It is, of course, easy to interpret these as purely cultic and ceremonial irregularities, the formal bowing down to stocks and stones. It is easy to equate them with externalized habits, the taboos of a mores-bound community. But such interpretations are far too hasty and superficial. Naturally, any people has both mores and taboos. And it is inevitable that it sanction these attitudes by appeal to its god. Idolatry does involve specific acts, and these acts take their meaning from contemporary prejudices. But the distinctive character of idolatry in the Bible becomes apparent in the fact that any act may be idolatrous and that the root of idolatry is located in man's intention. Even the ostensible worship of the true God may be idolatrous. Thus any list of idolatrous acts would be endless. Consider, for example, a small sampling from the Exilic prophets:

Pride in one's wisdom;
Trust in one's beauty;
Self-sufficiency in power;
Reliance on horses and chariots;
Trust in foreign alliances;
Claims of personal innocence;
Confidence of security — " I shall not be moved ";
Immunity to God's demands — " Thou wilt not require it ";
Immunity to God's vision — He " will not see ";
Denial of God's reality — " There is no God ";
Denial of God's power — " He shall not see our latter end ";
Denial of God's control over present happenings;
Measurement of God by human standards;
Deceitfulness of speech;
Indifference to fatherless and needy;
Gaining wealth by social injustice.

These are but a few of the protean forms which idolatry assumes. As a concrete possibility in every moment of decision, the sin of idolatry creates dread on the part of man as he stands naked before a God whose thoughts and ways are higher than his. Man shudders before its power and pervasiveness. It threatens his prospect as it has perverted his retrospect. For, looking toward the past, he sees the futility of behavior that cuts across the grain of divine intention, and looking toward the future, he anticipates the punishment of divided loyalties. He sees the idol as a dynamic historical influence which infects and aborts the fulfillment of hopes.

APPEARANCE OF THE DEVIL

The role which the idol plays in the Old Testament is taken in the New Testament by Satan. Demonology develops late among the Jews, as shown by the infrequent references to Satan in the Old Testament. When he appears in the Old Testament it is as a messenger of God, always acting at God's command and never on his own volition. He does not rebel against God's authority, and has no private reasons for tempting man or delighting in his downfall. His work is to accuse man, to try his patience, to put obstacles in his way, to test his endurance. Because of the important offices in the life of man, he has a place in the heavenly hierarchy. He is " Creation's errand-boy creator " who has " a proper place, which is, to push us into grace."

Poor cheated Mephistopheles,
Who think you're doing as you please
In telling us by doing ill
To prove that we possess free will,
Yet do not will the will you do,
For the Determined uses you,
Creation's errand-boy creator,
Diabolus egredietur
Ante pedes eius — foe,
But so much more effective, though,
Than our well-meaning stupid friends
In driving us towards good ends.[7]

Compared to the Old Testament, the New Testament mythos assigns to Satan a role far more dramatic, a role as prominent as that of God or Christ, as real as that of Peter or Judas.[8] He is at least a semi-independent prince of this age, under whose tyrannical authority men suffer. He is an enemy of God and the chief adversary of God's Anointed. His kingdom resists at every point the encroachment of God's sovereignty. The battle is joined in both heaven and earth. God casts him from heaven " as lightning," and sends the Messiah to banish him from earth and to give his followers release from their captivity to him. But Jesus' victory over Satan is not an easy one. At the outset, Satan tries to dissuade him from his mission by most alluring bribes. Surmounting this temptation through reliance on God's word, Jesus invades the enemy's province and " by the finger of God " casts out Satan from his strongholds. Satan retaliates by counterattacks, by deceiving the disciples, by planting in their minds false expectations, by tempting them to treacherous betrayals and denials. He finally strikes his deadliest blow on Calvary. But God turns this apparent success into Satan's final and irretrievable defeat by exalting Jesus to new power and authority in heaven.

This victory is decisive for those who, in dying with Christ, find his power channeled through their lives. To them the Kingdom comes with power to quench " all the fiery darts of the evil one." Yet against them, Satan turns all his wiles, his deceptions, his violence. He tries to foment civil war within the Church and bitter persecution from without. Though his power is overcome wherever men call on the name of the

---

[7] W. H. Auden, *Collected Poetry*, p. 277. Random House, 1945. Reprinted by permission.
[8] Cf. my essay " Satan Returns from Holiday," in *Religion in Life*, 1943, Vol. XII, pp. 187 ff.

Messiah, his control over this age continues undiminished until the end when Jesus Christ returns from heaven to banish him into the abyss. The nearer that event, the more energetically he roams about as a lion " seeking whom he may devour." Until that final defeat, the Church stands on the firing line, suffering and triumphing through a power not its own.

On this point we must agree with David Friedrich Strauss:

" The whole idea of the Messiah and his kingdom is as impossible without the counterpart of a kingdom of demons with a personal ruler at its head as the north pole of the magnet is impossible without the south pole. If Christ has come to destroy the works of the Devil, there would be no need for him to come if there were no devil." [9]

Of this elaborate mythology there are only scattered intimations in the Old Testament, and they occur in the latest writings. It would be quite false to maintain that the whole Bible shares all these views. Paul used a vocabulary and a set of conceptual images far different from those of Jeremiah. But it would be wrong to underestimate the continuity between the Testaments in this area of thought. If one focuses attention upon the conceptual form of beliefs, the differences are magnified; but if one focuses attention upon the existential content of faith, the differences dwindle in importance. In terms not of *what* man believes but of *how* he is related to idols or demons, the testimonies of Paul and Jeremiah radiate from the same center. Analyzed by *Religionsgeschichtliche* methods, the origins of Christian demonology may be traced to Iranian and Babylonian mythologies, mediated by the apocalypses of late Judaism. But analyzed in terms of personal experience, the origins lie in the perspective center of divine-human intercourse. Immediate awareness of Satan's power is basically akin to the prophetic apprehension of the history-long conflict between God and his rebellious sons. From man's side, demonology is but the form for expressing the interior struggle between the evil and the good intention, so central to Jewish anthropology. From God's side, it expresses the perpetual struggle with idols, which finds enduring expression in the Decalogue itself. The radii of theological ideas diverge, but the center in experience remains the same. Fuller treatment of the divergent development appears in Chapter 14, for that development keeps pace with shifting eschatological expectations. Here it will suffice to suggest the thesis which is more fully expounded there. New

[9] *Die Christliche Glaubenslehre*, Vol. II, p. 15. 1840–1841.

Testament apocalyptic simply makes explicit what was already implicit in the prophetic view of history; likewise the later demonology, which is everywhere in the New Testament dependent upon eschatology, makes explicit what was already implicit in the understanding of the human situation. When God confronts men they become aware of rebellion, occasioned by the activity of purposes contrary to the Creator's purpose. As this rebellion continues century after century in more aggravated form, men are forced to reckon with its pervasiveness, its persistence, its interrelatedness, and its power. Recourse to a more elaborate myth is thus a product of historical experience, seen from the vantage point of faith. It is as if a ray of light were passed first through a prism with a narrow refraction and then through a prism with a wide refraction. The bands of refracted color may be wider and more sharply distinguishable, but the colors may be the same and the origin of the light the same.

SATAN'S KINGDOM

One mark of the underlying unity throughout the Bible is the continuity of Satan's functions. In both Testaments, Satan accuses, tempts by making evil appear desirable, tries faith by making the good appear offensive, deceives and confuses, encourages pride and complacency, tests patience and endurance, paralyzes man's energies and perverts his loyalties, undermines his confidence in the covenant. The goal of his activities remains the same — the testing of man's dependence upon God. The results of his efforts are the same: in some cases the strengthening of faith; in others the demonstration of the shallowness of faith.

Another noteworthy coincidence is the kind of pseudo reality which is assigned to Satan in the New Testament: the demons are as real and as unreal as are the idols in the Old Testament. In neither case is the reality defined in metaphysical or ontological categories. The point of emphasis is the actual allegiance of men to invisible but potent forces. The earlier discussion of theoretical and existential monotheism is paralleled here by the contrast between the theoretical and existential definitions of idols and demons:

" We know that no idol is anything in the world, and that there is no God but one. For though there be that are called gods, whether in heaven or on earth; as there are gods many, and lords many; yet to us there is one God, the Father, of whom are all things " (I Cor. 8:4-6).

Still another mark of the characteristic Biblical perspective is the fact that alien demonologies, when transposed into Jewish and Christian thought, were radically changed to bring them into harmony with the basic dualism of Biblical experience. The tendency to identify the devil with the flesh, in the antithesis flesh versus spirit, is everywhere resisted by the Biblical awareness that the source of rebellion lies within the will. The spirit is not considered as wholly good nor the flesh as wholly evil. The sins attacked by Paul and John are perversions of the soul as much as of the body; God is the Creator and Redeemer of his whole creation.

Nor is belief in Satan permitted to absolutize the antithesis between God and the natural world. The development of Gnostic mythology is vigorously opposed. God creates the world and calls it good. To be sure, the term " cosmos " is used of the territory that lies under Satan's power, but the interchangeable " aion " indicates that it is the present *age* which manifests rebellion rather than what we call the order of nature. Similarly, the Biblical seers rejected the all-too-human tendency to equate the devil with human adversaries, to draw the line between good and evil men, and to absolutize this distinction. One must note that, even in periods of bitterest persecution, New Testament writers hesitated to identify Satan with a particular emperor. The contrast with Zoroastrian thought is remarkable.

"Zarathustra never perceived the opposition within his own bosom. He fought against outward enemies and their spiritual helpers; the thraldom of guilt and corruption were unknown to him. He never penetrated to the problems of the soul. . . . The enemies of the prophet were the enemies of God. That is why the conquest of self never entered into his ethical programme." [10]

Another significant change made in borrowed demonologies by the Biblical writers is the insistence upon Satan's ultimate subordination to God. We have noted that Satan grew from an errand-boy to a rebel tyrant, becoming semi-independent in authority and power over this age. His kingdom is organized to carry on vigorous warfare. But it is important to note that he never achieves full independence and full freedom of action. Even in the book of Revelation he exerts only such authority as has been *given* to him. It is God who permits him to sell his wares, who limits the bounds of his dominion, who terminates his age, who precipitates the final struggle that reveals both the present power

[10] Söderblom, *The Living God,* p. 210. Oxford University Press, 1933.

and the final impotence of the rebel king. God " is the Ruler yet " and Satan may challenge but not coerce him. At the peak of his career, the devil remains but one of those principalities whose tyranny is terminated " for us " by knowledge that God is all in all, and that " to them that love God all things work together for good, even to them that are called according to his purpose." For this reason we must deny the contention that the acceptance of demonology represents a modified monotheism. Monotheism is modified at this point no more completely than it was modified by the Old Testament recognition of the historical potency of idols.

The existential perspective of Scripture is also reflected by the fact that history remains the primary sphere within which Satan operates. His power is thought of only in connection with the present interim which separates the promise of God from its fulfillment. Very noticeable is the absence of attempts to explain his origin. Interest in his genealogy and family connections is extra-Biblical, as is the effort to locate his position in space, to define his ontological status in relationship to God. Equally scarce are the data in which the speculative curiosity delights: his names and numbers, his anatomy and private affairs. To know the name of demons is important, for the name represents authority and character; but such knowledge is needed, not for satisfying curiosity, but for establishing personal mastery. The logic underlying the myth moves from experience to description rather than from speculation to experience. The problem faced by men is not that of definition but that of defeating the power which leads them into rebellion. The existence of Satan is coterminous with his actual sovereignty over men, and is thus limited to the present age. He is banished in the future judgment when the Messiah's sovereignty is made effective, and in the present " time between the times " wherever Christ's sovereignty is operative. Entering into the sphere of this higher sovereignty, Paul finds that the " rudiments " have become " paltry and weak " (Gal. 4:9).

This throws light upon an observation of Johannes Weiss. In his treatment of Paul's world-view he points out that the apostle " fails to develop a complete cosmology." " In this his gospel differs from the Gnostic systems." " We know but little concerning the details of Paul's cosmological views." [11] To Weiss this seems to indicate philosophical

[11] *The History of Primitive Christianity*, Vol. II, pp. 595, 596. Wilson-Erickson, 1937.

immaturity on Paul's part. But why insist that a man's thought must begin with cosmology and be oriented within this cosmology as the primary frame of reference? Did not Paul begin with man's historical experience, and subordinate cosmology to personal apprehensions of historical reality? Does not Paul's cosmology seem inchoate and inconsistent precisely because it is entirely secondary to his confessional interpretation of man's history, viewed from within? No book in the Bible presents a systematic cosmology; every book in the Bible stems from historical struggle, and therefore assumes the divine-human dialogue as the frame of reference.

Satan never becomes alpha or omega; he remains a creature who falsely claims to be Creator, and who deceives men into attributing to him a false eternity and a false ultimacy. His work is always a reaction to God's deed and not a spontaneous emergent. Men are troubled, therefore, not by the logical contradiction between God's sovereignty and Satan's freedom (the philosophical problem of evil) but by the actual contradiction between the Creator's purpose and creation's response. Satan appears in a negative role, using his wiles to confuse men over each positive disclosure of the divine will. It is men whom God has called whom he tests by making rebellion attractive and loyalty obnoxious. The immediate sequel to Jesus' anointing is the wilderness temptation, to which he is driven by the Spirit. In Paul's experience, it was when he was exalted to the third heaven that a messenger of Satan was sent to buffet him. God's claim to exclusive sovereignty and his call into the coming Kingdom is what unleashes the power of Satan. It is God's word that incites rebellion; the more decisive the word the greater the rebellion.

" It is the native property of the Divine word, never to make its appearance without disturbing Satan, and rousing his opposition. This is the most certain and unequivocal criterion by which it is distinguished from false doctrines, which are easily broached when they are heard with general attention, and received with applause by the world. Thus, in some ages . . . the prince of this world . . . gave himself up to his ease and pleasures in perfect peace. . . . But when the Mighty One alarmed and assaulted his kingdom, then he began to shake off his wonted torpor, and to hurry on his armor." [12]

[12] Calvin, *Institutes,* trans. by J. Allen. Seventh American edition, Vol. I, p. 37. The Westminster Press, 1936.

REBELLION AND JOY

This existential connection between revelation and rebellion explains a little-observed but important axiom in Biblical thought: Awareness of rebellion is an occasion not for despair but for hope (Rom. 8:18–20). What seems to outsiders to be morbid obsession with the pervasiveness of evil becomes for insiders the ground of confidence and joy. Recognition of sin is the first step in a return to first loyalty, to the intended relationship to the Creator. The remedy for the warped results of destiny requires realization of rebellion and a return. Not only is diagnosis of illness the prerequisite of a cure; it is also a sign that the doctor has begun his work. God initiates his cure with a call to repentance, which itself serves to locate the infection. Recognition of sin leads to faith; faith prompts a keener recognition of sin. This interaction is a hallmark of both faith and repentance. Neither is found apart from the other. There is a Biblical tone in George Fox's counsel to a man in despair:

> "I told him that which showed him his sins, and troubled him for them, would show him his salvation; for he that shows a man his sin is the same that takes it away." [13]

Similarly, when Ezekiel predicts coming restoration of the exiles to their homeland and the reformation of their heart and spirit, he pictures their first reaction thus:

> "Then shall ye remember your evil ways, . . . and ye shall loathe yourselves in your own sight for your iniquities" (see Ezek. 36:22–31).

One corollary of this viewpoint is that every evidence of Satan's power is to be met with joy. Jesus' temptation is ground of confidence, his battle with demons leads him to rejoice, his cross is the point for transmitting his joy. The ostracism and violence which greets Christians, which they interpret as the work of Satan, is understood to mark the beginning of judgment. For this reason, the hosts of martyrs unite in singing praise to Him who alone is "worthy" to unroll the scroll of destiny. In their "call" into the Church, Christians experience both hatred by the world and the love of God. Jesus brings to the believer

[13] *Journal,* ed. by W. Armistead. Seventh edition, Vol. I, p. 50. 1852.

three things: the Kingdom, tribulation, patience — all of them interrelated (Rev. 1:9). Pascal's statement fits into such a frame of reference:

" The most cruel war which God can make with men in this life is to leave them without that war which He came to bring. 'I came to send war,' He says, 'and to teach them of this war. I came to bring fire and the sword.' Before Him the world lived in this false peace." [14]

Suffering in this war becomes the touchstone of participation in God's battle with the devil, and is therefore to be accepted in thanksgiving and joy.[15] But we must remember that this joy remains proleptic in character, always grounded in hope. Patient acceptance of tribulation is proof of one's faith, but the validity of that faith depends upon the imminent outcome of the dramatic struggle between God and his adversary. The forces of rebellion are dynamic and purposive in character; only a final defeat can resolve the present tensions. Idols and devil alike " have their day and cease to be "; their power is limited by time; they are creatures *within* history. Wherever God's word interrupts Satan's time and men order their decisions by that word, they conquer the tempter; this conquest is a foretaste of that final day when all the times of rebellion are ended. Thus is the problem of rebellion related to the problem of time.

A modern Biblical scholar, representing a large segment of contemporary opinion, has dismissed Biblical demonology with this verdict: " Though full of quaint interest from the point of view of folk-lore, the subject is not an edifying one." [16] Early Christians would agree neither on the quaintness nor on the absence of edifying value. They assumed the existence and sway of demons as implicitly as Oesterley rejects them. Struggle with "the principalities and the powers" was integral to their whole perspective. Apart from this presupposition, they would have found little meaning in the grace of God, in the coming of his Kingdom, in salvation through his Anointed. And though their vocabulary was far removed from that of the Law and the Prophets, there is clear continuity between them. Apostasy, adultery, and idolatry con-

[14] *Pensées,* No. 498, trans. by W. F. Trotter, p. 162. The Modern Library, 1941.
[15] Cf. S. Kierkegaard, *Journal* No. 638, trans. by A. Dru, p. 196. 1938.
[16] W. O. E. Oesterley, *Jews and Judaism During the Greek Period,* p. 278. The Macmillan Company, 1941. Entirely different judgments of the truths in demonology are expressed by C. S. Lewis, *The Screwtape Letters,* 1943, and by Denis de Rougement, *The Devil's Share,* 1945.

tinue to be the realities of the immediate human situation whenever God speaks to men and calls them to love him with their whole heart. No interpretation of the Bible is adequate that does not do justice to the intrinsic experiential realities which were expressed in such terms as sin, idolatry, death, and Satan.[17]

[17] Cf. E. M. Carlson, in *Journal of Religion*, Vol. XXV, pp. 247–250. 1945.

5

GOD CREATES A PEOPLE

WHEN God visits, he calls a particular man; in his speaking to and through that man he creates a community, an inheritance for his own possession. In his relation to an individual, he is also acting toward other individuals. And their relation one to another, in Toynbee's terms, " consists in the coincidence of their individual fields of action." [1] This common ground created by this distinctive source of action constitutes the Biblical community. To the spectator, the source of action may appear to be located in one of the individuals, a political or social leader, a seer or a saint. But the actors themselves assume a source beyond themselves to which they respond.

" Look unto Abraham your father, and unto Sarah that bare you; for when he was but one I called him, and I blessed him, and made him many " (Isa. 51:2).

This divine source of action is underscored by the fact that every new beginning is marked by miracle: the creation of Adam, the promise to Noah, the choice of Abraham, the birth of Isaac, the marriages of the patriarchs, the guidance of Joseph, the selection of Moses, and all the strategic events down to the births of John and Jesus, the exaltation of Jesus, and the new births of Christians through his Spirit. The list is a long one!

Isolated man, the " natural man," man *per se*, man considered apart from his community and from his Creator — such a man does not ap-

---

[1] A society " is a relation between individuals; and this relation of theirs consists in the coincidence of their individual fields of action; and this coincidence combines the individual fields into a common ground; and this common ground is what we call a society. . . . A field of action cannot be a source of action. . . . The source of social action cannot be the society." *A Study of History,* Vol. III, p. 230. Oxford University Press, 1934–1939.

pear in the Bible. No definition of man that breaks his essential nexus with the Creator's purpose is conceivable in the Biblical setting. And precisely the same can be said of community. It cannot be understood in itself and of itself and by itself, but only in its living relationship to Him who brought it into existence. " I . . . will be your God, and ye shall be my people." Because of this continual reference to the mystery and miracle of election, the mesh of modern categories is scarcely adequate to sift out the distinctive aspects of Biblical solidarity.

The most nearly neutral categories in our language are loaded with presuppositions and connotations which betray the century and culture in which they were spawned. When we apply the categories of modern sociology, we presuppose the existence of universal types of community, pigeonholes into which every human association may be filed. Then we place Judaism and Christianity under appropriate racial or cultural captions, and try to determine under which subspecies each belongs. We tend to forget De Maistre's warning:

"There is no such thing as ' man ' in the world. I have seen Frenchmen, Italians, Russians, etc., in my life . . . but as for ' man,' I declare that I have never met him anywhere; if he exists, I am quite unaware of it." [1a]

And even though we may observe that warning and recognize the particularity of each racial group, we may still miss the true character of Biblical community, unaware of the subtle complex of meanings which members of that community sensed as the true ground of solidarity. From within the context of divine-human intercourse they knew their community to be *sui generis*.

We find it difficult to describe any historical phenomenon without using the terms " social " and " society." Yet these terms or their equivalents scarcely appear in the Bible. This does not mean that Biblical thought is not pervasively " social," for no literature is more saturated with all that we mean by that term. But there is in the Bible no distinct or explicit philosophy of society. There is no antonym by which to distinguish " society " from what is not " society." There is no attempt to abstract " society " from the concrete entities, communities defined by existing relationships to particular gods.

There must be an explanation of this striking silence, an explanation

---

[1a] *Considérations sur la France,* edited by R. Johannet and F. Vermale, p. 81. Paris, 1936. (I am indebted for this quotation to Richard A. Schermerhorn.)

founded on subsurface attitudes. We have already pointed to one set of axioms: the grounding of community in its election by God. The totalitarian sovereignty of a single Creative Will destroys all the compartments of life, breaking down the wall between social and nonsocial, between the individual and the group. Every event involves a particular individual, for he is confronted by a demand that necessitates immediate personal response; but at the same time every event involves a particular community, because man is man only within the context of mutual relations, and his response to God affects and represents the entire web of mutuality. To be sure, this interpenetration of individual and group is never fully consummated within history, but it is implicit in every visitation of God, as that meeting discloses the original impulse and the final promise of creation.

THE BASIS OF SOLIDARITY

Little needs to be said to illustrate the intense solidarity which in the Old Testament binds the individual to the group, which makes Israel a single unit of responsibility and freedom.[2] The covenant is made with the nation as a nation; sin, judgment, salvation apply to the nation as realistically as to the individual. When God addresses David, he addresses the entire community; when he promises fulfillment to David, he has in mind the destiny of the nation (II Sam. 7:8 f.). Writers may frequently draw distinctions among the various factions, singling out a special segment for special blame or duty (Isa., chs. 53; 54). But never does the concern for the individual or the segment serve to separate either from the ultimate social integumentation within which all life finds its meaning.

Some modern analysts ascribe this solidarity to a primitive tribal collectivism, which other societies sloughed off with developing culture, but which Israel alone preserved as the basis of social religion. Some ascribe it to an unusual prophetic sensitivity to the corporate affiliations of human personality as such. These explanations are partly true, but they fall far short of adequacy. They make religion a product of social awareness, reducing God to the status of immanent natural forces. To Jews and Christians the sense of mutuality stems from consciousness

---

[2] The substance of this chapter appeared in my article " The Biblical Consciousness of Community," in *The Journal of Religious Thought*, 1944, Vol. I, pp. 82 ff.

of common election. Communal experience does not produce knowledge of God; rather, it is produced by such knowledge as God may reveal. It is only when he is confronted by the Sovereign of history that man becomes aware of solidarity with God's people.

Ezekiel's individualism is often cited as breaking away from primitive collectivism in such a way as to break the nexus between self and society. It is clear that he repudiated the adage, " The fathers have eaten sour grapes, and the children's teeth are set on edge," in favor of the axiom, " The soul that sinneth, it shall die." But Ezekiel is not trying to sever the ties between generations, to tear the self away from its social moorings, to claim an autonomy for the self in its solitariness. Rather, he proclaims the inescapable responsibility of every generation before God, the absolute need for repentance, the immediate call for personal decision. To exiles in the abyss of despondency, he speaks a word of the Lord which assures them of forgiveness and a new heart. The word of the Lord prompts the prophet to reject the current despair which undercuts present responsibility by maximizing the quantitative guilt inherited from the sins of previous generations. The same word impels him to call for a renewal of covenant obligations; and he is the channel through which this word is communicated to the people of the covenant. It condemns the qualitative guilt expressed in the present choices of the present generation, and invokes in the present a repetition of the conditions constitutive of the true Israel. It holds forth both threat and promise to Israel as Israel, and through Israel to the world. The despair over the present suffering and bleak prospect of the nation is countered with a vision of God's power to reverse the process of decay. The discussion centers, not in theories of sociological causation, but in the fact of man's unchanging responsibility to God. Ezekiel is not an anarchistic atomist, nor a modern libertarian, but a Biblical existentialist. For him, as for both Jews and Christians, individualism of election heightens the solidarity of election. In relation to men, individualism may be the antithesis of collectivism; but in relation to God, the two may be quite inseparable.

As it has been a mistake of modern criticism to exaggerate the collectivism of the Jew, so has it been a mistake to exaggerate the individualism of the early Christian. The sense of solidarity among early Christians is as strong as that among the Jews, if one keeps in mind that in both cases he speaks of the solidarity of the elect community. Signs of this solidarity are on every page of the New Testament. Judgment is judgment upon the world; the resurrection of Jesus and his followers is part of the general resurrection of the end-time; the realm of salvation is a Kingdom, wherein the covenant promises to a community are fulfilled.

All the metaphors applied to the Ecclesia stress this communal aspect. Some are drawn directly from the social and political realm: The Church is a new race, born after the pattern of Abraham; a new nation; a royal priesthood; a Kingdom, with its King elect and incumbent; a heavenly city; a new family, the brothers of Jesus. There are many analogies drawn from plants and animals: the olive tree; the grapevine with its branches; the flock of sheep with its shepherd; the plantation with its seed, its workers, its harvest. There are also architectural metaphors: the house; the temple, with its foundation, cornerstone, and building blocks. More personal and vivid are the descriptions of table fellowship, the guests participating in the hospitality of the host, sharing with him the covenants of bread and salt. Full use is made of the similarities between the Church and the body: its head and members, its animating spirit, its directing mind.

" The Body . . . is neither the sum of its particular members, nor the consequence of their interaction. The Body confronts the members, establishes them and makes them one. . . . They are not a mass of individuals, not even a corporation, a personified society, or a ' totality,' but The Individual, The One, The New Man." [3]

The ground of this community (the Word of God in Christ) determines its structure (the Body of Christ), empowers it with hidden dynamic (the Spirit), and transforms all areas of its experience. Each of the metaphors points to Christ as the source of solidarity. The believer lives, suffers, loves, triumphs, in association with other believers in a common dependence upon a living, suffering, loving, triumphing Lord.

It is worth noting that these metaphors were not used for purposes of propaganda, and only occasionally do they appear as pedagogical tools for social control. They are not flowery, romantic claims of what men have accomplished, nor nebulous dreams concerning what they would

[3] K. Barth, The Epistle to the Romans, trans. by E. C. Hoskyns, p. 443. Oxford University Press, 1933.

like their society to become. They spring forth spontaneously as irrepressible testimonies to what God has done to them and for them.

Christian solidarity is always a matter of present experience, but an experience which repeats past events and anticipates future events. These events which mediate the divine *agape* — Christ's death and resurrection — are events in which the community continues to participate. The ethos and ethic are thus functional, in that *agape* is always an immediate demand upon the individual to live according to the needs of the Body, the new organism which God creates. " Love edifieth " (I Cor. 8:1). They are dispositional, in that this love is always a reaction to the energies which God has released in Christ. " We love, because he first loved us " (I John 4:19). They are eschatological, in that *agape* is defined and directed by reference to the end of faith, salvation in the coming age. " Love your enemies, . . . and your reward shall be great " (Luke 6:35). Jesus Christ, as a single personal reality, encompasses primal intention, historical manifestation, and final return; his Body shares now in his eternal contemporaneity, and the love which animates it points to a solidarity, not only in the present, but also in the past and future. Let us look more closely at these distinctive aspects of Biblical community.

ISRAEL: PRESENT AND PAST

The character of Israel is defined by its oneness with preceding generations; the germ of present mutuality is the purpose of God, and the continuity of the generations stems from the consistency of the divine design. In the Kingdom men will sit down with Abraham and Isaac and Jacob (Matt. 8:11).

The vitality of the ancestral tradition is manifested by its contemporaneity.

" The Lord made not this covenant with our fathers, but with us, even us, who are all of us here alive this day " (Deut. 5:3; cf. ch. 10:15).

In the observance of the Passover in the Jewish home, when the son asks the meaning of the ceremony, the father replies:

" We were Pharaoh's bondmen in Egypt: and the Lord brought us out of Egypt with a mighty hand; and the Lord showed signs and wonders . . . before our eyes; and he brought us out from thence, that he might bring us in, to give us the land which he sware unto our fathers. And the Lord commanded us to do all these statutes, . . . for our good always " (see Deut. 6:20–25; cf. chs. 5:15; 9:6 f.; 15:15; Josh., ch. 24; Neh., ch. 9).

This quotation shows how carefully the consciousness of the living past was inculcated. But the corporate unity with the past is not merely a psychological phenomenon. Whether or not people recognize the bond (and frequently they do not), the bond remains firm, sustained by God's invincible purpose. God's action in the past encompasses his action in the present; to be a son of the covenant is more decisive than to be a son of the clan or a son of the land.

This quotation also shows that social memory reached its peak of intensity when focused upon the most strategic events of the past, " that part of our inner history which illumines the rest of it and which is itself intelligible." [4] Through such events " we understand what we remember, remember what we have forgotten, and appropriate as our own past much that seemed alien to us." [5] Such a memory is far more than natural recollection but is preserved in spite of its absurdity. As W. J. Phythian-Adams points out, the events were those of a dim and legendary past, separated from the present by more than a millennium. It is as if a modern Englishman based his faith and hope on stories of special divine assistance to King Arthur. " A man who in these days was prepared to base his life on such a memory would be set down without any hesitation as an erratic." [6] Yet Israel's faith was so deeply anchored to those events that, had memory of them been lost, the identity of the community must have vanished with it.[7]

The fact and momentum of this tradition-consciousness is well established, but it is difficult to explain *why* and *how* it developed among the Jews alone. Undoubtedly various racial and economic factors aided in forging the chain: for example, the conservative defense of nomadic culture against the infiltration of Canaanite mores, the desire of such men as Ezra for racial purity as a means to national unity. But such factors are not adequate in themselves to explain the unique phenomenon; they operated as well on other communities without producing similar results. We should remember the strange fact " that Israel, the most

[4] H. Richard Niebuhr, *The Meaning of Revelation*, p. 93. The Macmillan Company, 1941.
[5] *Op. cit.*, p. 110.
[6] *The Call of Israel*, pp. 17. 18. Oxford University Press, 1934.
[7] *Op. cit.*, p. 40.

ancient of living nations, has never been homogeneous." [8] Yet century after century, Jews returned " to . . . the pit whence . . . [they] were digged " in spite of catastrophes which among other peoples destroyed memory and splintered cultural unity. Strangely enough, among the Jews the tradition was most virile at those very moments when on empirical grounds it should have been weakest. Jews themselves were thrown back upon the confidence that the persistence of tradition could be understood only in connection with the persistence of God's purpose. Such persistence testifies to the creative power of memory to shape the present and future.

"It is a strange thing to trust one's memory; its hold on us is stronger than our hold on it; it carries us into its own world which is the very reality of the movement of our past, and we must obey it whether we will or no, must retrace those paths of time which are henceforth not only irrevocably fixed, but in which all things are bound together so that any particular moment conjures up all the past that has gone before it." [9]

The sense of corporate identity with the past did not produce among the Jews the same tendencies which appear in similar cultures. Except in erratic tangents, it did not lead to a romantic idealization of the past, a cult of ancestor worship, the apotheosis of human heroes. It did not attribute to the patriarchs unique virtue or wisdom; nor did it call for slavish emulation of an archaic Golden Age. It did not use the dead hand of the past to constrict present freedom, nor provide a dreamworld for sentimental escape from pressing dilemmas. Rather, it sharpened the horns of those dilemmas, leading men into, and out of, the valley of decision.

Jews did not come to such memory by way of a recollection of pristine innocence à la Rousseau, nor by way of a recollection of primal being à la Plato. Nor did they express their interest in the past by objective historical reflection and research. It is not primarily the prod of curiosity or of utilitarian need that impels them to preserve the stories of the patriarchs. The past lives in the present, not simply as a body of sacred tradition or a collection of chance memories, but as a contemporary power. Adam, Abraham, Moses, and Elijah are never merely hu-

---

[8] A. Guillaume, *Prophecy and Divination*, p. 85. Harper & Brothers, 1939.

[9] R. Maritain, *We Have Been Friends Together*, trans. by Julia Kernan, p. viii. Longmans, Green & Company, 1942. Cf. also J. Hempel, *Gott und Mensch im Alten Testament*, pp. 33–44. 1936.

man examples evoked from ancient lore to buttress current conceptions; they are living manifestations of divine will, revealing the present demands of a living God. Each of them " is at once himself and the race." The past is appropriated as contemporaneous, not by treating time as unreal or as a cyclical movement, but by hearing in the present moment the word of the same God who spoke to our fathers, and thus a word which transcends time because it creates time. To use Kierkegaard's distinction, we can understand the Biblical outlook only by using the category of repetition, not the categories of eternal recurrence, of Platonic recollection, or of historical continuity.

Christians appropriated the living past as completely as the Jews. They knew themselves to be heirs of all the ages, and especially of the covenants made with the Jews. The Church was the sphere of fulfillment of Israel's hope. The speech of God in Christ was a continuation and fulfillment of his speech in the prophets. Sometimes each scene in the drama of salvation was found predicted in a particular prophecy. At other times, the stress lay, not on literal anticipations of future events, but on the faith of the fathers now vindicated (Heb. 1:1 f.; 11:39, 40).

Deeply woven into all the titles ascribed to Jesus is the consciousness of his contemporaneity with the past, the entire past. He is the pre-existent and primordial Word, through whom God had made and upheld the world. Many of the titles applied to Jesus are drawn directly from history. He is a second Adam, creating a new humanity; a second Moses, giving a new Law. Like Jonah, he preaches repentance; like Elijah, he prepares the way for the Kingdom; like Solomon, he is the source of wisdom. A Priest after the order of Melchizedek, he is also the anointed Son of David. These are more than colorful descriptions of his role; they point to a real presence in Christ of these characters; in him God's purpose as it had been revealed in them is repeated anew. He had been a contemporary of every preceding epoch.

Inasmuch as the Church shares the powers of Christ, it shares his relationship to history as a whole. Christians participate constantly (by repetition) in the events of Jesus' career: in the despair and faith of Peter; in the fear and cowardice of Judas and Nicodemus; in the offense, mystery, and victory of the death and exaltation. They share his authority and mission. They even share through him in the events preceding his incarnation: They are sons of Abraham. Their solidarity with the ancestral community is thus secured and reinforced through Christ.

But while Christ made them contemporaries with Israel he at the same time dissolved any dependence upon the empirical institutions of Israel. His work fulfills John's warning, " God is able of these stones to raise up children unto Abraham." To become a son of Abraham through faith is implicitly to cancel all earlier social arrangements. Thus when Christians compared Jesus' work to that of Adam or Jonah, they always insisted upon a differentiation: " a second Adam "; " a greater than Jonah." [10] God's message in Christ repeats and fulfills his earlier communications, but its finality destroys further need for revealers such as his predecessors. The Church is Israel, but an Israel after the Spirit. This explains the tenacity with which, as " spiritual Semites," they held to their Jewish heritage; it explains, too, the bitterness of Jewish antipathies, once the claim of the Ecclesia is uttered. It explains why as a Pharisee Paul persecuted the Church, why as a Christian he affirmed the importance of ancestral covenants, and why he met death as a result of Pharisaic opposition. Though rejected by Israel, he remained an Israelite. The form of his memory, his identification with the past, persisted, but it was transformed by the fresh impact of God's action.

ISRAEL: PRESENT AND FUTURE

Biblical solidarity is also constituted by participation in the future. God is One who declares the end from the beginning, his word has gone forth and will not return void. He has sworn and will not break his oath. It is his promise that supports the community. He has already acted to redeem his elect, even though this act has not yet become manifest on the plane of observable results. Future destiny is thus a prime determinant of present experience.

This attitude is particularly clear in II Isaiah (especially chs. 44 to 47). A recurrent motif is found in the words: " I have purposed, I will also do it " (Isa. 46:11). In the *present* situation wherein the community faces an either-or decision, God reveals through the prophet the *promise* for the *future* which has already been made in the *past,* and this promise calls for man's obedience. From man's point of view the present

---

[10] This phrase, however, needs to be interpreted in the manner of B. W. Bacon, *Studies in Matthew,* pp. 387–396. 1930.

is still sharply distinct from the hidden future; but from God's point of view past, present, and future are all comprehended in a single purpose. His chosen people therefore shares this synoptic point of reference. Thus the community of the *word* is at once the community of the *fathers* to whom the promise was made and the community of the *end-time* when the promise will be fulfilled. Its members share in a common memory and a common hope.

" When the past is made to function as a project for the future, tradition itself becomes a form of prophecy. Past and future are welded into one on the forge of life, with its ties and loyalties of man to man." [11]

Christians as well as Jews sensed this contemporaneity with future events. The Church is a colony of heaven, a Messianic brotherhood of the last days. The gift of the Spirit marks the approach of the end; through the Spirit new powers operate in driving back the kingdom of Satan. " We are not of the night, . . . but . . . of the day." Yet the day which has dawned on them has not yet dawned on the world. They have been caught up into the divine realm, where things have happened which have not yet happened to history as a whole. Here they experience the end of history before the end of history. Already judgment has begun among them; already they have been born again after the pattern of the Risen Lord. The hidden mysteries of God's plan have been revealed to them. Soon that secret will be shouted from the housetops. The day is dawning when heirs will receive their inheritance and their sonship will be openly declared. Christians live at the point where that future makes its impact upon the present. They live with " one foot in heaven." And it is the dawning age which really determines their behavior and hence their destiny. Strangers and refugees here, they must still walk by faith and not by sight.

ISRAEL AND THE INDIVIDUAL

Thus the unique consciousness of election produced a unique sense of solidarity with the past and the future. At the same time it conveyed a unique attitude toward the function of the individual within the group, welding leaders and followers into a unit within which authority did not mean privilege, and obedience did not mean subservience. The estab-

[11] F. Kaufmann, in *Philosophy and Phenomenological Research,* March, 1944, Vol. IV, p. 296.

lishment of fellowship did not depend on authoritarian government or on a doctrine of natural rights, did not depend on a particular mode of political or economic organization or on a system of checks and balances, on the power of an elite minority or the articulate will of the masses. God's word at the same moment separated leaders for special functions and strengthened the bonds of communal unity.

The prophets do not gain special privilege or a separate status. They become focal points in the tradition, but they do not inherit a fate separate from that of the community. The call of God intensifies their consciousness of solidarity with the group at the same moment that it leads them to revolt against prevailing mores. The prophet's mantle is not to be sought as a mark of social standing or unusual wisdom, but is to be shunned as a wearisome burden. Similar are the attitudes toward ancestral heroes. In Jerusalem is no hall of fame for Joseph or Elijah or Moses as individual persons. They were not geniuses, to be revered as the most successful or the most virtuous. Their only claim to special importance is what God said and did through them to the community. Some were undoubtedly very able political leaders, but their chief significance, in later tradition, at least, lies in their typological, representative, universal character. Adam, Israel, Jacob, Moses — each of these represents all spiritual descendants through the span of centuries. When God addresses David or Abraham, he addresses the entire community, past, present, and future. Yet these figures remain more than symbols; each is a distinct individual facing a concrete situation. Their place in tradition remains unique, unrepeatable, their very own. The respect for historical reality is not dissipated in abstract, timeless concepts concerning their symbolic meaning. Nor do they serve as perennial paragons of virtue to be emulated by succeeding generations. (The moral and pedagogical exploitation of their biographies as found in the Testament of the Twelve Patriarchs is quite un-Biblical.) Their significance remains grounded in the divine purpose which God revealed through them to his covenant community. Other Jews are related to them horizontally only because they are related to the same God vertically.

The same observations may be made of the role of the individual Christian in the Ecclesia. One's inclusion is signified by his rebirth. Called by the Spirit, believers participate in the Spirit; they pray by it and are guided by it. It is the Spirit who directs the division of the Church into apostles, prophets, and teachers. Because of this vertical dimension, every Christian has a vocation all his own, which includes his entire life. The motives of ambition and imitation are thus limited. One should imitate the patience of Paul but not envy him his authority or compete with him for prestige. One should accept the role of teacher but not seek it. One should speak with tongues but not claim superiority because of it. Pride over one's place in the community is ruled out by the fact that whatever prestige one holds is the gift of the Spirit, and that Spirit moves in channels of love for the brothers. "What hast thou that thou didst not receive" (I Cor. 4:7)? Every vocation is unique, yet the goal of each is the same: sharing the ministry of reconciliation. No man can communicate vocation to another; only God can do that. Thus are the egoistic and gregarious tendencies in men fulfilled and transcended. Isolation is overcome in a new fellowship stronger than any found elsewhere; yet the self is not lost and absorbed into the communal life so as to lessen its unique responsibility before God. Both selfhood and the impulse to fellowship are expanded. Possession by the Spirit means identification with the Body of Christ and a unique vocation as his servant (I Cor., chs. 3; 4; 12; 14; Rom., ch. 12).

That Christians experienced a new burst of spiritual freedom and power needs no documentation. That this freedom coincided with stronger social ties is more often ignored. But the fact stands clear that the Church had greater cohesive power than any other institution of its day. It could defy all existing social institutions, it could demand that converts break away from family, race, religion, and nation; — all this it could do, but only because it could replace these ties with stronger ones. The most strongly entrenched units in ancient society gave way before the adhesive power of the Gospel. They persecuted the Church, but the very persecution cemented the persecuted into greater unity.

ISRAEL AND THE WORLD

But at the same time that the consciousness of being chosen created a unique sense of inclusiveness, it created a unique sense of exclusiveness as well. The call separated the called from the world.

" There is an exclusiveness in God's love. This idea of exclusiveness in God's love has been part of 'the offence of the Gospel' since almost the first days. Such an idea must necessarily be involved in some degree as soon as the word 'choose' is used. We may not like this word 'choose' or its companion 'election.' They may be abhorrent to us, but they are firmly embedded in both Old and New Testament. Either we must accept this idea of choice on the part of God with its necessary accompaniment of exclusiveness, or we have to hold to a doctrine of the Love of God other than that which is Biblical." [12]

The God of love is a jealous God. Consequently the Hebrew tradition is highly particularistic. Individuals do not win places for themselves by effort of thought or will. Only God's call can bring one within the commonwealth. And there is no salvation outside his "*people.*" Outsiders are excluded by divine fiat. But the absoluteness and conservatism of this exclusivism are modified in two directions. In the first place, the ground of exclusion is *God's* choice and not *human* prejudices. Even in creating races and nations with separatist histories, he transcends their boundaries. He can and does include in his community those who cannot claim racial or national purity; he can and does exclude those whose pedigree by human standards is unimpeachable. No *man* can draw the line between the chosen group and outsiders.

" Scripture everywhere sets the counsel of God, on which is founded our salvation, in opposition to our merits. Hence, when Peter calls them elect according to the precognition of God, he intimates that the cause of it depends on nothing else but on God alone, for he of his own free will has chosen us. Then the foreknowledge of God excludes every worthiness on the part of man." [13]

In the second place, each community is defined by contemporaneity with the future. God's community is an order of redemption as well as creation. Its constituency is determined by future direction as well as by past projection. It is not only a saved remnant but also a saving remnant, an *elect* and not an *elite* minority. As a result, the boundary is never closed, never frozen, never within the province of men to determine. Fresh manifestations of God's activity always indicate that man's understanding of the boundaries of the covenant community is mistaken. Only the future can declare the exact make-up of the group. Until then, " the wind bloweth where it will."

From this angle we may understand the radical change in ideas brought about by the mission of Christ. In revealing his purpose God offended most men; their blindness was evidence of their exclusion from

[12] N. H. Snaith, *The Distinctive Ideas of the Old Testament*, p. 139. The Epworth Press, 1944.
[13] John Calvin, in *Commentary on I Peter*, comment on ch. 1:1.

his remnant. In fulfilling his promises through the gift of the Spirit he was actually selecting the community to inherit his Kingdom. The Christian can observe the sword of the Spirit separating the saved from the lost, but he cannot explain the mysteries of election. The basis of division is so new, so unpredictable, so different from all the orders of creation, that the sense of mystery is all the greater. Thus the line between the Church and the world becomes even sharper than the line between Israel and the Gentiles. The precise location of the line can be discerned only by noting the results of election: either faith or unbelief. Men may try to control the decrees of divine judgment, but the movements of the Spirit cannot be traced and the power of God's forgiveness cannot be restricted. God is now about the business of revealing the *true Israel,* the Israel of the promise, the Israel of faith. As a result he disavows the pretensions and claims of those who claim to be of Israel, and creates new sons of Abraham through his Word in Christ, *a new Israel.* Yet his purpose is not to bestow privilege but to secure responsible witnesses to his love. The Church is needed as his herald to the world. And the conflict between the Church and the world is a symptom of " the real, final divorce between profane and hallowed existence." Lines between insiders and outsiders are not drawn by some men acting against others but by God acting on men. And God's purpose ultimately envisages the salvation of all men.

The boundary between the Church and the world is thus defined according to an instrumentalist view of the historical process: that is, the human community is God's tool for realizing his purpose. This may be distinguished from the symbolist view, in which the community serves the individual by symbolizing eternal meanings, which may be appropriated by the individual in his very solitariness. Events which happen are merely symbols of the divine nature, communicating truths that are truer in their abstractness than they are in concrete particularity. The criterion of exclusion becomes that of personal acceptance of the truth so conceived, and the very definition of the truth of the symbol serves to define the constituency of the Church. Paul was not setting up this kind of creedal test when he wrote: " No man can say, Jesus is Lord, but in the Holy Spirit " (I Cor. 12:3).

The instrumentalist view may also be contrasted to the pragmatic conception of social life. According to this view either the group functions to conserve values for the individual member or the individual member serves to enhance social values by subordinating his will to that of the group. In either case religion becomes an instrument by which man realizes his end, his particular Utopia. Events are significant only as they increase the welfare of individual or group. The criterion of membership becomes the size of the contribution of the individual to the group or the subordination of the individual to the authority of the group; or else the worth of the community, and the ground of the individual's obligation to it, is assessed in terms of the community's contribution to self-realization. Paul's saying quoted above can be interpreted in neither of these ways.

In the Biblical view the history-long life of the elect community is an instrument in God's hands to manifest his glory and to reveal his power in redeeming his creation. Every event derives its importance as a sign of God's activity, indicating that he is at work through created life to achieve his purpose. Every such event involves election, and indicates (to those with seeing eyes) the men who have been chosen for participation in the promised redemption. An individual enters the Church, not when he accepts certain abstract ideas of eternal truth, nor when he promises to contribute certain values to the Ecclesia, but when God, active in Christ, bestows faith as a gift of the Spirit. " No man can say, Jesus is Lord, but in the Holy Spirit." Extreme hostility to the world is thus thoroughly compatible with preaching the Gospel to all men and with accepting men from all quarters without any requirement other than faith. The barrier is so high as to be impassable by human effort, but God stands at the boundary with his Word, and at any point in the wall he may open a gate to him who responds to the Good News.

To sum up, Israel is a reality, unique because it is molded from within by the invisible activity of God. This invisible activity lies beyond the gaze of casual spectators, but is revealed in concrete historical events to men of faith. In these events, the secrets of the future as well as the meaning of the past are disclosed. But the mystery remains a secret, hidden from human reason and historical measurement. As Stählin [14] insists, this mystery is the life principle of the Church. The Church is the place in the world " where this mystery is experienced." To live with Christ as a member of his Body is to partake in the mystery of God's act on the cross. Only the divine presence can lead one to recognize that event as " the one, once-only, once-for-all-time happened mystery," and

[14] Cf. W. Stählin, *The Mystery of God,* trans. by R. B. Hoyle, pp. 47–52. 1937.

the repetition of that mystery within the worship and sacraments of the Church is another mystery, as is the anticipation now of the future glories of history's end. The first century Christian found it impossible to communicate the mystery of the Church to an outsider by any means whatsoever. So also the modern Christian may despair of finding any rational method of classifying the Church as a social institution. Yet such failure does not lessen the reality of the new Israel; it simply points to an irreducible mystery of divine election, which is found wherever faith in Jesus as Christ is found. As Edwyn Hoskyns wrote:

" The church is the concretion in a living organism of the grace of the Lord Jesus Christ and the love of God and the fellowship of the Holy Spirit." [15]

[15] Cf. George Johnston, *The Doctrine of the Church*, p. 75. 1943. The above may be applied to the Israel of Old Testament times by substituting the mystery of the Passover for the mystery of the cross.

6

GOD APPOINTS TIMES

THE pivotal category in every philosophy of history is the *concept* of time; the pivotal reality in every perspective of life, whether or not it has been articulated in a conscious and systematic philosophy of history, is the *sense* of time. That strange history which appears in the Bible is permeated by a time consciousness inherently unique, so much so, in fact, that it almost eludes description. The difficulty lies in part in its remoteness from our time sense. At few points is the Biblical perspective more alien to modern forms of thought. The failure of modern interpreters to recognize this means that their interpretations of Biblical eschatology are inherently anachronistic. The difficulty also may be attributed to the fact that in the Bible the sense of time is assumed rather than discussed, and is therefore hidden from the casual glance. So axiomatic is it that it is easily overlooked. It is for this reason that writings permeated by a unique sense of time do not present formal doctrines of time. From the first prophet to the last, historical *consciousness* is primary and determinative; historical *knowledge* is secondary and derivative. In this respect, the mood of modern intellectualism illustrates almost the reverse emphasis.[1]

Because of this marked contrast in time sense, it may be forever impossible for us to apprehend in its fullness the strange consciousness of the prophet and apostle. But knowledge of the contrast may decrease the inveterate tendency toward anachronisms in this area. At least, it should warn us that we must not begin our evaluation of Biblical revelation by assuming that we know what time is, by supposing that our time sense is an ultimate reference by which to measure the validity of prophecy.

[1] Cf. P. Tillich, *Review of Religion,* Vol. III, pp. 255 f.

"Time varies with and is determined by the time sense; while the time sense varies with and is determined by the sense of life. The very contents of time gain their temporal structure in accordance with one's basic outlook." [2]

Humility with regard to our own chronometers, and imaginative openness to Biblical attitudes, may be fostered by personal reminiscence. Where is there a man whose sense of time has not been revolutionized by a particular crucial event in his life? Recall that moment when time has stopped, or has raced by at whirlwind rate, when time has been forgotten, when every second seemed a year or the whole year seemed a second? Any profound conversion involves a transformation of calendar as much as of character; it may be described as the receiving of a new, inner chronometer, the adopting of a new calendar. And with a shift in the sense of time, our whole universe shifts into new focus. In Ignacio Silone's *The Seed Beneath the Snow*, Pietro describes his conversion thus:

"From my first moment in that stable I lost all sense of time, a thing that exists only for those desiring or seeking something, or for the bored, whereas I had nothing more to seek — I had arrived — and I have never known boredom. Time simply disappeared for me." [3]

This illustrates at the outset the contrast between two different rhythms: the movements of solar and lunar bodies, which are fixed and constant; the impacts of events in personal history, which are fluctuating and variable. [4] In the Bible, time is primarily a category of history rather than of nature. To be sure, there are frequent references to hours, days, months, and years, but the basic reference is to successive human events and not to astral cycles. Even Old Testament narratives purporting to be histories are not organized into the framework of objective calendars, which were available and could have been used, as in the court annals of other peoples. The precise dating of events according to objective calendars is only rarely a concern of Biblical writers. After centuries of painstaking historical research, Biblical chronology remains the despair

[2] F. Kaufmann, in *Philosophy and Phenomenological Research*, March, 1944, Vol. IV, p. 294.
[3] Trans. by F. Frenaye, p. 50. Harper & Brothers, 1942.
[4] Cf. Minear, "Time and the Kingdom," in *Journal of Religion*, 1944, Vol. XXIV, pp. 77–78; the discussion of this chapter is drawn in part from this article, which is used by permission of the publishers.

of investigators. For this reason, in the writings that are composite in character, the original editors seldom arrange the materials in chronological order. The literary critic who attempts to rearrange the prophecies of Jeremiah, the events in the life of Jesus, or the visions of Revelation in the order of chronological origins, finds obstacles at every turn. These observations underscore the fact that in the Bible God's activity is not defined by time; on the contrary, his activity is the basis for the only genuine measurement of time.

For men of the Bible, the sense of time is dependent upon the interweaving of the three dynamic purposes (and there are only three) that constitute the essence and content of human life. (1) It is dependent upon the purposes of man, whether an individual, a group, or a nation. Time is used to measure the crucial stages in the destiny of a particular societal unit. (2) Inasmuch as this destiny is everywhere assumed to be " given " in creation, time is relative to the purposes of the Creator. Sequence in time is sequence in the maturing of his intention, a sequence punctuated by continuing calls and judgments. (3) Inasmuch as God's purpose is everywhere opposed, inasmuch as his call always reveals rebellion, man is aware of conflicting purposes that threaten his destiny. His time sense is thus engendered by the movements in the plot of this dynamic drama. Because of these three affiliations of historical consciousness, the present discussion will follow these three paths to the point of convergence.

THE TIME OF MAN'S PURPOSE

The first path is the one most easily charted, for the dependence of time sense upon human purpose is so universal a fact in experience as to be recognized in many philosophies of history. Because the history that matters is *our* history, the time that concerns us most is *our* time. Time is " a dimension of our life "; the kind of duration we feel is " the time of our lives." This duration is qualitative rather than quantitative, internal rather than external, personal rather than impersonal. " To every purpose there is a time." Our time is not something abstract and universal into which our lives are inserted, but a duration that is particular, and located within the span of our purpose. Although in the maturation of purpose, as in the execution of a legal contract, quantitative time " is of the essence of the matter," the qualitative purpose is that which creates the need for measuring the distance between two events.[5]

Among recent philosophers, Henri Bergson is noteworthy for his insistence that time becomes in the deepest sense real and living only when it is seen as a personal perception of duration, in which the feelings of movement, freedom, frustration, and fulfillment are prominent.

"Pure duration is the form which the succession of our conscious states assumes when our ego lets itself live, when it refrains from separating its present state from its former states . . . Nor need it forget its former states: it is enough that, in recalling these states, it does not set them alongside its actual state as one point alongside another, but forms both the past and the present into an organic whole, as happens when we recall the notes of a tune, melting into one another. . . . Pure duration might well be nothing but a succession of qualitative changes, which melt into and permeate one another . . . without any tendency to externalize themselves in relation to one another, without any affiliation with number." [6]

Bergson contends that the reduction of personal duration into an external, homogeneous, and measurable time debases the self and replaces the ego with its own shadow. Time made extensive becomes " nothing but the ghost of space haunting the reflective consciousness." To substitute quantitative measurement for qualitative duration breaks up the synthesis of the fundamental self and " corrupts at its very source our feeling of outer and inner change, of movement, and of freedom." [7]

Calendar time implies endless and infinite extension, a process for which no beginning and ending can be posited. It implies that all events must be fitted into a single external framework. Thus considered, the time process becomes

" a negative, gravitational tug, diminishing the personal and depriving the human of its creative significance by sucking events and meanings down into its 'objectivity,' its 'order,' its circularity." [8]

But where purpose defines duration, then the realities of a beginning and an ending become not only possible but necessary. And the character of imagination concerning the alpha and omega will be dependent upon the character of the purpose. In a child's mind it is impossible to

[5] Cf. R. Klibansky, in R. Klibansky and H. J. Paton, *Philosophy and History*, p. 329. 1936.
[6] *Time and Free Will*, pp. 100, 104. The Macmillan Company, 1910.
[7] *Op. cit.*, p. 74; cf. also pp. 98, 111–133.
[8] S. Hopper, *The Crisis of Faith*, p. 195. Abingdon-Cokesbury Press, 1944.

conceive of a beginning apart from his own consciousness. What happened before his birth just does not exist for him. In the mind of an octogenarian, whose purposes have begun to wither but whose memories of the distant past begin to live again as more real than the present, the conceptions of beginning and ending are found to be radically different. The full meaning of another man's beginning and end is incommunicable to us whose purposes differ from his. Time as a dimension of our life has both a beginning and an end, and its center moves in accordance not so much with the days of our years as with the momentum of our dominant desires.

This implies that our time varies in tempo, whereas calendar years march " with unperturbed pace." Like Ignacio Silone's hero, we feel the passage of time

" as if it were the flowing of a river, not in the uniform, artificial, abstract manner of a clock, but in the manner of a living stream, intermittent and irregular, first slow and then fast, according to the slope of the ground." [9]

Arthur Koestler, in his diary of days spent in a Spanish prison awaiting execution, depicts the dramatic struggle with time. " Time crawled through this desert of uneventfulness as though lame in both feet." Riveting his eyes on the second hand of his watch, resolving to think of nothing but pure time, he found the hours interminable. But later on, as he looked back upon those hours, he found his perspective radically reversed.

" The greater the sum of blank days, the lighter their weight in the memory. The time that, when it is present, passes most slowly, passes swiftest of all in the memory. And the converse is also true. . . . It is in flight that time leaves behind the most visible traces. . . . The only time that is unforgettable is that time during which one forgets that time exists. Only that time is fertile which remains chaste and unsullied by the touch of consciousness." [10]

Measured by the calendar, time becomes a single, all-inclusive process; measured by our history, time is seen to consist of multiple and exclusive processes. Viewed existentially, there are only separate histories, not one single world history. Greenwich time, with its exact division of the globe into zones, with their E.S.T., C.S.T., et cetera, is a human invention which submerges true individuality under apparent mathe-

[9] *The Seed Beneath the Snow*, trans. by F. Frenaye, p. 50. Harper & Brothers, 1942.
[10] *Dialogue with Death*, pp. 120 f. The Macmillan Company, 1942.

matical equivalence. For those whose sense of time is defined by Green-wich, it is almost impossible to conceive the sense of time innate to those who lived before such an innovation. For workers whose existence is punctuated only by the time clock or by meeting the schedule of appoint-ments, time becomes a tyrant that enslaves the soul; self-consciousness for them can be revived only by breaking this tyranny and reasserting the independence of the will to act in accordance with its own quiet pur-pose rather than as directed by that most subtle of all modern dictators — one's watch.

It is no wonder that Thoreau could establish a spiritual independence of time only by taking captivity captive: "Time is the stream I go a-fishing in." It is no wonder that Thomas Mann often pictures his char-acters as beginning to recover their selfhood by first destroying both clocks and calendars.[11] To disjoin the sense of time from its native con-text in human purpose is to destroy the significance of both. Time be-comes a highway running forever in either direction, divided by mile-stones into years; the self views itself, in Karl Heim's metaphors, either as a traveler along that highway, a diminutive point wearily trudging from one milepost to another, or as a supertemporal spectator, sus-pended above the road in the car of a captive balloon, and watching the endless procession.[12]

In the Bible the intrinsic nexus between time and purpose preserves the vitality of each.

"There is . . . a time for every purpose under heaven: a time to be born, and a time to die; a time to plant, and a time to pluck up" (Eccl. 3:1 f.).

It is this grounding of time in purposes that gives vitality to the tenses: past, present, and future. Torn loose from the basic concerns of the self, each tense loses its meaning. The past is gone, irretrievably vanished as a way station far back along a one-way road. The future has not yet come, and can be charted only as a projection of the same line infinitely in unilinear direction. The present moment is a split split second of transition where the unreal future becomes the real but inert and rapidly receding past. Every human expectation, whether fulfilled or not, is swallowed up in the abyss of the past. But in the time which is organic

[11] Cf. Kaufmann, *op. cit.*, p. 292.
[12] *God Transcendent*, trans. by E. P. Dickie, pp. 110–122. 1936; also N. Berdyaev, *Slavery and Freedom*, pp. 254 f. 1944.

to our history as duration, the past and future remain real constituents of present existence.

The past is present as our memory, following us at every instant. It is dynamic in us, seeking to direct our future. To lose this memory by amnesia shatters the meaning of present decisions. When memory is dominated by the sense of guilt we want to lose it, but can't; when it is dominated by remembrance of primary loyalties, it may stimulate a repetition of previous choices, each choice witnessing to the power of our past. Likewise, the dimension of our actual life includes the future as a real determinant of present performance.

The hope by which we live is as fully present as the past from which we seek to escape. The future is present as both hope and fear because it confronts us now with freedom and potentiality. When that potentiality is fully recognized, it produces immediate reactions of anxiety or trust, and usually an uneasy balance of both. Volition is by nature future-regarding; apart from the future it ceases to be volition and becomes the flickering impulse of the moment. The present forms the real center of the time of our lives. Both the past and the future are *now,* vividly unforgettable to him who is struggling toward a decision.

This interrelatedness may be illustrated negatively by what happens to a person when all his purposes dry up, as in the case of complete ennui or nervous exhaustion. When one's will loses its spring, the future loses its pull and becomes a nightmare of unending, empty motions. It becomes wholly impersonal, a continuing routine of dull, gray days. The past also dies and ceases to provide any push toward meaningful activity. The sense of loyalty and the sense of guilt are both sterilized, and one views his life as but another drop of water going over Niagara Falls, forever and forever.

And because both future and past die, the present dies also. There is no duty, no enjoyment, no fear, no hope — nothing that distinguishes today from any other day. The anguish is that one's body goes on functioning, as if in sleepwalking, while one's heart and will are inert. One wants to die but cannot even match the desire with an appropriate action; he does not want to die strongly enough to *will* to die, for it is his will which has already atrophied. Thus even a destructive purpose is disarmed and impotent. When a living purpose returns, it brings with it a sharpened sense of time. The past and future — and in turn the present — begin to live again. Throughout this cycle of death and rebirth of purpose there has been no variation in calendar time, but real time stops, and then, perchance, begins again at a different tempo. The reality of both tempo and tenses depends upon the readiness of the will to be itself, to accept its responsibility of standing here and only here, where a concrete future meets a concrete past in present decision.

In no other literature is there so acute a sense of time as in the Bible, so acute a sense of purpose, so acute a sense of decision. Man is constituted by his will; his experience is therefore viewed in terms of history rather than nature; his history focuses upon the frustration and fulfillment of purpose; the significance of life and death stems from this attitude. So far considered, however, the difference between the sense of time that is Biblical and that which is universally human appears as one of degree rather than of kind. Wherever men reflect upon the deeper desires of the heart, their time sense is sharpened. Are there disclosed in the Bible more distinctive determinants of historical consciousness?

THE TIME OF GOD'S PURPOSE

The answer must be in the affirmative. Apprehensions of time are unique because they stem from encounters with God wherein he asserts that *it is he alone who appoints times and seasons.* Men come to full consciousness of themselves as purposive creatures only through contact with the Creator's purpose; they shudder before the necessity of decision because of the impact of his impatient demand; their sense of time records the interim between his word and his deed, between creation and fulfillment. Time derives its momentum from the impulse of revealed purpose. The content of the present is transformed when he says, " This is the day." No longer a fleeting point in succession, like every other dot on an endless line, the present annuls this succession because of an ultimate command. God's voice fills " infinitely full " a moment which had been " infinitely void "; at that moment a new past and a new future are created.

" I have showed thee new things from this time, even hidden things, which thou hast not known. They are created now, and not from of old; and before this day thou heardest them not " (Isa. 48:6, 7).

A proverb runs: " Jahveh hath made everything for *its own end* "; the alternate reading suggests the same meaning in different terms:

"Jahveh hath made everything for *his own purpose*" (Prov. 16:4, margin). It is his purpose which defines its end; his intention which determines the time of his creature, its history from inception to fulfillment. This explains why the Bible regularly speaks of time in the plural (so different from our practice). Each nation receives its particular time of flourishing (Acts 17:26). Each plant is given a cycle of growth and harvest; each wind has its appointed time (I Clement 20:4, 10). There are thus as many times as there are creatures.

Time's arrow thus loses its uniformity in direction and speed. There are countless arrows moving in countless directions and speeds, and their only unity is to be discerned through God's overarching purpose. The plurality of purposes cannot be reduced by men to a single time. Only he whose purposes encompass all the various times can provide unity. Thus is the unilinear and the endless character of calendar time destroyed.

"God overarches the whole course of time. Time is a whole in Him and through Him. He is the beginning and He is the end of time. . . . The purpose of God frames time. . . . Time becomes an instrument in the hand of God: it becomes eschatological."[13]

Through his purpose man transcends chronological time by realizing the unity and continuity of past, present, future. But his tragedy lies in the fact that he nevertheless remains subject to chronological time. Through His purpose God transcends chronological time without losing his sovereignty over all times and seasons. The Biblical forms of expressing this attitude are diverse but consistent. "I am the Alpha and the Omega," "the beginning and the end," he "who is and who was and who is to come."

Because of this supertemporal reference, for those who by faith and obedience subordinate their wills to that of the Creator the time process loses its character as *pure succession* and assumes the antithetical character of simultaneity.

"Inspiration, psychologically interpreted, is a sudden simultaneity of the ordinarily sequential. Accelerated associations crowd together; the horizontal becomes vertical; the activity of the soul takes contrapuntal pleasure in itself. The almost divine self-consciousness of one inspired is based on this overcoming of the homophonic, of the 'bourgeois' progress of time."[14]

[13] R. Kroner, *Anglican Theological Review*, April, 1943, Vol. XXV, p. 208.
[14] F. Werfel, *Between Heaven and Earth*, p. 153. Philosophical Library, 1944.

For the man of faith, the time process also loses its irreversibility and becomes the scene of *repetition*. This repetition gives to Israel its distinctive mark as a community which is identified in the present with the past formation of the covenant and the future fulfillment, and which exhibits an inner solidarity that bridges the generations.

" ' Repetition ' for Kierkegaard meant (if one may coin the word) *Preminiscence*, the ' remembering in advance ' of that restoration, and more-than-restoration, of the original Paradise, the anticipation by experiencing faith of that consummation when all created things shall find fruition in the presence and glory of God. Kierkegaard saw this as fundamental to the New Testament." [15]

The illusory infinitude of time is thus overcome by the revelation of God's will, for the whole span of times and seasons is included within the parenthesis of divine purpose. Knowledge of that purpose relates man directly to pretemporal and posttemporal reality. God creates time with his word and ends time with his word, his word being simply his revealed purpose in action. The pre-existence and postexistence of this word is assumed throughout the Bible, though it appears most clearly articulated in the New Testament. [16]

The time sense of Biblical writers does not, therefore, accent time as " the time in which things happen " (*Geschehenszeit*). More important in their consciousness is time as " the time in which things are ordered " (*Ordnungszeit*). But because God's purpose is contemporaneous and never simply a past act of creation, the real consciousness of *Ordnungszeit* is derived from time conceived as the time of destiny (*Schicksalzeit*), though this destiny is not considered as merely the future outcome but the future constituent of contemporaneous decision. [17]

A time sense so oriented can only be expressed in a story that tells of those divine deeds which reveal the purpose that determines destiny. To scholars who attempt objectively to relate Biblical religion to other religions, this aspect seems definitely to justify the classification of Biblical stories as mythological. One scholar defines myth as

" the dramatization in temporal terms of things seen from the non-temporal standpoint of eternity. . . . A myth is not about something that once hap-

[15] G. O. Griffith, in *Expository Times,* March, 1945, p. 155; cf. also T. H. Croxall, in *Expository Times,* August, 1945, pp. 292 f.
[16] Cf. below, pp. 246 ff., 275 f.
[17] Cf. R. Klibansky, *op. cit.,* p. 330.

pened, but rather about something that is always happening: the narration of a divine event. . . . The myth-maker starts not with the particular, but, by illumination of the spirit, with the abstraction of something timeless. . . . The mind sees the whole process at once . . . its dramatic sequence enables anyone meditating on the myth to reverse the analysis, to synthetize and to share the eternal perception from which the myth-maker started." [18]

If one tests these statements by the Biblical accounts of the fall of Adam or the temptation of Jesus, one notes a general appositeness. But the divergences are crucial. In the Bible there is no " myth-maker," no individual who consciously starts with " the abstraction of something timeless " and dramatizes this in temporal terms. It is not accurate to speak of God's purpose as nontemporal. And in the Bible, consequently, the myth purports to tell something that once happened as well as something that always happens; it never distinguishes the particular event from the timeless abstraction. The initial perception includes both, the sense of time itself being engendered by divine activity. It is impossible therefore to " reverse the analysis."

Professor White describes the myth further:

"Every event has a double significance appropriate to the duality of his experience. He enjoys two modes of perception, two distinct but simultaneous ways of viewing each phenomenon; he has two types of information, not drawn from time and eternity respectively, but seen from them. He likewise uses two methods of expressing these parallel perceptions: one is history; the other is myth."

But one must demur again. The prophet is not conscious of his view as bifocal; his perceptions are not parallel alternatives but fused from the beginning. He does not see the event respectively from time and from eternity, nor use two methods of narration. To the extent that God's activity is revealed, to that extent it constitutes the only true history. It is we who draw a line between history and myth. And what we call " myth " is to the prophet the only genuine history, while what we call history is to him a dangerously deceptive " myth," which expresses and reinforces man's self-confident blindness and sin. To draw the line between myth and history in terms of the distinction between time and eternity, and thus to become aware of the use of myth as a means of describing the eternal happening — all this smuggles in Hellenistic patterns of analysis and perverts the Biblical perspective. Herein lies the

[18] Lynn White, Jr., in *Journal of the History of Ideas,* Vol. III, pp. 145 f. 1942.

real ground for objection to the easy application of the term " myth " to the Bible and the legitimate basis for dissatisfaction with current efforts to justify Biblical theology by defending it as true myth. As Hamann observed, if revelation belongs inherently to the history of creation, then all history is mythology.[19] And if all history is mythology, the term myth loses its meaning.

To return to the discussion of time, we must underscore the fact that in the Bible the Hellenistic antinomy between time and eternity does not appear. Since God appoints the times, they are neither meaningless nor evil. To emphasize will is to emphasize time, because time is simply the manifestation of will.[20] Time is will's creation; duration is significant, but it is a derived significance that ceases when the dynamic intention is fulfilled, i.e., when the Kingdom of God comes. Within this perspective, time cannot be viewed abstractly as an impersonal continuum for it has no objective reality per se. Time neither depreciates nor appreciates the value of things. The essential conflicts within which both God and man seek their ends are not conflicts with time. Time is an expression of spirit; its momentum marks the pressure of spirit seeking its goal.[21]

If time is thus an ever new instrument of God's creative purpose, it can hardly be spoken of as a reality over against God *into* which he enters and *with* which he struggles. God ordains the entire chain of times which interweaves man's life (Eccl. 3:10–14); he seizes, and gives, and changes the times. The question therefore arises: In what sense does the Bible speak of an evil time?

THE TIME OF REBELLION

We have seen that history is the story of human rebellion, the arena of conflict between the Creator and the created. We have noted that the sense of time is derived from the awareness of crucial stages in this conflict. How does this derivation color man's experience of duration and change?

[19] Cf. Wendland, *Geschichtsanschauung und Geschichtsbewusstsein im Neuen Testament*, p. 1. 1938.

[20] Cf. Bevan, *Kingdom of God and History*, ed. by H. G. Wood, pp. 54–57. 1938.

[21] The discussion of Professor Kroner, in *Anglican Theological Review*, April, 1943, should be studied with care. For thorough documentation one should consult the article on " *Kairos,*" by G. Delling, in Kittel, *Theologisches Wörterbuch zum Neuen Testament*, Vol. III, pp. 459 f. 1938.

As we have noted, it is the inherent character of each purpose, whether of man's or of God's, to create a time. In his encounter with God, man perceives his rebellion against God, he becomes conscious of contrary purposes and of the evil character of the times which those purposes create. To speak of one's own time is to claim an autonomy for one's own purpose. The evil time in which man lives is the time appropriate to his own stubborn intention (cf. John 7:6).[22] Whereas birds know their appointed times, men refuse to recognize theirs. " The earth teems according to his will at its proper seasons " (I Clement 20:4), but men blind themselves to the signs of their times. Jesus condemns Jerusalem for preferring its own time to God's time (Luke 19:44). Likewise, Ezekiel complains of the sin of his city:

" Thus saith the Lord Jahveh: A city that sheddeth blood in the midst of her, that *her time may come,* and *that maketh idols against herself* to defile her! Thou art become guilty in thy blood that thou hast shed, and art defiled in thine idols which thou hast made; and thou hast caused thy days to draw near, and art come even unto thy years: therefore have I made thee a reproach " (Ezek. 22:3, 4).

To seek one's own time is tantamount to idolatry. But he who is living in idolatry is enslaved to a false time based upon a fictitious autonomy. Men consult oracles to learn the future, to enhance their security, but God drives their diviners mad (Isa. 44:25). Those who prophesy " out of their own heart," i.e., in line with their own desires, are false prophets who deceive the people with their interpretation of the times. They " follow their own spirit, and have seen nothing " (see Ezek. 13:1–7). Idols can declare the meaning neither of the past nor of the future, nor of the demands of the present (Isa. 41:21–24). Slavery to the illusory time of the idols leads men to doubt the true prophet who does not serve their interests. They are made skeptical of former visions, because " the days are prolonged," and of present predictions: " The vision that he seeth is for many days to come " (see Ezek. 12:21–28). Their sense of time deafens them to the contemporary word of the Lord (Ezek. 14:5). Thus rebellion, idolatry, and their corresponding times forge the chains with which man is bound.

In the New Testament the present age is evil precisely because it lies under the authority of Satan. Satan has his own time, but it is *given* to

---

[22] Cf. G. Delling, *op. cit.,* p. 461.

him and can be ended by a word. Satan is a pseudo creator of time; those who share his purposes dwell securely in his age, but their security is also limited as his: it may be ended with a word. God has a controversy, not with time as such, but with this evil time, the age of rebellion. He ever struggles to redeem the evil time by transferring erring creatures from their own pursuits to their true end, knowledge of God and reliance upon his time.

Thus we approach the point of convergence of the three paths of investigation, tracing the sense of time to its three sources in man's will, God's intention, and ever-present rebellion. Viewed from the point of standing of Biblical writers, the important question is not, What is time? but, What time is it? What time is it for us now? And the hands of this clock are set by reference to three existential relationships: What time is it by *my* purpose? by *God's* appointment? by the illusory *idols* under whose tyranny we live? The true answer to all three of these questions is communicated to man in a single moment when God speaks and acts. It can never be computed by objective calculation but only by inner receptiveness and obedience. The true "time of our lives" is revealed to us only from the contemporaneous center where God visits us.

THE YEAR OF VISITATION

The understanding of God's time for us, the ultimate dimension of our lives, stems from two focuses of God's purpose: his revelatory deed and his redemptive deed. The two constitute the beginning and end of God's *kairos*.[23] " As I live, saith Jahveh, I will . . ." The Day of the Lord belongs to him alone; its essential element, maintained with countless variations, is the operation of his sovereignty in destroying his adversaries and completing his strange design (Zeph., ch. 1).[24] No one can appoint him a time (Jer. 49:19). He binds himself by an oath speedily to terminate the period of rebellion and restore creation to its pristine end.

" My righteousness is *near,* my salvation *is* gone forth, and mine arms *shall* judge the peoples; the isles *shall* wait for me. . . . The heavens *shall* vanish

---

[23] Because of the wide divergence between the Biblical and non-Biblical connotations of the term "time," it is necessary in the following discussions to use the Greek word *kairos* to indicate the Biblical connotations of a purpose-created and purpose-charged time.

[24] Cf. A. B. Davidson, *Theology of the Old Testament,* pp. 367 f. 1912.

away like smoke, and the earth *shall* wax old like a garment; and they that dwell therein *shall* die like gnats: but my salvation *shall* be for ever" (Isa. 51:5, 6, margin).

In such a quotation the oscillation from present to future tense and their nearness to each other is worth pondering.

This year of visitation always involves judgment upon the evil *kairos,* a day of wrath, frequently described in metaphors of the harvest, the refining of metals, the crumbling of Babels, and the shaking of the sieve. In the day when God is exalted, the *day* of idols will cease (Isa. 2:5–18) and Satan's *leave* will be canceled.

"An end is come, the end is come; it awaketh against thee; behold, it cometh. Thy doom is come unto thee . . . : the time is come, the day is near. . . . Now will I shortly pour out my wrath upon thee." (Ezek. 7:6–8).

The Day of the Lord, whether in the Old or the New Testament, is thus envisaged as the true time that ends false times, as God's time that ends Satan's. In his act God manifests his sovereignty over all times.

The year of visitation always brings blessedness and joy to those whose lives, once imprisoned in a sin-full time, are now timed by God's appointment. They are children of the day (I Thess. 5:4–6). The divine *kairos* is characterized in terms of *coming to pass,* whereas the *kairos* of sin is characterized as *passing away* (Zeph. 1:14–18). The future of rebels is already past; in its beginning, sin carries with it inevitable frustration. On the other hand, the future of servants is always just beginning, for the act of obedience is the beginning of assured fulfillment. To the servant, the certainty of this fulfillment is always expressed in the nearness of *his coming.* "His salvation is nigh them that fear him" (Ps. 85:9; cf. Zeph. 3:17 f.).

"Jahveh is nigh unto all them that call upon him,
To all that call upon him in truth.
He *will* fulfil the desire of them that fear him;
He also *will* hear their cry, and will save them"
(Ps. 145:18, 19).

Man therefore always enters God's *kairos* by a forward step; he always steps backwards when he trusts the *kairos* of false purposes.

" The future is the incognito in which the eternal, as incommensurable for time, would nevertheless maintain its relations with time." [25]

The attraction of this future *kairos* impels man into a race, hurrying toward the goal, which is always present as call-and-response and is always coming near as promise-and-hope. The response of the runner is often described as repentance and trust. By repentance, he repudiates the competing purposes which permeate the defeated and retreating *kairos*. By trust, he ardently appropriates " with heart and soul and mind and strength " the single purpose which rules the victorious and advancing *kairos*. Synchronization of man's obedience and God's demand marks the way that alone leads to life (Deut., ch. 30; Mark 10:17–22). By trusting in God's word, man anticipates " the dawning of the morning " (Ps. 119:147). And in the darkness before the dawn he suffers, caught in the vortex of the surging " times ": his own, those of idols and demons, and that ultimate *kairos*. He endures by hoping in God's promise: " Blessed are ye that hunger now: for ye shall be filled."

We may return for a moment to the question, What time is it for us now? and suggest that the answer always involves an *interim,* but that there are several interims to be considered. First, there is implicit in every choice of man an interim between an act and its end — either in emptiness or fullness. Secondly, there is implicit in every situation an interim between the advent of God's word and its return to him. Thirdly, implicit in every situation is the *kairos* of evil, deceptive and alluring, with seemingly objective evidence of its ultimacy, but nevertheless an interim bound to end in futility. Man's destiny requires him to choose that interim within which he will stand. By obedience to God's command, man stands within God's *kairos,* renounces the evil time by repentance, and lives by hope in God's promise. By rebelling, he takes his position within the evil time, obeys the command of false lords, and lives by false hopes in the illusory promises of idols or Satan. The more fully his decision is determined by the enemy, the less power he will attribute to Jahveh to fulfill his promise soon. Will he live as one who is " born of blood . . . the will of the flesh . . . the will of man " or as one " born . . . of the will . . . of God " (John 1:13)? By which

[25] S. Kierkegaard, *Concept of Dread,* trans. by W. Lowrie, p. 80. Princeton University Press, 1944. Such a sharp contrast between eternity and time is not wholly Biblical, but may be traced to Kierkegaard's conscious use, in the pseudonymous works, of Greek modes of thought. The above quotation remains, however, an apt characterization of Biblical thought.

kairos will he orient his purpose? This alternative is seen in its sharpest form in the New Testament where God sets forth the cross as the final turning point, the point where Satan's *kairos* is ended and God's new age begins. But the same alternative is posed in both Testaments: when God speaks, he calls man, now enamored and enslaved by a dying age, to return to a new beginning in the *kairos* which the Creator appoints.

7

MAN BUILDS A HOUSE

"Ye have built houses of hewn stone, but ye shall not dwell in them; ye have planted pleasant vineyards, but ye shall not drink the wine thereof" (see Amos 5:10–13).

W E HAVE engaged in elucidating the inner structure of human existence as apprehended by prophets and apostles, that hub of the wheel on which their experience revolved. We turn now to analyze an aspect of their viewpoint that peers through the lines of every book, i.e., the ultimate issues which are involved *for man* in his encounter with God. Who can enter into this strange history without being struck by the intense seriousness of the writers? Every moment is crucial, every scene is decisive, every act has personal and historical implications that are laden with total destiny. When God invades man's consciousness, man's reliance on "peace and security" vanishes from every nook of his existence. His life as a single whole becomes vulnerable. Broken down are the bulkheads between the chambers which confine explosions to one compartment. When God chooses man, he invests him with full responsibility for total obedience to an absolute demand. In man's rebellion and allegiance, the destiny of the community is at stake as well as that of the individual. Caught up in the immediate battle are all the interests and influences that are waging war in global proportions. A shift in the battle line involves a major shift in strategy and in time schedules, but the war continues. Each incident in each battle raises the question of ultimate defeat or victory in the total war.

To use such dramatic terms may appear to exaggerate and romanticize life's petty choices. To the dilettante spectator, the vocabulary of the Bible must appear filled with homiletical pomposities and rhetori-

cal hyperboles. " A man cannot always be in a crisis of this sort." Yet
the Bible does not read as if it were written by preachers striving for
effect by exaggeration. The depth of concern is genuine. Nor does the
Bible present the crises of life as a means of glorifying man's trivial
actions or of expanding his self-importance. Before God, man is made
more conscious than ever of the microscopic littleness of both himself
and his systems. And yet this same man, before God, is overwhelmed
by the macrocosmic implications of a single response to God's call. It is
not so much that man overestimates the possible consequences of his
act upon other men, and judges his act accordingly. He does not reason pragmatically: " A single vote may swing an election; a single election may swing the nation; a single nation may swing the world."
Neither prophet nor apostle is so motivated. Rather, he is compelled
before God to realize that in one particular decision are bound up the
ultimate issues of all decisions. The one choice he must make is a total
choice: " Choose you this day " life or death. At every moment man
finds himself suspended between oblivion and salvation, because every
act relates him to a *kairos* — either of God or of a false god.[1]

THE AREA OF DEEPEST NEED

Rightly or wrongly, the Biblical sense of need is far more compre-
hensive and compelling than that of most modern readers (especially
those in a classroom). The urgency that permeates these writings is not
limited to the desire for conceptual knowledge, however ignorant one
may be. It is not comprised by the craving for emotional satisfaction,
however impoverished one may feel. It is not restricted to the need for
moral or social improvement, however wicked may be either self or
society. The need for deliverance is assumed to be as great among the
very wise as among the very ignorant, among the well-adjusted as among
the ill-adjusted, among the good as among the bad, among the successful as among the failures. Improvement in these areas of human association does not diminish the sense of need, unless it leads one to complacency and self-reliance. Before God, one is made aware of needs
more profound than any of these.

[1] This grounding of obedience on time is directly connected to the accent on self-
regarding motives and sanctions, as discussed above, pp. 51 f.

Before describing this awareness further, it may be well to stress an oft-neglected axiom of theological discussion. Any universe of discourse may be entered and understood only by keeping central the fundamental need which provides the axis on which that universe rotates. Efforts to build a bridge between different worlds get nowhere until some common point of standing can be located in terms of man's ultimate need. *From* what does man seek salvation?

For some of us, the sense of need is most acute in the field of ethics. The enemies which anger us most are those vices that destroy moral integrity and social fellowship. In this case, the good news over which we wax enthusiastic is that which provides knowledge and power to extirpate these vices. Primary obstacles to salvation will likely be found in the prevailing ignorance of correct moral standards, the relativity of the various systems of ethics, the selection of appropriate and effective means, the necessities and hazards of compromise.

Again, some of us locate the chief enemies in the area of nervous and spiritual equilibrium. Struggling with obsessions and complexes, burdened with guilt and anxiety, we seek mental peace as the *sine qua non* of happiness. But the present conflict is a touch-and-go affair. Psychological tensions keep us dangerously near the insanity which seems so endemic in our age. Boredom, ennui, despondency, estrangement, keep thrusting us from one difficult mental state into another. A crisis in external affairs unnerves us. Deliverance into poise and peace is no small boon. The way to salvation must include means for banishing the legion of demons that inhabit our armchair. If this be our deepest sense of need, if this be our real battleground, we will measure all religions by their ability to produce victory on this front.

The universe of discourse populated by professors usually revolves about another axis — the never satiated craving for accurate, objective knowledge. If this be the task about which we are most enthusiastic (perhaps an unsound assumption), then we will tend to locate the source of evil in ignorance, in subjective prejudices, in authoritarianism and obscurantism. Believing that knowledge is power, we will try to locate and harness that power. We search for the sharpest tools, refine epistemological and scientific procedures, and long for the day when our system of knowledge will be perfected. The Bible may then supply grist for our mill, providing methods of analysis or concepts to be assimilated within our total ideology. The historian may be immediately concerned with the infiltration of Hellenism into Biblical thought, the theologian with the relation of reason to revelation, the psychiatrist with the psychic health of Paul and Jesus, the sociologist with the techniques of social control employed by minority leaders. The danger most feared by the scholar may be that he will be caught by other scholars in naïve acceptance of Biblical beliefs or in hasty reliance upon unsound deductions.

A perennial source of misjudging the Bible lies at this point. A world of moralists, a world of theologians, a world of historians — each is preoccupied with problems of acute import to his work, but of subsidiary import to men of the Bible, and each claims the final right to interpret the Bible. It is not strange that in the process the Bible should pass through a radical metamorphosis. Proclamations which originally illuminated the struggles of a shepherd of Tekoa or a fisherman of Galilee lose much of their pristine power when domesticated into the narrow confines of ecclesiastical usage, where they become the peculiar property of clergy and earnest laymen. They may lose even more of their initial relevance to the whole of human existence when they are made the special possession of academicians who exert monopolistic control over their interpretation. The measure of relevance now becomes their contribution to the solution of problems of *thought* rather than to problems of *destiny*. And measured by this criterion the worth of the Bible may diminish steadily. Every problem of thought receives a baffling diversity of treatment in the Bible: the cosmology of Amos was not that of Paul; the psychology of Elijah was not that of Peter; what were moral virtues to David were not virtues to Job; attitudes toward economic and political problems in Deuteronomy are not paralleled in Revelation. Before the bewildering jumble of moral, social, philosophical, political problems that emerged during the millennium of Bible history, what else can be done but surrender all claim to unity, all pretense of normative finality? A return to the Biblical conception of need in any of these areas would necessitate atavistic idolization of antiquated and unscientific ideas of early Semites. Their answers to these questions can only be incorporated into our systems of thought by violently tearing them out of their original context and pushing them forcibly into a modern set of pigeonholes. But such questions were not the primary concern of the Biblical writers! Their quest was motivated from a different source. In an effort to describe positively the sense of need that persisted throughout the tradition, we begin by summarizing hundreds of passages under four words.

1. Precariousness. A clear delineation of this aspect of man's existence may be found in Isa., ch. 40. In God's sight men are but grasshoppers: the strongest of them faint, the speediest become exhausted, the wisest are " as vanity." Powerful empires are drops in a bucket. To be sure, all these creatures try to become creators, the trowel seeking to become the architect.[2] They build systems, organize laws, found empires, trying desperately to establish permanence and immunity to misfortune. They create idols of the most costly, beautiful, and enduring materials, elaborating a religious cultus that will sanctify their efforts. But the same epitaph marks every tomb: " The whirlwind taketh them away as stubble." Nor is this a particularly morbid or melodramatic passage. Elsewhere Isaiah pictures men as gnats. Job views them as spiders trusting in their web and as moths that are crushed between morning and evening (Job 4:19; 8:14). The psalmist knows how many there are who stand in " slippery places "; the seer of Proverbs lists many sins besides pride which go " before a fall." Everywhere God is found humbling those who deceive themselves into thinking that they " shall not be moved."

The precariousness of all men is heightened in the New Testament with the expectation of impending Judgment. Rich men build barns, traders plan their journeys, Dives feasts in luxury, people occupy themselves with their normal routines — sleeping, baking bread, marrying, cultivating their farms — when the lightning strikes. The sieve is shaken, the ax is laid at the root of the tree. Destruction falls while they are saying, "'Peace and safety'" (I Thess. 5:3); the bridegroom returns while the virgins are sleeping; the thief comes in the night; the lord of the vineyard demands his rental; floods beat against the houses. The tenuous uncertainty and instability of all human structures is disclosed by the approach of God's time. Whatever one's wealth or wisdom or prestige, that disclosure finds him on the edge of the precipice.

2. Transiency. Man's precariousness is not, however, a matter of occasional or accidental misfortune. His permanent status is that of a transient being, whose days fly swifter than " a weaver's shuttle " (Job 7:6). When Johannes Brahms was composing his *Requiem,* he turned for texts to his well-worn Bible, selecting them from widely scattered parts

[2] De Maistre.

of Scripture. Through some genius of sensitivity, he chose the most poignant and typical elegiac passages and blended them perfectly with music:

> " Behold, all flesh is as the grass, and all the goodliness of man is as the flower of grass;
> For lo, the grass with'reth, the flower thereof decayeth. . . ."

> " Lord, make me to know the measure of my days on earth, to consider my frailty that I must perish."

> " Here on earth have we no . . . continuing place. . . ."

> " All my days here are as an handbreadth to thee. . . ."

> " Verily, mankind walketh in a vain show,
> And their best state is altogether vanity. . . ."

The writer of The Wisdom of Solomon, drawing upon the proverbial wisdom of the Old Testament, described man's life in the following metaphors: a shadow, a passing rumor, a ship passing through the sea, a bird flying in the air, chaff blown by the wind, hoarfrost, an arrow speeding on its journey, smoke carried on the breeze, the memory of a guest who stays but a night (Wisd. of Sol. 5:9–14). The stress upon such metaphors is not homiletical melodrama but simple realism that describes the limits of human existence at its best, and not at its worst. This stress does not stem from hypochondria or hysterical imaginings of dreadful evils but from a sober recognition of the irrevocable limitations of human life.

3. The frustration of achievements. It is not alone the insecurity and brevity of man's lifetime that makes his situation desperate; what intensifies the shortness of his days is the potential pointlessness of his efforts. That life ends so quickly and abruptly is tragic enough, but this tragedy is heightened by a fruitless harvest. Men who sow the wind must live on wind (Hos. 12:1); not all " that sow in tears shall reap in joy," but only those to whom God grants a harvest. Man builds a house, but in vain " except the Lord build " it; he watches the walls of the city, he prepares the horse for battle, but all in vain apart from God's blessing. When man sees all the travail of his soul, will he be satisfied, or will he moan, " ' I have spent my strength for nought ' "? Everywhere he observes unpredictable reversals. It is possible for God to lead one in the way everlasting, so that his works " follow after him," but fre-

quently man's glory is put to shame. Those who die and rest from their labors are blessed *if* their works actually follow them, but how often God frustrates their desires (Hos. 4:6–10)! Men heap up riches but do not have power over them (Ps. 39:4–6). Their pride is but "labor and sorrow; for it is soon gone, and we fly away" (Ps. 90:10). None of the things in which man glories is immune to this destruction (Ps. 103:14; 144:4; 146:3). This anxiety is a continuing *a priori:* "What hath a man of all his labor?" How may one know that his house will stand?

It is no wonder that the metaphor of harvest should be so prominent in Biblical speech, that eschatology should become such a crucial problem. Man's purpose, the core of his existential selfhood, requires an end; the justification of all his efforts must await the consummation of that end. The planter lives by a future which he can neither know nor control; that future alone will disclose the fruitfulness of his labor. Men cannot live without laying up something in store for themselves; the question of prime importance is how good this foundation is "against the time to come" (I Tim. 6:19). That verdict belongs to the Judge of all men, who alone can fulfill or frustrate their hope.

4. *The vanity of hope.* Man's sense of need is oriented around his fear of futility and his hope of fruitfulness. Present precariousness, transience, and frustration may be replaced by an enduring house; present success and security may be as evanescent as smoke from the chimney. Some assurance of coming vindication is therefore essential. In Ecclesiastes we find an elucidation of the human situation when all faith in the future vanishes — not typical, perhaps, in the degree of skepticism, yet this book shows the inevitable reaction when the spring of hope is broken. It indicates the most deplorable state conceivable. The writer of Ecclesiastes is led to admit that "a man cannot find out the work that God hath done from the beginning to the end." God has made prosperity and adversity side by side "to the end that man should not find out anything that shall be after him" (Eccl. 7:14). There is no memory of former or latter generations (ch. 1:11). "Of the wise man, even as of the fool, there is no remembrance for ever" (ch. 2:16). Every man "cometh in vanity, and departeth in darkness, and the name thereof is covered with darkness. . . . All the labor of man is for his mouth, and yet the appetite is not filled" (ch. 6:4, 7). The prophet had proclaimed the inevitable frustration of sin and idolatry: "They shall eat, and not have enough" (Hos. 4:10). In extending this frustration

to all human hopes, the Preacher arrives at the extremest formulation of human agony: "Vanity of vanities, all is vanity." He thus articulates the Biblical sense of need in its sharpest form, unless it be exceeded by the early Christian apprehension of the law of sin and death that infects the whole groaning creation (Rom., chs. 1; 8).

In this word "vanity" is comprehended evil at its maximum, salvation from which is most desperately needed: the cancellation of one's efforts, the final alienation from continuing purpose, the eternal deprivation of destiny. With an empty future, man has no present; with no fruits, the planting is wasted labor and the day of death becomes better than the day of birth.

THE SUPREME PUNISHMENT

We may note that the fact of mortality, which places a limit upon one's lifetime, is a factor in all four definitions of the sense of need, but it is not the central or dominating factor. In facing the termination of their own earthly existence, Jews and early Christians were free from morbid introversion and gloomy sentimentalism. Fear of the Reaper's scythe was not a source of hysteria or of frantic search for assurances of immortality. Both Testaments refuse to share a hope for survival that is spawned simply by the death of the body. It was not the fact of mortality that tormented the writers of Job, Ecclesiastes, or Romans. The time of death is appointed to men; to seek to evade it is sinful rebellion. To be sure, premature death is a manifestation of precariousness, of transiency, of frustration of efforts, and perhaps of the emptiness of hope, but the cessation of life does not necessarily coincide with the verdict of vanity. One may lose his life and yet save it. Death is an ambiguous event; it may or may not be an expression of the futility of man's life; it may or may not mark the collapse of the house which he has built. Postponement of one's demise does not appear in itself as the major goal of effort.

Death is a category similar to time in Biblical thought — it is not a single universal reality with a single meaning that can be stated in objective terms. No single definition can be made to fit all Biblical uses of the term. Its meaning is derived from the central meeting of God and man; each specific instance receives its significance from man's purpose, from God's purpose, from the convergence and conflict of those purposes. This explains why *vanity* better defines man's sense of need than *death;* only to the extent that death coincides with vanity (in each individual case) does it move into the area of basic concern. At times the term " death " is used without any reference to the religious relationship, just as there are occasions when reference to time is purely chronological. In these cases the fact of death does not enter the problem of salvation. But when the God-relationship provides the context in which the experience of death is set, then death becomes significant as the object of human choice and the punishment of sin. In this context, and here again the analogy with time is instructive, death receives a double focus. It is viewed from the standpoint of both contemporaneity and futurity. One is dead while he lives, if his purpose is estranged wholly from the Creator's intention (Eph. 2:1–5). But the reality of this death will be manifested only when future oblivion shrouds this idolatrous purpose. By the act of rebellion, by the choice of his own *kairos,* man seeks and receives death. The branch is sundered from the Vine; no longer does it receive its true sustenance and its only destiny is to shrivel up into a nullity. It is in this sense that death and vanity become coterminous. Man's greatest need is to be delivered from this vanity-death, conceived as both contemporaneous and future. And it is axiomatic with Biblical writers that such oblivion is always the punishment for a heart alienated from God's will and for a *kairos* determined by this evil heart. A corollary presupposition conceives the ultimate problem of human existence in terms of perfect obedience to God and the fulfillment of his promise in his appointed time. Varying concepts of salvation thus become virtually equivalent: man receives salvation and fulfills his true destiny by escaping this vanity-death, by knowing and glorifying God, by deliverance from sin, by inheriting the promises.

One should not, of course, ignore the vast changes that develop in the concept of punishment during the millennium of Biblical history. The threat to the continued existence of wandering nomads took a form very different from the threat to the existence of the Christian Church during the reign of Domitian. The specific prophecies of Hosea envisaged different types of catastrophe from those of the specific " woes " of Jesus. Such events as the murder of Abel or the Noachic flood were reinterpreted differently in each successive century to illustrate the penalties of sin. During one epoch the frustration of tribal hopes was the chief threat; during another epoch the frustration of national hopes became predominant.[3] But the basic assumptions remained unaltered. Unaltered, too, was the double orientation of fruitlessness in terms of contemporaneity and futurity. God's word in the present promises coming retribution. The threats of Amos coincide at this point with the woes of Jesus:

"The Lord Jahveh hath sworn . . . the days shall come upon you" (Amos 4:2).

"I . . . hate . . . ; therefore will I deliver up the city" (ch. 6:8).

"The end is come upon my people Israel; I will not again pass by them any more" (ch. 8:2).

"Woe unto you, ye that are full now! for ye shall hunger" (Luke 6:25).

"Except ye repent, ye shall all likewise perish" (ch. 13:5).

"Woe unto thee, Chorazin! . . . It shall be more tolerable for Tyre and Sidon" (Matt. 11:21, 22).

These warnings are more than a vague guess of some coming retribution; they are a revelation of present alienation from the will of God. The existing situation is precarious because present decisions are in themselves vain; the impending future will simply disclose their inherent emptiness. Where vanity is defined in terms of purpose, its present and future are integral parts of the same reality. Present and future are different aspects of the same *kairos,* the *kairos* of iniquity. Before God this *kairos* is judged as a whole. To live in rebellion is to live in suspense between the two poles: God's word wherein he condemns existent sin, and his deed wherein his promised penalty is meted out. This remains true even when the postponement of the penalty lulls the rebel into a false sense of security.

THE SUPREME REWARD

What has been said of the punishment of sin can be said as well of rewards for obedience. The righteous are delivered from precariousness to a place where they " shall not be moved "; from transiency to an abiding heritage; from frustrated works to a " way everlasting "; from an empty hope to an assured rest; from vanity-death to a life wherein

[3] Cf. P. S. Minear, *And Great Shall Be Your Reward,* Ch. I. 1941.

existence is fulfilled coincidentally with the fulfillment of God's creative goal. As in the case of the term "death," "life" is a word with multiple meanings. But here again the central connotation is that which is derived from a context in the God relationship. And during the epochs of Biblical history there develop as many variant conceptions of life as in the case of death. But throughout this history the basic attitude is that of existence in relation to God. Life comes from God and returns to him; life is fulfilled when its primal thrust is carried out to the glory of God. Such an existence is oriented around the present revelation of God's will and the future fulfillment thereof. "Seek ye me, and ye shall live" (Amos 5:4).

This promise was more than a promissory note to be fulfilled at a date in the future. It was a covenant undergirding present struggle, defining existent relationships. Thus alone could the psalmist testify:

> "My flesh and my heart faileth;
> But God is the strength of my heart and my portion for ever"
> (Ps.73:26).

Encompassed by darkness and misery he could sing, "Jahveh is my light and my salvation." Surrounded by enemies that appear invincible he abides in his "refuge and strength," finding God "a very present help in trouble." From the depths of anguish burst the most exalted affirmations of God's continuing help. With him is the fountain of life; he daily bears our burdens; he alone can keep our souls. The presence of God in a heart inclined to do his will remains the ground without which hope is inconceivable.

> "These wait all for thee,
> That thou mayest give them their food in due season.
> Thou givest unto them, they gather;
> Thou openest thy hand, they are satisfied with good.
> Thou hidest thy face, they are troubled;
> Thou takest away their breath, they die. . . .
> Thou sendest forth thy Spirit, they are created;
> And thou renewest the face of the ground"
> (Ps. 104:27 ff.).

We should not forget, however, that this consciousness of the nearness of God as "my portion for ever" strengthens the awareness of the precariousness of all existence apart from his word.

"The grass withereth, the flower fadeth; but the word of our God shall stand forever" (Isa. 40:8).

Those who worship idols are encouraged to hope for an easy escape from insecurity and frustration, for a false assurance of permanence. But they feed on ashes (ch. 44:20). The word of the Lord proclaims in the same breath that men shall die like gnats and that his salvation shall be forever (ch. 51:6). This recognition of man's utter dependence upon God, with the accompanying awareness of man's transiency as a creature, is occasion, not for despair, but for hope.

Nor should we forget that the sense of God's nearness is always expressed in terms of the nearness of his coming salvation. "Blessed are ye poor: . . . for ye shall be filled" (Luke 6:20, 21). Blessedness is always a present anticipation of future promise. Men are saved in hope. And "hope that is seen is not hope." In this sense, the writer of II Timothy gives voice to the longing and the confidence of both Testaments:

"I know full well Him in whom my trust reposes, and I have complete confidence that He is able to guard securely my faith and my fortunes, which I have placed in His keeping until the Great Day" (II Tim. 1:12; translation by Falconer).

In stressing the hope-full character of faith, the writer of Hebrews is also true to the entire tradition (Heb., chs. 10 to 12).

We pointed out how accurately Johannes Brahms caught the note of desperate need in his *Requiem* texts. We should point out, too, how well he articulates the faith and hope which enabled men to look down into the depths of need:

"Blessed are the dead, which die in the Lord . . .
That they rest from their labours, and their works follow after them."

And how aptly his music rises to its climax in the triumphant witness to the sufficiency of God's promise:

"I am the beginning and the end, saith the Lord."

Franz Kafka is not far from the Biblical outlook in his profound saying about suffering:

"Only here is suffering suffering. Not in the sense that those who suffer here are ennobled somewhere else because of their suffering, but in the sense that what is called suffering in this world is, without any alteration except that it is freed from its opposite, bliss in another." [4]

Each man builds a house, but only houses built by God may be expected to stand. That, in fine, is the Biblical perspective with regard to man's destiny. That is one response of those whom the Lord visits with his call and his demand. It is a response nerved by obedience to revelation and by hope for the promised fulfillment. But it is a response that is scorned and derided by the majority of men in every generation. And not only is it ridiculed by opportunistic self-seekers and by the complacent self-sufficient, but it is also contradicted ever again by the external movements of human affairs. It is a faith that proves itself by the obstacles it must overcome; a confidence in the invisible that is ever denied by the visible; a commitment to heavenly purposes which are apparently thwarted by earthly forces. It is natural that this testing should be most severe at the two points where by human standards the faith seems most vulnerable. God's word and deed are challenged at the two most crucial points: the present revelation of his intention; his promise of imminent salvation. The hovels of the righteous appear so much more flimsy than the mansions of the rebels. Are these hovels after all built according to the design of Almighty Power? Will they, as a matter of record, stand after the substantial edifices of the mightiest men have crumbled to dust?

The servant is justified by his faith, but the question inevitably arises: Is his faith justified? Is the servant's faith met by the faithfulness of God? When man accepts the time appointed another problem is set: How soon will God's promise, now spoken in the ear, be shouted from the housetops? How certainly will the anticipated morning dawn? Only in the coming of the goal can the race be justified. It is this interim between the revelatory act and the redemptive act that subjects the servant's faith to its greatest strain. The greater the agony of frustration, the greater the tension; the greater the tension, the more radical must be both the repentance and the trust. Under increasing trial, man can diminish the tension by surrendering either the revelation or the promise. But to give up either is to give up both. Man can treat the revelation as something in the past, the more and more distant past, and thus adjust himself more comfortably to the present. Or he can treat the promise

---

[4] *A Franz Kafka Miscellany,* p. 55. Twice a Year Press, 1940.

as something limited to the future, the more and more distant future, and thus reduce the immediacy of God's salvation. These were perhaps the tendencies represented by the extreme legalists and extreme apocalyptists of Jesus' day. But those who confronted God's *kairos* in full contemporaneity of revelation and full imminence of redemption, and who, in response, yielded their heart's deepest longings in repentance and trust, must accept the bent spring as a necessary concomitant of their situation.

But still the spring might break at any moment. Over and over again they were tried to the point of despair. The revelatory act is hidden now; perhaps it is a delusion. The redemptive act is still deferred, the promise is contradicted at every point; perhaps it too is an empty dream. Does our God actually appoint the times? Can we continue to trust our destiny to him? These two questions, phrased in myriad forms and probed in myriad directions, will occupy most of the remaining chapters. On their satisfactory solution, albeit a solution in terms not of speculative theory but of actual experience, rests the validity of the entire structure of Biblical faith. What was more important, on their solution in immediate decision rested the destiny of each man and each nation.

THIS RELIGION says that men are in darkness and estranged from God, that He has hidden Himself from their knowledge, that this is in fact the name which He gives Himself in the Scriptures, Deus Absconditus. . . . *It endeavors equally to establish these two things: that God has set up in the church visible signs to make Himself known to those who would seek Him sincerely, and that He has nevertheless so disguised them that He will only be perceived by those who seek Him with all their heart.*

— Pascal, *Pensées,* trans. by W. F. Trotter, No. 194. The Modern Library, 1941.

8

GOD CONCEALS HIS WORD

" Surely the Lord . . . will do nothing, except he reveal his secret unto his servants the prophets. The lion hath roared; who will not fear? " (Amos 3:7, 8).

IT IS God's visit that precipitates the strange angle of vision, the unique point of standing, which we have depicted in Part I. It is the impact of his purpose that creates a distinctive awareness of vocation, duty, conflict, community, time, and destiny. The revelatory act changes the eyes of him who beholds it. In the preceding pages, we have noted how the tensions of man's relations to the world place in jeopardy the validity of this revelatory act. That " lion's roar " which is most convincing to the prophet is least convincing to the nonbeliever. It is now necessary, therefore, to examine more closely the nature of that act. What is the character of this occasion in the foreground, on which the prophet focuses his vision, and which provokes the dilemmas of faith?

If God were not Creator, but a part of creation, this question might be answered with greater ease. But as Creator he is wholly other than his works. Man can see his works, but cannot see their Author.

" I beheld all the work of God, that man cannot find out the work that is done under the sun: because however much a man labor to seek it out, yet he shall not find it " (Eccl. 8:17).

We must therefore, at the outset, inquire into the character of this hiddenness (ch. 8). His voice is inaudible; yet he speaks. How does that voice enter the range of human audition (ch. 9)? When he speaks, the servant is commissioned to speak the word to others. What means are most appropriate for the executing of this commission (ch. 10)? But God speaks through his works, and the prophet must convey his message by his actions. What is this strange medium by which actions speak more loudly than words? What is the form and import of signs (ch. 11)?

Taking up the first of these questions, we begin with a brief résumé of the angle of vision to show the centrality of the revelatory act in the entire perspective. Then we move into a study of the hiddenness of God by noting the relative positions of the hearer and the Speaker. Finally, comes an analysis of the juncture between speaking and hearing.

CENTRALITY OF COMMUNICATION

Ordinary life becomes meaningful existence before God when God visits man, Subject meeting subject in personal communication. True selfhood as an " I " presupposes the free self-disclosure of a " Thou." Apart from a personal word of God, this meeting does not take place. Awareness of God's call alone precipitates a sense of the dynamic and ultimate possibilities of this concrete situation. A new self-consciousness and historical consciousness stem from the revelation of Him who creates the self for a particular destiny.

Each encounter with God is viewed from within by a particular creature, who is at once himself and his community. This creature senses that his total existence is involved in the encounter, focused in the moment of revelation. The word is addressed especially to him, not to " all those whom it may concern." Disclosure is granted, not through general and universal principles and laws for all times and places, but through a distinct word and deed at a single time and place, here and now. Man is confronted, not with revelation in general nor with many revelations, but with this revelation, i.e., what God is saying to me now.

The living God speaks to living men always in the *present*. He speaks through " remembrance of things past " and points back to covenants disclosed to the fathers, but his voice provokes a contemporaneous repetition of the covenant. He makes promises and threats concerning forthcoming judgment, but these predictions constitute by anticipation a crisis which forces men to make an ultimate choice now. The only compass that indicates true direction is that which is oriented by the two poles of what God has said and will say, a needle that rotates on the spindle of what God is now saying.

Revelation is thus inseparable from demand for immediate decision. Because the disclosure manifests the purpose of *God*, man finds himself in a situation in which his decision is an absolute either-or. Fully responsible, man faces the possibility of obedience, the possibility of rebellion. Postponement or compromise are in effect prime instances of rebellion.

The decision to which man is summoned is the most serious business of all, for on it depends the futility or fruitfulness of his life. Apart from an understanding of God's active purpose, destiny is immediately and totally jeopardized. His time is in God's hand. God's *kairos* must be disclosed if it is to be shared. Such disclosure includes a vision of the future sufficiently clear to avert the threatened catastrophe but not so obvious as to compel acquiescence, sufficient to command faith but insufficient to insure its fulfillment. Man is called to venture everything for an end which by revelation is made subjectively certain, but which must await the time of fulfillment for objective certainty. This coming event alone will bring perfect knowledge of God. And such knowledge will be communicated through an ultimate judgment wherein God's purpose is seen to be triumphant over every obstruction, and through an ultimate salvation wherein the goodness of his creation is manifested and the faith of his servants is vindicated. During the interim before that consummation his word is the primary power propelling each particular creation toward that end.

This, then, is the necessary point of departure for a discussion of revelation. But we cannot rest satisfied with this minimal statement of the area of consensus; we must seek to expand the area by probing the implications of these skeletal statements and by inductive study of the relevant evidence. Much evidence justifies the conclusion that a larger area of consensus may be found.

THE SITUATION OF THE HEARER

In extending this area, we may begin by observing that it is generally assumed that apart from God's self-disclosure, man is hopelessly ignorant of God's will.

" For man also knoweth not his time: as the fishes that are taken in an evil net, and as the birds that are caught in the snare, even so are the sons of men snared in an evil time " (Eccl. 9:12).

" As thou knowest not what is the way of the wind, nor how the bones do grow in the womb of her that is with child; even so thou knowest not the work of God who doeth all " (ch. 11:5).

Consciousness of ignorance comes perhaps to sharpest expression in Ecclesiastes, where the spring of faith is most severely bent and where the word of the prophet is no longer heard. Even this extreme skeptic, however, refuses to relinquish the conviction that all is the work of God and that destiny is in his hands (ch. 9:1). Though this book may be relegated to the circumference of Biblical tradition, it shows that the arrows of the skeptic are directed, not against the power of God, but against the blindness of men. And here the skeptic's doubt is not far removed from the testimony of the prophet. Jeremiah, for instance, received as compelling a word from Jahveh as any; yet he cries (or should we say, *therefore* he cries), " O Jahveh, I know that the way of man is not in himself; it is not in man that walketh to direct his steps " (Jer. 10:23).

Both Ecclesiastes and Jeremiah imply that this ignorance is inherent in man's status as creature. God's ways and thoughts differ from man's, simply because God is God and man is man. Man's understanding of the meaning of a situation is always relative to his involvements. No one within history can detect its meaning clearly or experience fully its consummation, for his judgments are based on appearances and on a fragment of God's work. His inferences are colored by self-interest, limited by inability to disentangle the permanent from the transitory, the source of energy from the manifestations of energy, the divine from the demonic. His standards of judgment are derived in part from observing the external course of history rather than from unmediated contact with the source of history. He cannot escape his status as creature by initiating a process of self-transcendence or by accumulating a vast store of knowledge through observation, experimentation, and reason. It is to the wise men of his day that the fourth Evangelist repeatedly insists, " No man hath seen God at any time " (John 1:18).

Such ignorance as is native to man as creature does not, however, condemn him to futility. Salvation does not require an obliteration of the distinction between God's knowledge and man's ignorance. Rather, it requires the recognition of that distinction as ineradicable. But man is not satisfied with that recognition. He seeks to erase the distinction, seeks to extend his knowledge beyond the limits appointed to him, and trusts his security to such illegitimate extensions of knowledge.

He is persistently tempted to trust in his own thoughts and powers. Not knowing his own heart, he acts as though he does, and is progressively deceived (Jer. 17:9). Not knowing the source or goal of his history, he assumes that he does, trusting his power to deduce such knowledge from his analysis of exterior events. He fights the tenuous insecurity of his life by seeking to establish within himself or his community a basis of security — in swiftness, prowess, wealth, wisdom, or power — but his trust in himself or his group never becomes stronger than a "spider's web" (Job 8:14; cf. Amos 2:13 f.). He devours the fruit of the tree of knowledge of good and evil, in the hope of becoming like God. But his confidence that he can discern good and evil deceives him and estranges him from God's initial purpose. Assuming that his own purposes are ultimate, he relies upon a cause-effect analysis of experience to yield the techniques for realizing those ends. The eyes by which he measures men and events have been injured by the glasses he has worn from birth, which have been given to him by a sinful community, and which therefore warp every picture of so-called reality. When God reasserts his sovereignty, man discovers how astigmatic his vision is, how he is enslaved by social criteria of judgment, how he relies upon proximate and deceptive goods, how he trusts his own power to coerce conditions to his ends. He discovers, in short, that his blindness is as deep as his sin.

Man's status as creature, when corrupted by trust in his own knowledge, always provokes a famine of the words of God (Amos 8:11). Blindness and self-deception are a manifestation of sin, a punishment for sin, and a warrant of coming judgment.

"Jahveh hath a controversy . . . because there is no truth, nor goodness, nor knowledge of God in the land. . . . Therefore shall the land mourn. . . . Thou shalt stumble in the day, and the prophet also shall stumble with thee in the night. . . .
"My people are destroyed for lack of knowledge: because thou hast rejected knowledge, I will also reject thee " (see Hos. 4:1–10).

Yet consciousness of this famine is not sufficient to provide food. Frantically men may seek God's word and not find it; helpless they may fall and there may be nothing to help them rise (Amos 8:11 f.). Consulting the prophets for guidance, they hear the false assurance, " ' Peace, peace; when there is no peace.' " The prophets also stumble.

Throughout the Bible man's contemporary blindness is seen to involve a flaw in memory, a perversion of the covenant relationship. The current situation is distinguished by a dangerous declension from the initial directness and clarity with which man apprehended and accepted God's will. Eyes have been blinded, perhaps by adversity (Israel in exile), perhaps by prosperity (settlement in Canaan), perhaps by the lack of vindication of God's power (the psalmists), perhaps by the apparent superiority of other gods (Elijah), or by the strangeness of the signs of God's activity (the Gospels). In any case, ambiguity and uncertainty cloud the previous understanding of God's purpose, and apostasy is at the point of triumph. The covenant becomes a closed book, inert, static, unreal, outworn.

Present blindness also involves a flaw in hope, a defective attitude toward future fulfillment of the covenant; it jeopardizes prospect as well as retrospect. God's power to complete his promises becomes dubious, and other expectations become more alluring and convincing. The blind man substitutes his own conception of future possibilities for God's revealed Word, and tries confidently to lead others in his chosen direction. He finds blind prophets to strengthen his own guesses, and together they fall into the pit.

Such blindness can be healed, but not without a radical correction of vision. The blind man must become aware of his blindness and of his inability to heal himself. And that is no easy step. Repentance may be less than total, and partial repentance may inhibit true repentance. It may follow the path of archaism, a retreat to a previous golden age. Impelled by disillusionment with the present, men may affirm the superiority of the ancestral covenant, and may seek to return to former conditions of glory. The massive witness of the past overbalances the confused witness of the present, and is hailed as providing the authority and certainty needed for salvation. A call is issued to reform self and society into conformity with this received tradition. Previous revelation of God's will is eulogized as adequate ground on which to build anew. This tendency to archaism may be discerned everywhere in the Bible, but it is everywhere *resisted* by the prophets and those who remain true to their perspective. Pharisaism and rabbinism overcome the resistance and move definitely in the direction of archaism by codifying the Law and the Prophets, by affirming the adequacy of this previous revelation in canonizing it, and by assuming that the Holy Spirit and prophecy have ceased to guide the destinies of Israel. The New Testament represents the rejection of this archaist interpretation of revelation. Repentance meant for Jesus and Paul something different from what it meant for Shammai and Hillel, in that for the former it involved the cure of a distorted memory.

On the other hand, men who are dissatisfied with the present status may select the path of futurism. Aware of contemporary blindness, they may attribute this epidemic to a particular set of environmental conditions or to popular acquiescence in them. Leaders arise with a vision of renewed independence and righteousness, and call for vigorous social reformation to establish a new set of conditions when once again the covenant may be enforced. Here belong some of the Zealots of the Maccabean and Herodian days. By prophetic and Christian standards, their analysis of the extent of blindness, and hence the depth of needed repentance, is faulty. The Zealots are confident that they can see, but in fact they too are blind leaders of the blind. Or a second type of futurism may be chosen: the prevalent blindness may be attributed to a predestined scheme for this age. Only in God's own time, at last near at hand, will a renewal of pristine perfection be granted. A new covenant will be made, justice will be executed, knowledge will again return to earth. Only then will true prophets arise again to provide the needed guidance. But the extreme apocalyptists in weaving dreams of future redemption trusted their own eyes, and envisaged a happy land in which they would be blessed and their enemies would be punished. Though they could not establish justice, they were confident that their *own standards* of justice would be respected.[1]

But the cure of blindness was viewed by Old Testament prophets and New Testament apostles in more profound terms. Man cannot cure himself, and the conviction that he can is but the sharpest example of his blindness. Repentance must be more than a self-chosen return to conditions of the past, for man's blindness has infected his vision of the covenant itself. The process of *recollection* is invalidated by the sin of those who seek to return down the corridors of the past. The covenant must be *repeated* rather than recollected, and repetition can come only by a fresh act of God, manifesting his purpose in new clarity. Repentance must likewise be more than a self-chosen and self-defined leap into the future. Blind men dream dreams, but the content of the dreams reflects their blindness. God alone knows the riddle of destiny; his future

[1] A thorough study of archaism and futurism is provided by A. J. Toynbee, *A Study of History*, Vol. VI, pp. 49–132. 1934–1939.

is the true future, and that future becomes realized only within the orbit of present revelation. Prophets are false if they predict a future in accordance with their dreams of glory, or if they postpone to the future a revelation that does not radically alter the present existential reality.

To return to the metaphor of the compass: Archaism tries to realign the needle to the pole of previous revelation, and futurism realigns it to the pole of coming retribution, but both fail to place the needle on the true pivot of the disclosure of God's power — now — of the miracle of healing now, whereby new eyes can discern the present working of God. Repentance is actual only in the present; it is adequate only when it is total, i.e., when it confesses the need for a new heart, new eyes, new patterns of judgment and expectation. Only the transformed mind can see what is the true and perfect will of God (Rom. 12:1 f.); and only a fresh, immediate revelation of God's initiative can so transform the mind. In a sentence, revelation heals blindness by revolutionizing man's understanding of the critical situation wherein he now stands. Man's ignorance cannot be removed by himself because he is ignorant with regard to the depth and source and form of his ignorance. God alone can give him true knowledge of his ignorance.[2]

Early Christians understood the mission of Jesus in these terms — the radical character of blindness, of repentance, and of God's activity in restoring true vision:

" For judgment came I into this world, that they that see not may see; and that they that see may become blind " (John 9:39).

In our day, T. S. Eliot has reiterated the requirements of a restored knowledge of God:

" In order to arrive at what you do not know
    You must go by a way which is the way of ignorance.
In order to possess what you do not possess
    You must go by the way of dispossession.
In order to arrive at what you are not
    You must go through the way in which you are not.
And what you do not know is the only thing you know
And what you own is what you do not own
And where you are is where you are not." [3]

[2] Cf. Paul Ramsey, in *Christianity and Crisis,* 1943, Vol. III, No. 6.
[3] *Four Quartets,* p. 15. Harcourt Brace & Co., 1943.

THE SITUATION OF THE SPEAKER

The self-concealment of God's word is the precise counterpart of the blindness of human eyes; the epiphany of God is the precise counterpart of restored sight. The transition from hiddenness to open manifestation coincides with the transition from blindness to sight. The objective miracle of God's act is inseparable from the miracle of human response. From the standpoint of the blind man who now sees, the activity of God is the primary source from which his new sight is derived. He becomes the light by which we see.

From this standpoint, too, the ultimate source of blindness is the act of God in hiding himself from men (Amos 8:11). He sends false prophets; he drugs his people, shuts the ears of the prophets, stops the eyes of the seers, reduces his instruction so that " they may go, and fall backward, and be broken, and snared, and taken " (see Isa. 28:9–13; cf. ch. 29:9–14). Parallels to these prophetic statements may be found throughout the New Testament: in Paul's letters, the Synoptics, the Fourth Gospel, and the Apocalypse. B. W. Bacon recognized this theme as " ancient," as " fairly stereotyped," as an " indispensable key," as " a commonplace of post-Isaian Judaism." Such central passages as I Cor. 1:18 to 2:16; Matt. 11:25–27; Mark 4:11, do not, according to Professor Bacon, advance " anything new." [4]

These observations may illuminate the ubiquitous Biblical references to Jahveh as one who hides himself. The God of Israel dwells in thick darkness. No one can see his face and live. No one can model an image in his form (Deut. 4:12–19) and any attempt to represent his presence in visible and tangible substance is gross blasphemy. His glory is by nature irreducible to human categories. To see his glory and salvation is to behold what has been hidden from the foundation of the world. To see his Messiah glorified is to behold him in clothes whiter than any human can make them. Phrased in a pungent proverb,

> " It is the glory of God to conceal a thing;
> But the glory of kings is to search out a matter "
> (Prov. 25:2).

[4] *Studies in Matthew*, pp. 202 ff., 378 ff. 1930. With these judgments we must agree, although dissenting from the explanation that Biblical writers were primarily interested in defending their special status, and in asserting their superiority over outsiders.

Nor does the general revelation of God in creation abrogate this in such a fashion that man can move progressively and unaided from a knowledge of nature to a knowledge of God. Every writer affirms with Paul that " the invisible things of him since the creation of the world are clearly seen, being perceived through the things that are made " (Rom. 1:20); affirms with the psalmist that " there is no speech nor language where their voice is not heard " (Ps. 19:3, King James Version). But these writers who stress the creative activity of God in all things also stress the hiddenness of God in what he has made. Man cannot find God by searching, nor create an epiphany of God by following a prescribed formula. His Kingdom is not to be taken by storm, nor is his glory to be reduced to the dimensions of mere human intelligence.

Other ancient peoples, to be sure, were impressed with the hiddenness of the divine Being, as, for example, the Sumerians. Between the Sumerian and the Hebrew thought worlds are many common strands, but, if we may accept the witness of Alfred Guillaume [5] there are major differences in the way in which these two peoples conceived of God's hiddenness. For the Sumerians, the concealment of God is an irrevocable fact designed without reference to any concern for man, who therefore must respond to this fact in a mood of terror and despair. The scrolls of fate are forever closed to him because of his natural status rather than because of his historical alienation via sin. If he is to avert the dread consequences of an inscrutable fate, he must use special esoteric techniques and magical practices. Traces of these attitudes may be found in the Bible, but the prevailing accent and mood are different. Here the hiddenness of God has a positive meaning derived from his purpose for men: the glory of God will ultimately be manifested throughout his creation. God's hiddenness produces fateful results, not because of man's status as creature, but because of his status as *fallen* creature, whose actual historical sin has blinded him to the Creator's intention. And this blindness can be removed, not by trust in techniques or practices that enable men to exert control over God, but by wholehearted return to their true status. To the penitent, the hiddenness of God becomes, not the curse of an irrevocable decree, but the blessing of a loving Father. Trust in the invisible God leads him to see that the pagan effort to establish a direct relationship to God is idolatry, that " to walk humbly with

[5] Cf. *Prophecy and Divination*, pp. 19–49. 1939.

thy God " is possible only when God hides himself. He knows that " Nature . . . is the work of God. And yet God is not there." [6]

SPEAKING THROUGH AN EVENT

But the decisive difference between Biblical and Sumerian perspectives lies in the fact that in the former God is constantly disclosing his secret to those with eyes of faith. His power is manifested in strategic events as the power underlying all events. His promise is vouchsafed in epiphanous moments as a promise that determines the destiny of all epochs. God tells man what time it is. But this telling is not simply the conferring of information from the central telephone exchange; in itself it has the power to shift man from one time to another time. Only a creative deed can thus change the *kairos,* and the change in *kairos* is the sign that something momentous has transpired. Within one *chronos* (the time in which things happen), revelation acts to transpose men from one *kairos* to another. And this transposition is precisely the meaning of revelation. God creates with his word by appointing a new time. Men enter this new time by repenting of their blindness, trusting in his purpose, by seeing and obeying (I Thess. 5:4–6; Zeph., ch. 3).[7]

Any event, person, or method may be the signal for this revolution. The event may be ordinary and trivial or it may be a crisis in the affairs of nations; the person may be a shepherd or a king; the method may be conventional or exceptional. The " ways and means " of God's disclosure are so various that any list would be endless and any systematic formulation of " laws " would be an oversimplification.

God always speaks through an event of history. Such a statement, however, is either a truism or a deception. It is obvious that a person's will is most surely manifested in his activity, that his deed is his speech, and that his word is itself an act. It is clear that in the Bible God's word and his deed are inseparable, both combined in a single emission of authority and power. But to be content with the glib statement that he always speaks through a historical event does not advance understanding. All depends upon the definition of *event.* What makes an event eventful? Which are the significant events in history? Are men able to judge what happenings are epoch-making and what happenings are unimportant?

[6] S. Kierkegaard, *Concluding Unscientific Postscript,* trans. by D. F. Swenson, pp. 220–221. Princeton University Press, 1941.
[7] See above, Chapter 6.

Do men say, " Here is a world-shaking catastrophe; ergo, God must be speaking here," or do men say, " God has spoken to us here; *ergo,* this is an event that marks a new epoch "? If the latter alternative be chosen, then it becomes tautologous to say that God always speaks via events. And this latter alternative is surely the one chosen by Biblical writers.

Taken as a whole, the chronology of significant events narrated in the Bible is vastly different from the chronology of significant events recorded in secular histories of the same period. Many events of tremendous importance to secular historians pass almost unnoticed in Biblical histories, and the pivotal happenings in the Bible are often wholly ignored by secular historians. Nor is this due to accidents in the process of preservation of documents; rather it is due to the different criteria of importance which prevail in the two types of literature. To be sure, there are some coincidences in the estimates of significance. An epidemic, a war, an exodus may be recorded in both types of historical narrative because of its impact upon both faith and national fortunes. But in this case the prophet's interpretation of the inner meaning of the event always differs from the interpretation in other circles. By its very spectacular character, an occurrence may impel men to examine it for signs of the times, as a surface eruption of subsurface currents. But only when God discloses his purpose therein does the true relevance of the occurrence appear. And this relevance may be quite the reverse of normal deductions.

On the other hand, the moment of revelation may be so ordinary and trivial as judged by human standards that it escapes the notice of commentators on public affairs. It may appear to have only a private reference, with no public significance whatever, yet to the eye of faith it looms larger on the horizon than a world-shaking catastrophe, more definitive for social destiny than the movements of huge armies. God speaks through events, but an occurrence is made eventful precisely by the power of his word. His action is the only source of genuine history, determining the course of genuine history. And apart from knowledge of the source, which comes only by revelation, man cannot understand the course of that genuine history, since his estimates of the significance of events are distorted by quantitative measurements of horizontal and spurious history.[8]

[8] Cf. H. Thielicke, *Geschichte und Existenz,* pp. 1–35. 1935; H. Wendland, *Geschichtanschauung und Geschichtsbewusstsein im Neuen Testament,* pp. 81–84. 1938.

The sharpest expression of this revaluation of judgment may be found in the New Testament. The stories of the birth of Jesus reflect a double motivation: to affirm the cosmic and historical importance of the Advent, and to accent the hiddenness of this importance from contemporary gaze. The crucial events in the ministry of Jesus, on which the salvation of men depends, escape the notice of those whose eyes are fixed on public happenings which they falsely suppose to be important. The baptism, the temptation, the transfiguration take place quietly outside the area of public acclaim. When disciples penetrate his incognito, Jesus assures them, "'Flesh and blood hath not revealed it'" (Matt. 16:17). Jesus appears as man, and only the Father can reveal who the Son is. (The whole of Matt., ch. 11, is instructive at this point.) The "Messianic secret" is a necessary expression of the fact that the Messiah participates in the hiddenness of the One who anointed him. As E. Lohmeyer writes of the transfiguration incident: "He is revealed man and hidden Lord, and becomes in this moment revealed Lord and hidden man." [9] The conflict between the two standards for measuring historical importance finds its climax in the death of Jesus. How could a bystander in Jerusalem, watching one of the innumerable executions beyond the city wall, detect that scene as one decisive for all human history?

Revelatory events, therefore, are always ambiguous and paradoxical. They reveal what is hidden, and hide what is revealed. At least two explanations of every happening are always possible: in the one case the interpreter judges by the standards of horizontal and spurious history; in the other he judges by the eyes of faith, which have been opened by the act of God in revealing the reality of vertical and genuine history. Only in the final reckoning will this conflict be resolved, when God's purpose will be made known to all creation. Until then, the servant of faith lives by the promise, "There is nothing . . . hid, that shall not be known." Then will men of faith "know as all along we have been known."

SPEAKING THROUGH A MIRACLE

The event by which God reveals himself is, to the eye of faith, miraculous and awe-inspiring: A miracle is the natural way for the supernat-

[9] *Das Evangelium des Markus*, p. 179. Göttingen, 1937.

ural to express itself.[10] His activity is always more than men can discover unaided, always inexplicable in terms of observed cause and effect. Wherever man's life is invaded by the divine Presence, there it is touched by miracle.

"The miracle is the peculiar way in which the divine mystery reveals itself in the midst of everyday life. Against the background of this life the appearance of the divine discloses unusual events which prove the presence of a power infinitely superior to nature and ourselves. . . . The spirit and the hand of God shine through these events. They interpret the purposes and motives of his will. Thus they become as it were transparent. And they assume the character of miracles . . . proofs of the existence of God — of that God whose existence cannot be proved by rational means."[11]

But to say that God reveals his power in a miracle is apt to deceive, for we are prone to define the term "miracle" by categories drawn from an alien thought world, by reference to a system of natural laws defined by contemporary scientific knowledge of cause and effect. That the Biblical perspective resists reduction to these categories should be obvious. For over and over again, the prophets and apostles protest that incidents that appear to be miraculous, as judged by objective standards, are not miraculous at all; they do not truly disclose God's purpose but are the stock in trade of false prophets and magicians. And repeatedly the Scriptures present as wholly miraculous incidents that are neither extraordinary nor inexplicable by natural and rational means. In their thought the scientific distinction between miraculous and nonmiraculous incidents is wholly lacking. The prophets did not proceed logically from the observation of an inexplicable phenomenon to the question concerning its cause; rather, a fresh apprehension of God's activity led them to a radically new understanding of the hidden purport of an incident. Viewed speculatively, to pronounce an event miraculous implies a *subsequent* judgment upon it from the *outside*. To the prophet that which appears miraculous is seen *simultaneously* with the event and from *within it*.[12] For those who sense the hand of God in an occurrence, it ceases in one sense to be a miracle at all, and in another

[10] M. Dibelius, *Gospel Criticism and Christology*, pp. 90–96. 1935.
[11] R. Kroner, *Religious Function of Imagination*, pp. 41, 42. Yale University Press, 1941.
[12] I am indebted for this acute observation to J. Leslie Dunstan.

sense all occurrences become equally miraculous for "there is no moment in history which has not been touched by that Hand." [13]

"To say that they (the miracles) run counter to the laws of nature is to misinterpret; for they happen on a level of meaning where the laws of nature have no meaning at all. Miracles can be rejected or verified by means of scientific thought as little as the laws of nature can be comprehended with the power of religious imagination; they occur and are meaningful in a sphere quite different from that of science and thought." [14]

A miracle is not to be considered as one event in nature distinguished from other events in nature by having an inexplicable and *ab extra* cause, but something wrought *on* creation by the Creator. It is not to be viewed as one event in history, isolated from other events by a unique origin, but as a contemporaneous manifestation of the genuine history within which man perceives the true ground of existence and the true end of all social destinies. It is a clue by which men are led to understand all nature and all history as subsumed under the transcendent purpose of God. [15]

The line between the miraculous and the nonmiraculous coincides with the line between events which disclose the Creator and those which hide his purpose. A single act may be at once miraculous to the believer and nonmiraculous to the skeptic; a single event may have ultimate importance to one man and have no importance to another. The genuine history which is the story of creation is at once wholly miraculous and wholly natural because it contradicts the spurious history of the blind; the genuine history of the chosen people is likewise wholly miraculous from the inception to the fulfillment of the promises which constitute the existence of that people; the genuine history of the Messiah participates fully in this divine mystery, "which hath been hid for ages and generations: but now hath it been manifested to his saints" (Col. 1:26).

THE OCCASION OF OFFENCE

No matter how miraculous in this sense an event may be judged, it remains ambiguous and confusing to the onlookers. Satan appears and

---

[13] W. J. Phythian-Adams, *The Call of Israel*, p. 175, Oxford University Press, 1934; cf. also R. Kroner, *op. cit.*, pp. 45–47.
[14] R. Kroner, *op. cit.*, pp. 42–43.
[15] Cf. J. Haroutunian, in *Religion in Life*, 1943, Vol. XII, pp. 381–382.

reveals himself at the same moment and in the same event as God. In fact, the more decisive the revelatory event, the more contradictory the possible explanations. The Exodus does not reveal the truth to the Egyptians or even to all the Israelites; the deeds of Jesus provoke both unbelief and faith; the cross is a stone of stumbling and a cornerstone of salvation. A miracle becomes a miracle only within the specific context of divine-human encounter, wherein God's word is heard by the ear of faith. The miracle is at once subjective and objective, and neither is possible without the other. Hence, the believer attributes both the opening and the closing of human ears to the purpose of God.

The hiddenness of God's acts always has provoked many questions whenever the Biblical witness is uttered in a non-Biblical world. Why does God so conceal his will? Why are the channels of disclosure so obscure and baffling? If he causes blindness, is he truly good and are men truly sinful? How can such knowledge be called knowledge without objective verification? These questions will continue to occupy our attention in subsequent chapters, but here we may suggest some answers that may throw light upon the problem.

First we note that these questions are all stated from a point of view outside the sphere of revelation. The prophets and apostles do not feel them so acutely as do their critics; something has happened to them which shifts these questions to the margin of their concern.

The astute suggestions of Pascal have relevance:

" If there were no obscurity, man would not be sensible of his corruption; if there were no light, man would not hope for a remedy. Thus it is not only fair, but advantageous to us, that God be partly hidden and partly revealed; since it is equally dangerous to man to know God without knowing his own wretchedness, and to know his own wretchedness without knowing God." [16]

If God revealed himself by miracles which were clearly miraculous to everyone, by events which bear on the surface their ultimate significance, man would not be led to a distrust of his own powers of observation and deduction. His repentance would not be total, for it would not include his own and his society's standards of judgment. His faith would not be faith, but an application of his own knowledge. He would not need to depend wholly upon God, nor break away wholly from the illusions of wisdom and virtue which yield fictitious security.

[16] *Pensées,* trans. by W. F. Trotter, Nos. 585, 565, 555, 229. The Modern Library, 1941.

" The consciousness of man's moral frailty can no longer be preserved, when he claims self-sufficiency in the realm of knowledge. The intellectual and moral limits of the human mind are parallel if not identical. When man believes that his intellectual powers are great enough to enable him to open the shrine of ultimate truth, then he must lose eventually the respect for an intellect higher than his own. He must lose the awe of the unfathomable, that is, the basis not only of faith, but of moral humility as well." [17]

Or, following the suggestions of Kierkegaard, we may say that even God must adapt his methods of communication to the state of the hearers. To those who confess their own blindness and who seek him with their whole heart, he can speak directly, for their repentance marks a rejection of spurious, self-motivated history and a return to their true status in genuine, revealed history. But to the others he must adopt other means of communication, for though they are blind yet they are confident that they can see; though they have become alienated from the true Israel yet they rely upon their sonship to Abraham. To speak to them directly in terms readily grasped would confirm them in their blindness and make salvation less possible. He must communicate with them indirectly in such a way as to provoke " double reflection." The first step must be to make the blind recognize their blindness, to make the apostates recognize their apostasy. He must, therefore, " wound them from behind." Their confidence that they already possess an objectively valid revelation must be shattered. He cannot do this by following the pattern of revelation required by their expectations. They must first suffer from a famine of the words of the Lord. Until they repent, he must, for their own good, cause them to stumble. He ordains punishment for them, predestines them to condemnation, in order that they may ultimately be redeemed. Yet even the precise nature of this punishment must remain ambiguously connected to their historical fortunes; otherwise their repentance would be compelled and would not be *their* repentance (cf. Rom., chs. 9 to 11).

The very hiddenness of God marks his superiority to idols. It is his hiddenness that requires that men must seek him with their whole heart. They must seek him in a different way from that in which they seek an idol. As Subject, God calls for men to seek him; an idol is an object which men themselves decide to seek. As Creator, God claims sole sovereignty and is jealous of his competitors; as a creature of man,

[17] R. Kroner, *How Do We Know God?* p. 31. Harper & Brothers, 1943.

the idol cannot be so exclusive and intolerant. God, as invisible Spirit whose ways are "past finding out," requires a different quality of faith and uses a different mode of communication. When men ask questions of an idol, their questions presuppose the answer which they seek. They set the limits of possible answers by the pattern of expectation which they have adopted; a word from the idol merely confirms their hopes and buttresses their illusions; he is used to enhance their security in terms of their current understanding of security, without challenging or destroying that understanding. But to seek Jahveh with the whole heart calls for raising questions to which man cannot presuppose the answer. His thoughts and his ways are qualitatively different; man who would learn of him must dispossess himself of expectations modeled according to the world's judgments.

For God not only reveals the answers but revolutionizes the form of the questions. He reveals what eye has not seen and ear has not heard. He who seeks God with his whole heart must confess his blindness and his dependence upon God for a knowledge that passes understanding. For him, the moment of revelation is a moment of revolution, marking a new turning point in his life and producing a new center, a new goal, and *new eyes*. An idol is less hidden than God, but *because of that fact* an idol cannot reveal himself to men with so decisive an impact. An idol can neither create nor judge by his word; that prerogative belongs to God alone. The hiddenness of God underscores this demand for total repentance. To be true to his purpose, he must withdraw himself from those who deal treacherously with him. He must make their search futile, because they are insincere in their desire for knowledge of his will (Hos. 5:4-6). He must negate the confidence of counselors, priests, and princes, causing them "to stagger like a drunken man." But to those who return to him in full humility, "his going forth is sure as the morning" (see Hos. 6:1-3). To them, his hiddenness is seen to be an expression of his sovereign purpose to save men in the only way in which they can be saved — in giving to God the glory and the power, the wisdom and the mercy.

9

GOD REVEALS HIS WILL TO THE PROPHETS

A S MEN of the Bible viewed things, there is but a single world of experience, and this world is common to all men on precisely the same terms.[1] But the Source and Goal of creation must remain invisible; the ultimate Power behind phenomena reveals himself as a hidden God. If human thought and action would escape vanity, they must be aligned to his will, but knowledge of that will is not available by means of objective analysis of the external course of history. The gulf between man's wisdom and God's purposes cannot be bridged by reconstructing a chain of causes reaching back from an event to its origin in God. The *course* of history is not separated from its *source* by aeons of intervening time and by an infinite number of secondary and derived causes. In Hebrew consciousness, man lives within the orbit of God's immediate action, from moment to moment under the direct control of the divine Hand. God is the Creator who acts in every situation, whether in nature or history.[2] And in acting he seeks to call men first to understand his will, and then to proclaim it. This chapter is devoted to the first of these steps.

THE PROPHET'S VOCATION

God speaks; he acts. The prophet hears; he sees. He is propelled into the center of the dynamic sequence of events whereby the Creator's purpose is actualized. But this purpose can be fulfilled only when men respond to it and participate in it. In the present moment, this response and participation is only partial and potential. The prophet stands in the interim within which the word moves toward actualization and

[1] C. N. Cochrane, *Christianity and Classical Culture*, p. 238. 1944.
[2] A. Guillaume, *Prophecy and Divination*, p. 184. 1939.

fulfillment. The prophet's message is the medium through which this impulse is transmitted. Genuine history, consequently, is focused upon those occasions wherein God speaks to and through his servants, the prophets.

To be sure, since God is the Creator, he can and does act *through* all sorts of men and all sorts of historical occasions. His judgments determine the destinies of all nations. And often he speaks through them to Israel, using as instruments pagan rulers who are quite unconscious of their role (e.g., Cyrus, the Pharaohs). Evil men and nations serve to reveal his intention. Yet the understanding of this intention is his gift and commission *to* chosen servants. When he speaks to them, it is with instructions for them to proclaim the message to others. "From faith unto faith" is the direction in which revelation moves (Rom. 1:17). This word creates a chosen people, a spiritual Israel, and lays upon them the responsibility of giving appropriate witness to the nations.

In the true story of creation the accent therefore falls upon the prophet-revealer. And, in his case, the accent falls upon his God-given vocation and mission. Nowhere does it fall on his public status, his personal virtue, or his private sentiments. He may be a king, a priest, or an obscure tentmaker or carpenter, but, whatever his activity in the political and social world, it is his passivity in the role of revealer that is stressed. His personality and his private interests remain strictly subordinate in his consciousness. Any claim to privilege or sense of self-importance only impedes God's use of him. There is no place for pride in his own zeal for the Lord. When Elijah, after calling down fire to prove God's power over Baal, flees for his life, convinced that he alone of the faithful is left, God turns against his pride as withering a fire as had been used on the hated sacrifices (I Kings 19:1-14).[3]

The anonymity of many prophecies testifies to the unimportance of the speaker and the importance of his message. In the case of but few prophets are births and deaths narrated; only in rare cases can their biographies be reconstructed or the chronological sequence of their speeches be recovered. The records remain silent on their fate as persons, apart from their mission as revealers. As men they do not differ from other men; they are not branded as saints in the company of sinners; their lives are not encircled with legendary halos, so as to make them subjects of a sacred history untarnished by profane history.

[3] Cf. N. Söderblom, *The Living God*, pp. 289-298. 1933.

In and of themselves they exert no claim on others, and for that very reason they testify more clearly to an authority not their own.[4] In his story of Bernadette of Lourdes, Franz Werfel has recaptured this characteristic of prophecy:

" That men should praise her . . . for the spring of grace and healing remained incomprehensible to her. The Lady's reality grew sharper to her as time went on. But she was impatient of things being taken for what they were not. When people thanked her, she considered it as absurd as if one were to thank the postman for bringing money and not him who sent it." [5]

This insight of the novelist is in full accord with the careful deduction of the historical scholar. Consider, for example, two definitions of prophecy and two examples of prophecy drawn from the study of Alfred Guillaume. The prophet is

" one who is in the state of announcing a message which has been given to him. He is the passive recipient of something which is manifested in his condition as well as in his speech. . . .

" The subject is the object of action from without and retains the character or condition imposed upon it by that influence or action." [6]

" Nothing can undermine Moses' position as a prophet, a man who received suddenly and apparently unsought, a divine message as he went about his daily business." [7]

" The Beduin saw: Amos was made to see." [8]

One indication of the stress on the divine origin of the prophet's vocation is the frequent reference to foreknowledge. " Before I formed thee in the belly I knew thee " (Jer. 1:5). God " separated me, even from my mother's womb, and called me through his grace " (Gal. 1:15). Likewise the prophetic community is foreknown and called from the beginning (Isa. 41:4; I Peter 1:1, 2; Rom. 1:1, 6, 7; 8:28 ff.; I Cor. 1:1 f.; Eph. 1:3–12). As we have noted above (Chapter 2), such foreknowledge does not signify a prescience about all the facts of a person's life, an arbitrary fate that places antecedent limits upon free choice, a romantic providence that grants special immunity to the hazards of existence. It

[4] Cf. K. Barth, *The Epistle to the Romans,* p. 33. 1933.
[5] *The Song of Bernadette,* p. 438. The Viking Press, 1942.
[6] *Prophecy and Divination,* pp. 112, 113. Harper & Brothers, 1939.
[7] *Op. cit.,* p. 96.
[8] *Op. cit.,* p. 149; cf. also H. H. Rowley, in *Harvard Theological Review,* 1945, Vol. XXXVIII, pp. 22 f.

signifies rather the priority-sovereignty of the divine purpose in designating a person in respect to his function. It underscores the conviction that the divine commission was no afterthought, no sudden expedient suggested only by casual needs, no tentative experiment inspired by unusual merit on the part of man, but an integral factor in the original divine plan.[9]

This foreknowledge is not at all inconsistent with the stiff resistance which the prophet offers to the divine call; in fact, the two are complementary ways of accenting the divine initiative in the prophet's call. It is because the prophet struggles against God and finds himself overcome by a stronger One, that he comes to recognize that God has been preparing him for this special mission. Consciousness of being " foreknown " is thus a painful deduction rather than a pleasant presupposition. Prophets loudly protest their unwillingness and unworthiness to serve as God's messengers. Paul kicks against the goad; Jeremiah curses the day of his birth; Isaiah cries, " Accursed am I for I am a man of unclean lips "; Jonah flees the Hound of Heaven but cannot escape him.

It is the genuineness of this struggle that convinces the prophet of the authority of the word, that distinguishes him from false prophets, that separates him from the soothsayers of pagan cultures.[10] The prophet experiences the word as judgment, as a " hammer that breaketh the rock in pieces." His pain is no rhetorical device for impressing his sincerity on others, but a genuine agony that stems from an uncompromising demand for complete surrender. The prophet is torn loose from his own securities and from his own moorings in society. He does not talk of the joys of self-expression or the challenge of creative writing. He does not revel in his nearness to God or relax in perfect adjustment to his environment. The word brings not " peace, but a sword." The same sword falls likewise upon the elect community, the corporate servant of God. Their witness runs: " The time is come for judgment to begin at the house of God " (I Peter 4:17).

The tension experienced in the soul of the prophet is paralleled by strain between himself and the world, wherever the word meets resistance. He becomes a laughingstock. But he has anticipated this derision

---

[9] Cf. F. J. A. Hort, *First Epistle of Peter,* comment on ch. 1:1, 2. 1898.
[10] Cf. R. B. Y. Scott, *The Relevance of the Prophets,* 1944, pp. 88 f.; H. H. Rowley, *op. cit.,* pp. 23 f.

and rejection, for the conflict has already been waged within his own soul, and there the word has proved itself victor. (The effect of these tensions in producing the prophet's ecstasy and the " thorn in the flesh " has not been sufficiently stressed in psychological analyses.) He therefore sets his forehead " harder than flint " (see Ezek. 3:9–14) and fearlessly speaks " whether they will hear, or whether they will forbear " (see ch. 2:3–5). Though he recognizes the inevitability of such estrangement, it remains a constant source of bitterness and complaint which only the constraint of the Lord can overcome. As a man, he is loyal at heart to the interests of his community; as a prophet, he is forced to oppose the policies of rulers and the desires of the people. He becomes branded as a traitor. Almost always he is a harbinger of woe, proclaiming disaster and defeat as the punishment of God on a generation of rebels. Nor are these counsels of defeat idle guesses; each prophetic curse has power within itself to inflict damage. This characteristic of prophecy leads Mr. Guillaume to say, " Nothing like the prophetic literature of the Hebrews is to be found anywhere in the world's literature." [11] All that has been said underscores a single fact: nothing is permitted to obscure the vocation of the prophet, his call to communicate the message of God. This call opens his eyes and makes him the eyes of Israel (Isa. 29:10).

THE PROPHET'S KNOWLEDGE

What kind of knowledge is this which he receives for transmission? Certainly it is not a system of propositional ideas, it is not an all-inclusive wisdom concerning the nature of the cosmos, it is not a neat list of attributes of God, nor a complete scale of moral virtues and vices, nor a blueprint of all coming events. Rather, as Johannes Hempel writes, it is

" the making known of God's will which is to be performed in the particular and concrete situation, and of threats and promises of divine activity which also will be realized in the particular and concrete situation." [12]

In executing this task, human ignorance provides no exemption from responsibility, as Jeremiah discovered (Jer. 1:6). There is no suggestion

[11] Op. cit., p. 171.
[12] In H. W. Robinson, Record and Revelation, p. 67. Oxford University Press, 1938.

in the case of Amos and the other prophets that the revealer must have an unusually clear mind, unusual preparation in the way of moral growth or devout meditation. Contemporaries did not speak of the prophets as being outstanding either in their piety or in their human wisdom.

It is therefore germane to note that there are many kinds of knowledge, and that revelation deals, not with all kinds, but with only one — the revealed knowledge of God's purpose. We may begin by distinguishing accumulative from nonaccumulative knowledge. Many misunderstandings of revelation come from the false supposition that it conveys accumulative knowledge, in competition with other methods of extending that type of knowledge. This knowledge is of the kind that can be stored up in the mind as money is deposited in the bank for future use. It is information held and utilized by a subject in his understanding and control of an object. Each tomorrow marks the possibility of advances in such understanding. Each month adds a few pages to one's mental encyclopedia. The memory is progressively stocked with data and concepts; habits are progressively conditioned by techniques and methods of control; speech and writing are gradually brought under recognized rules of effective articulation. The mind seeks actively through observation and inference to discover new contents, e.g., a new chemical formula or a new use of atomic energy. A teacher is one who knows more, and one who is equipped to transfer that plus of knowledge to the student. When he has communicated his fund of knowledge, when the student has equaled his mental inventory, the teacher ceases to exert authority over the student. The test of this process of transmission is an " Information, Please " examination, or mastery over a field of techniques, or proficiency in a given area of historical research. In extending the boundaries of this knowledge, the full impartiality of the knower is essential; subjective concern is an impediment.

Nonaccumulative knowledge, by contrast, does not follow the analogy of a bank or an encyclopedia. One person communicates his message to another person without necessarily adding to his fund of concepts, habits, or techniques. The experience does not require a previous accumulation of factual information, nor does it yield a pragmatic confidence that tomorrow's possibilities will surpass those of today. One leaps or is thrown with his whole being into a new dimension, is introduced to a new standpoint that alters his entire perspective, and becomes aware of the structural laws which permeate this new world.[13] One's retrospect is enhanced; one's prospect is illuminated, but the change is not reducible to quantitative measurement. The recipient apprehends a new *direction* for his life. He understands himself with new acuteness, for full subjective participation is a *sine qua non,* but outwardly no change may be recorded. The experience may be repeated, but not in the sense of turning again to the same page of an encyclopedia or drawing resources from a bank. It may be repeated only as a genuinely new experience, one that again totally absorbs thinking, willing, and feeling.

"The distinguishing mark of secular truths is this: It is enough to learn them once, and to retain them well in the memory, so that there is no further need to be taught them again. Religious truths, on the other hand, can never be reduced to impressions in our memory. A person knows religious truths only in virtue of the inward operation of God's Spirit."[14]

The authority of the teacher in this area need not reside in more extensive knowledge or greater adeptness in manipulating techniques. The teachability of the student is not measured by intelligence quotient but by capacity for wholehearted response, alertness of imagination, and suppleness of spirit.

It is this second kind of knowledge that is communicated by revelation. It is the knowledge, not of an object, but of a Subject as he communicates His purpose. Its transmission is marked by a total change in the recipient, a shift in center of gravity, a deepening of roots, a broadening of sympathies, a transformation of perspective. The effect may be registered in an enlarged capacity for trust, patience, suffering, joy. The description of the change may require new verbs, new tenses and moods, rather than new nouns and adjectives. Knowledge *about* God may be couched in terms of accumulative knowledge, but knowledge *of* God must be described in terms of nonaccumulative knowledge. In fact, the impact of God's word brings under judgment the speculative and accumulative knowledge *about* God, convicting one of an ignorance that is not lessened by a large stock of theological concepts. When God confronts man, man is made to realize that he is neither damned by false concepts nor saved by true ones.

[13] For a more detailed description of the mode of being which characterizes this knowledge, cf. K. Heim, *God Transcendent,* pp. 73 ff. 1936.

[14] E. Cailliet, *Pascal, Genius in the Light of Scripture,* p. 76. The Westminster Press, 1945.

"The concepts involved in the image of a personal God, of His justice and kindness, of His creative power, of the world as His creation, of history as determined by His will, all these concepts are no concepts at all, if we take this term in its strict sense, demanding notions defined and controlled by logical procedure. These concepts are imaginative, used in biblical narratives and commandments and prophetic addresses which were not intended to teach a doctrinal or theoretical truth. The images do not have a strictly defined meaning. . . . [They] are akin to life and related to the ever-changing spirit of history. The images themselves are alive and therefore not determined and fixed. We do not regard this character of vitality as a defect in them; on the contrary, we feel it to be the source of their strength and a guarantee of their inner truth." [15]

THE PROPHET'S MESSAGE

Keeping this general distinction in mind, we raise the question: What does the God of the Bible say when he meets man? Is there any consistent pattern in the content of revealed knowledge? Does the recurring moment of revelation possess any inner structure? In the different periods, when the same God approaches men who possess radically different reservoirs of conceptual knowledge, does he communicate his purpose in images that yield similar responses?

The consistency of God's self-disclosure may be suggested by noting ten affirmations that recur constantly in both the Law and the Prophets.

1. "I am" (Deut. 5:6). When God speaks he uses a basic indicative to communicate the sense of his own reality. He is real, the only self-existing reality: "I am that I am." He is present, always contemporaneous with the moment of disclosure: He always *is,* and this *is-ness* is the ground of the whole past and the whole future, for he is Alpha and Omega, the One who is and was and evermore shalt be. Yet he is present only as ineffable mystery and majesty, whose existence cannot be subsumed under any external category or concept of existence: "I am that I am"; "the great I Am." The precise meaning of such statements baffles all interpreters, just as it baffles the immediate recipient of revelation. God dwells in thick darkness, yet he is the light by which men see.

"No better way of conveying the mystery of the words of God could be devised than that in which the Authorized Version with its use of capitals writes: 'And he said, Thus shalt Thou say unto the children of Israel, I AM

[15] R. Kroner, *How Do We Know God?* pp. 85 f. Harper & Brothers, 1943.

hath sent me unto you.' . . . Nothing that has been said or written . . .
conveys with such simplicity and reserve the majesty and incomprehensi-
bility of Israel's God." [16]

2. "I am Jahveh thy God" (Deut. 5:6). God always manifests himself as "thy God." His name is known and made known through his
chosen people. Only in direct relationship to particular men does he
speak. To them, he identifies himself, not as the ultimate Reality of
the philosopher or as the universal immanent Spirit of the pantheist
or as the mysterious mana of the animist, but as the God of their fathers
and *their* God. Whenever he thus identifies himself, he exerts an implicit but unmistakable claim that they belong to him, that he has an in-
alienable right to their total obedience. The experience of revelation
clinches in full intensity this unique, specific encounter with a Person.
The initial impact is expressed not so much by the concept "maker of
heaven and earth" as by the sovereign declaration, "I am thy God, thy
creator, thy judge, thy redeemer" (Isa. 44:24 f.).

3. "Thou shalt have *no other gods* before me." God always manifests himself as the One with sole and exclusive authority over his people: "The Lord thy God is *one* Lord." "Before me there was no God
formed, neither shall there be after me. I, even I, am Jahveh" (Isa. 43:
10, 11). He is a jealous God who will famish all the other gods of men
(Zeph. 2:11); who says, "Ye cannot worship two masters." Yet in every
situation, men ignore this command. In prosperity men assume their
independence; in adversity they run to other gods. In either case they
fall away into apostasy, idolatry, blasphemy. Ever and anon God calls
them to return: "That they may know that I alone am God." He seeks
a holy people who will know him as all in all, who will be to him for a
name, for honor and glory. All his judgments are directed to that end.
He battles other gods for dominion over men's wills. In the end he must
destroy the idols so that he alone will be exalted in the earth (Isa. 2:8–
18).

4. "I . . . brought thee out of the land of Egypt, out of the house
of bondage" (Deut. 5:6; cf. v. 15). Always in moments of revelation
God confronts his people as One who has done great things for them. In
part, this emphasis serves to make clear his identity; in part, it serves
to justify his claim for obedience and to show his power to save and to
destroy. The contents of memory, to which he appeals, are capable of al-

[16] A. Guillaume, *Prophecy and Divination*, p. 103. Harper & Brothers, 1939.

most infinite variety in different books and periods. Most frequent are those pivotal events in the fortunes of the elect community: the exodus from Egypt, the wonders of the Red Sea, guidance and food in the wilderness, infiltration into Canaan, success or failure in war. Frequently, the catalogue of signs and wonders includes more ordinary phenomena within personal careers: " I am . . . [he] . . . that frustrateth the signs of the liars, and maketh diviners mad; that turneth wise men backward, and maketh their knowledge foolish " (Isa. 44: 24 f.). The past of both deity and people is epitomized in these central activities of God. Revelation serves to clarify men's understanding of their own past, and to reveal what were the determining factors therein.

5. " Thou shalt remember." The experience of revelation crystallizes a new self-knowledge; and this self-knowledge revises and revitalizes memory. " When Israel was a child, then I loved him. . . . I taught Ephraim to walk; I took them on my arms. . . . I drew them with cords of a man. . . . I laid food before them " (Hos. 11:1 ff.). The existential reality of the covenant community is defined by that genuine history which is constituted by the sequence of God's activities in their behalf. Self-knowledge requires recovering lost memory, since rebellion has blurred the impression and the implication of these decisive events. A true sense of their destiny, and of the forces which actually determine that destiny, stems from renewed understanding of what God has done. The present disclosure of divine will demands the forgetting of what should be forgotten and the remembering of what should be remembered. This memory becomes in turn the basis of God's claim in the present, the ground of gratitude, of obligation, of understanding the hidden source of history, and of the hope of future salvation. Action now must be a response to divine action; otherwise it is vain. Inspired memory is essential, and such a memory arises only through revelation.

6. " Thou shalt." We have already discussed the focusing of God's word in his demand for obedience.

" What doth Jahveh thy God require of thee, but to fear Jahveh thy God, to walk in all his ways, and to love him, and to serve . . . [him] with all thy heart and with all thy soul, to keep . . . [his] commandments . . . and his statutes, which I command thee this day for thy good " (Deut. 10:12, 13).

This demand may endorse or countermand the prevailing standards of right action (I Kings 20:41 ff.; Gen., ch. 22). It may prescribe or proscribe the performance of regular cultic sacrifices. It may be couched in terms of very concrete and detailed acts, or it may speak in more general terms, " Seek ye me, and ye shall live." Even in the latter case, there is little doubt that specific decisions are involved. It may call for vigorous and heroic gestures, or it may call for more passive and subtle reorientation of the soul in resignation, trust, and patience. In every case, it is addressed to the immediate recipient of revelation: " Thou art the man." And in every case it calls for repentance and return. In every case the requirement is in the present tense and within the range of possibility.

" It is not too hard for thee, neither is it far off. It is not in heaven, that thou shouldest say, Who shall go up for us to heaven, and bring it unto us, and make us to hear it, that we may do it? . . . But the word is very nigh unto thee, in thy mouth, and in thy heart, that thou mayest do it " (Deut. 30:11–14).

7. " Thou hast rebelled." Consciousness of sin always stems from revelation, and when God speaks he manifests the stubbornness and pervasiveness of this rebellion. It is very difficult to find in the Bible an example of divine disclosure in which this consciousness does not ensue. It is perhaps safe to generalize this situation in terms of John 1:13. All that exists is born either of the will of man or of the will of God. Through his word, God discloses that which is born of his will, and this disclosure becomes the touchstone that marks off that which has been born of the will of man. Revelation is thus in itself judgment, for it brings into human consciousness the nature and extent of the rebellion against God's purpose. The light shines in darkness and manifests the darkness.

8. " I will judge." Judgment is thus always an aspect of revelation, the counterpart to the accusation of rebellion. No man is free from sin; no sin is immune to punishment. To be sure, the sinner may claim immunity: " God does not know "; " He cannot see "; " We are not guilty "; " He is asleep " and " will not see our latter end "; but God's voice confounds this complacency. The penalty is not coterminous with the sin itself; otherwise sin would be treated as an aesthetic or ethical category rather than a religious one. It is a Person who punishes sin. The connection between the sin and its penalty may be hidden from men, the time lag between the two may be short or long. The act of revelation does not always make plain the methods and the fairness of the judg-

ment, but it always impresses the recipient with the certainty and the fearsomeness of retribution. And it affirms an intrinsic relation of sin to penalty. Inasmuch as sin denotes an estranged will that seeks a destiny of its own, its punishment includes frustration of that will in terms of its historical outcome. Hence the present proclamation of judgment is normally in the future tense, but this threat increases rather than diminishes the immediate sense of guilt. The word, " I will judge," creates a mood different from the assertion, " There is a natural moral law which man cannot break with impunity."

9. " I will forgive." Inseparable from disclosure of God's wrath is disclosure of his mercy. No Biblical writer appears to feel any inconsistency or contradiction between these two activities. A lively sense of judgment is corollary to a lively sense of forgiveness. In fact, the same event precipitates both. The ultimate purpose of every judgment is that God may " heal their backsliding." Judgment is

" never merely punishment for sins, as though God were concerned simply to restore the balance between men by making those suffer who have inflicted suffering. . . . [It is] always primarily punishment of sinners who are to be chastened and changed in the character which produced the sinful acts." [17]

Since the motive underlying judgment is the return and restoration of man, one may accept judgment with hope and confidence rather than despair. To him who is ignorant of his sickness, the word speaks of an incurable disease; to him who recognizes his sickness, the same word speaks of healing (Jer. 30:12–17). The issue is decided by man's response; his repentance brings a revision of the divine disposition (Jonah 3:10). And such repentance is always possible; is always the *telos* of the encounter.

The precise form which forgiveness takes varies according to the condition of men. In his mercy God answers their penitent prayers (Judg. 3:6; I Kings 8:31 f.; 21:29); he relents and turns aside impending catastrophe (I Kings 21:29; II Kings 20:1 ff.; II Sam. 24:16; Isa. 1:18; Hos. 11:9); he moves them to repentance (Jer. 31:20); he refuses to " make a full end " (Deut. 4:31; Jer. 5:18; cf. ch. 51:5 f.; Hos. 11:8 f.; Micah 7:18); however faithless they become, he remains faithful to his covenant promise (Deut. 4:31; Micah 7:20) and manifests this fidelity in the justice of his punishments (I Sam., ch. 2). In time of exile he pro-

[17] H. Richard Niebuhr, in *Christian Century*, May 13, 1942, Vol. 49, p. 631.

vides a sanctuary for them (Ezek. 11:16); remembering his former mercies, he brings them back to the homeland (Isa., chs. 40 to 44; Ezek. 11:18; 34:11 f.). Punishing the wayward less than they deserve (II Sam. 16:12; Hos. 14:1 ff.; Ezra 9:13; Isa. 6:7), he raises up deliverers for them — prophets, judges, kings (Judg. 3:6; Neh. 1:10; Micah 5:2 ff.; Hos. 11:1 f.). However severe the chastisement may be, he persistently draws them and yearns for them, ever ready to make a new covenant with them (Jer., ch. 31). Even from beneath the load of ill fortune, he who hears God is impelled to testify: "He is good, for his lovingkindness endureth for ever toward Israel" (Ezra 3:11; cf. Hos. 14:4 f.; and many psalms). The situations are countless; and the forms and channels of mercy are likewise countless, but never is the situation hopeless and never does man pass beyond the range of God's help. Always the disclosure of God's promise realigns present possibilities, opening a door to hope, no matter how long the promise tarries.

10. "Ye shall know me." Both judgment and mercy, whether present or future, are oriented around an ultimate goal, a restoration of genuine history and a fulfillment of the separate moments of revelation, when knowledge of God will cover the earth "as the waters cover the sea." All the specific acts of judgment and forgiveness are directed toward the positive realization of "creation's story." The process of revelation itself will cease; for the blindness of men and the hiddenness of the divine purpose will together be erased, and men will know even as also they are known. Then will be manifested openly the secret which has been hidden through the ages; "for nothing is hid, that shall not be made manifest."

> "I will give them one heart, . . .
> I will put a new spirit within you; . . .
> I will take the stony heart out of their flesh,
> And will give them a heart of flesh;
> That they may walk in my statutes . . .
> And they shall be my people,
> And I will be their God "
> (Ezek. 11:19, 20).

RELATIVITY AND FINALITY

But the sharpness of this ultimate promise is not blurred by the fog of abstraction and infinitude. This all-inclusive will of God makes its impact in terms of specific predictions addressed to the immediate condition of his children. The ultimate end is mediated by the power at work within a restricted historical situation. It could never be dissociated from the current demand for obedience in the seemingly trivial acts of today. "Finality, the dismal end of all things human, is to be forever dissociated from the Hebrew conception of God." [18]

This explains the concrete character of prophetic prediction.

"There is no prophet in the Old Testament who was not a foreteller of the future. . . . They were feared because it was believed that they knew what was coming, and even had power to bring about the events which they prophesied. When a prophet ceases to prophesy in this sense he ceases to be a prophet and becomes a preacher." [19]

The prediction of the prophet always deals with a live option open to himself and his people. He does not spend his time in dreams of a perfect state in some far-off age. He does not have a map that shows the ultimate destination of the two roads which meet here where the next step must be taken. He does not guide the steps of men in Judea with a map of universal history.

Yet we must be careful not to assume that revelation was merely a matter of daily guidance, without reference to the total divine plan for creation. God reveals his promise through specific demands for the present crisis, but this promise is aligned to the basic promise of the entire covenant, and the promise to the elect community stems from the purpose underlying all creation. God is one Lord, who sees the end from the beginning, and all history lies within the purview of his purpose.

It is this perspective that saves the predictions of the prophets from being counsels of expediency of the sort provided by pagan seers and false prophets. It is this that gives their specific predictions such tremendous significance and makes the current decision so ultimate. It is this alone that gives continuity to their history as a whole, and enables previous predictions to retain a contemporaneity for each succeeding generation. God's purpose, always revealed *de novo* and "*for the time being*," is a continuing purpose which seeks a single end. The finality of this end is presupposed in revelation, but it is not disclosed in terms of a visualized historical situation. Each disclosure of the immediate

[18] A. Guillaume, *Prophecy and Divination*, p. 100. Harper & Brothers, 1939.
[19] A. Guillaume, *op. cit.*, p. 111; cf. also H. H. Rowley, *op. cit.* pp. 35 f.

direction of his will points toward an ultimate disclosure, when the need for revelation will cease, when the clouds will vanish away and God will be all in all. In the present moment, such salvation can only be apprehended as a promise, and as a secret which, though revealed, does not cease to be a hidden and invisible power. The history of the covenant community takes its dynamic qualities from this consciousness of a certain culminative pressure within the sequence of divine disclosures. The end is "nearer . . . than when we first believed." (It must be admitted, however, that this sense of pressure, this consciousness of the fullness of time, reaches its maximum in the New Testament and is only adumbrated in many sections of the Old Testament.[20]

Because each disclosure thus bears the stamp of absolute authority and invincible power, it produces a sense of finality. But this finality does not mean that the content of the message received today remains fixed for all tomorrows. The prophets protest against the tendency to stereotype forms of worship, to organize revealers into a closed shop, to codify the Law, to objectify previous messages in external and unchanging form. God is not bound by precedent; his Spirit is not confined to the past. Revealers do not encourage the identification of revelation with written scriptures. It may be true, as George Foot Moore insisted, that the development of legalism is "a logical consequence of the idea of revealed religion," but it is also true that the prophets themselves were impressed with quite a different logic. To be sure, as soon as revelation is embodied in writing, the tendencies toward legalism begin to operate: the word becomes law; the law becomes more and more extensive; its preservation demands codification; correct interpretation demands careful casuistry; the sanctity of the whole blurs the distinctions between lesser and greater commandments; defense of its authority produces a system of normative doctrines based on literal infallibility.[21] But Professor Moore recognized that these developments were only in their earlier stages in the age of the Tannaim. Such tendencies were resisted in the Old and New Testaments, wherever the voice of the living God spoke directly to living men. For them, revelation is always a divine activity directed manward and not a human code directed Godward. Its momentum points toward the future rather than the past. Viewed by the faithful in the present moment, revelation unveils the power

[20] See below, pp. 279 f.
[21] Cf. G. F. Moore, *Judaism*, Vol. I, pp. 235 ff. 1932–1940.

which is working toward a future consummation. It produces, not a final deposit of ideas or rules of behavior, but a strenuous reaching toward the goal, " a salvation ready to be revealed."

In this connection we may inquire what the New Testament says as to the content of this future revelation. What are the various things which men will know " when that which is perfect is come "? They will know God, " who the Father is." His " arm," his " wrath," his " righteousness," his " glory " will be revealed. Men will also see openly displayed the " man of sin," the devil and all his works. They will see the Kingdom of God and all who share that Kingdom: Abraham, Isaac, Jacob, Moses, Elijah, the prophets and kings. The Son of Man will be manifested throughout creation: who he is, who his servants are, the character of his judgment and of his triumph. Then also will the community of the elect be made known, their endurance, love, and joy. But until that time their " life is hid with Christ in God."

This context throws light upon the relation of reason and revelation. Reason may affirm, " There is a God," or, " God is," but this is different from the existential hearing of the word, " I am the Lord thy God "; reason may arrive at a conviction of an omnipresent Power behind and within all phenomena, but it scarcely confronts man with the personal claim, " I brought thee up out of the land of Egypt "; it may adduce the reality of a universal Spirit animating things, but it does not yield the awareness, " I have called thee from thy mother's womb "; it may insist that God is just and that justice represents the inner structure of history, but such affirmations have a strikingly different impact from the stern threat, " I will judge "; it may arrive at an assurance of a categorical imperative, but this is not the same as the stringent demand of the Biblical God, " Thou shalt "; it may even run ahead of experience and venture a prediction of things to come, but such a prediction must invariably be distinguished from the divine promise, " All shall know me."

The contrasts are so sharp and so consistent that one must conclude that the two terms belong to two different vocabularies, each integral to its own universe of discourse. Each is inherently meaningful within its normal habitat; each is indigenous to its own perspective center; but nothing but confusion results from trying to transpose the two terms without regard for the particular histories in which each has meaning. Reason is a factor in that history in which man seeks to accumulate knowledge about his environment. Specific acts of revelation are events in that history whereby Jahveh creates, judges, and redeems.

Emil Brunner has accurately summed up the contrasts between the two types of knowledge and the corresponding types of history. The first kind of knowledge is

"first of all something over which I have disposal; secondly, something that does not essentially change me; and thirdly, something that leaves me solitary. But if the Word of God meets me in faith, this is all reversed. . . . I myself become disposable. . . . Faith . . . does change me in the very core of my person . . . is the radical overcoming of the I-solitariness. The monologue of existence . . . has become the dialogue of existence: now there is unconditional fellowship." [22]

GROWTH IN KNOWLEDGE

To describe revelation as a nonaccumulative form of knowledge, to distinguish it so sharply from reason, may seem to remove it entirely from the sphere of growth and advance. But that would be an entirely false inference. Both Testaments employ dynamic concepts that envisage progress toward recognizable goals. Yet this progress is to be sharply distinguished from ordinary concepts of mental or moral evolution. True progress is a native property of the *divine* will, stemming from the Creator's act, moving toward the Creator's goal, and at every stage being energized by the Creator's grace.

"No man ever finds Him until he has already been found of Him. Not to seek Him is to be abandoned by Him. Without God, man can do nothing: 'Perseverance of the faithful in the ways of justice is nothing else than the continuity of grace, it is not a single manifestation of grace which persists forever.'" [23]

At every point in this dynamic process man is called upon to make a total surrender to the purpose of God. Appropriation of one's election brings one within the magnetic field of the progressing plans of God.

If we take a typical passage in the New Testament, the first chapter of Colossians, we may detect the area within which increased knowledge is not only possible but required. Here we find such marks of growth as these: "to walk worthily of the Lord unto all pleasing, bear-

[22] *The Divine-Human Encounter,* pp. 88 f. The Westminster Press, 1943.

[23] E. Cailliet, *Pascal, Genius in the Light of Scripture,* p. 77. The Westminster Press, 1945.

ing fruit "; to be " strengthened with all power, according to the might of his glory "; to endure successive trials with " all patience and long-suffering with joy "; " unremovable from the hope of the good news "; to fill up the measure " of the sufferings of Christ "; to grow in gratitude to God, and to extend the sphere within which reconciliation is effective. All these increments are intrinsic to continuance in faith; all are signs of the fruitfulness of the initial word, implicit in the mystery of Christ; all are manifestations of God's purpose " to present every man perfect in Christ." The activity of God's word in Christ creates a new history, and refusal to share in the process of " growth " marks a rejection of this genuine, redemptive history in favor of a return to " the rudiments of the world," i.e., to the false history which enslaves men to spurious notions of progress (Col. 2:8 ff.). Growth is necessary and inherent; but it is a growth which springs from the seed of God's word, man " knoweth not how."

To be sure, in the Bible a premium seems occasionally to be placed upon the progress made by some individual in his knowledge of God. But these references are almost always *biographical* and *retrospective*. More frequently, the mind is directed *autobiographically* to the demand for progress in the *present,* a progress in response to the dynamic working of the Spirit.

" Not that I have already obtained, or am already made perfect: but I press on, if so be that I may lay hold on that for which also I was laid hold on by Christ Jesus " (Phil. 3:12).

Knowledge of God increases, but it increases by revelation, by preserving the character of its original impulse as a sign of God's address to men.

10

THE PROPHET SPEAKS PARABLES

GOD reveals his purpose to his servants with the compulsion to proclaim it. Immediately the question arises, How shall the prophet communicate the mystery of God's word? In what forms shall he give witness to what he has seen and heard? The source and burden of his message are not his own, yet he must express that message intelligibly in word and deed. The form adopted by the prophet must conform to the mystery, revealed in faith. It is small wonder that prophets and apostles, from Moses to Paul, quailed before the problem and bemoaned their inept and stuttering speech.

The basic demand laid upon the prophet is correctly defined by R. B. Y. Scott: " He must speak as befits an ambassador." [1] It is the responsibility of an ambassador to transmit the content of a message, all the while preserving its dignity and urgency. To convey the radical impact of a divine proclamation, the words must be charged with strong emotional force and must confront men with the authority which the prophet himself has found irresistible. God's word creates the prophet and sends him on a mission, and his words must remain appropriate to his status before God. The character of the message and the character of the audience combine to create a distinctive situation; this situation, in turn, conditions the forms of communication. As L. S. Thornton insists, " The contents of the revelation are mysteriously inseparable from the forms in which they are conveyed." [2] Even the vocabulary of revelation, according to E. C. Hoskyns,[3] must forever remain in a special sense the language of the Church. We shall try to indicate why and how this is so.

[1] *The Relevance of the Prophets*, p. 88. The Macmillan Company, 1944.
[2] *The Common Life in the Body of Christ*, p. 3. Dacre Press, 1942.
[3] *Cambridge Sermons*, pp. 90–97. 1938.

THE AUTHORSHIP OF THE WORD

One obligation in transmitting the message is this: The prophet must seek to prevent listeners from confusing his human authority with the authority of God. Men are saved, not by their relationship to the ambassador, but by their relationship to the King. They must get their sense of direction from the earthly signpost but must set their hearts upon a heavenly destination. Undue reverence for the prophet frustrates the very purpose of Him whose word is spoken. The author of human words is unimportant; the authority of the divine word is all-important.

In fulfilling this obligation, the ambassador may be called upon to repudiate his own wisdom and power. He therefore includes in his witness a candid confession of sin. In the speeches in Acts, for example, the apostles insist, "We also are men of like passions with you" (Acts 14:15). After the cure of the lame man, Peter cries, "Why fasten ye your eyes on us, as though by our own power or godliness we had made him to walk?" (ch. 3:12). In the anecdote about the sons of Sceva, the narrator takes pains to show the disastrous results of treating the apostolic power as a transferable human capacity (ch. 19:14 ff.). In the Synoptics, Jesus is provoked to deny misdirected praise and to repudiate knowledge of the exact date of coming events (Mark 13:32). He rebuffs those who revere him as either a genius or a judge. In the Fourth Gospel, he insists, "I can of myself do nothing" (John 5:19, 30).

Paul refers to his credentials as a Pharisee of the Pharisees only to repudiate them (Phil. 3:4–9). He is sent, not by men, but by God (Gal. 1:1). His claims to the loyalty of his converts are everywhere qualified by his discrimination between human and divine authority. When his followers confuse the two, he sets them right. When they are led astray by the superiority of other leaders, as measured by external criteria, he defends his own rights but makes it clear that he is speaking as a fool (II Cor. 12:1–12). He carefully discriminates advice given as a man from the commands issued by the Spirit (I Cor. 7:6–12). At these points the New Testament is in full accord with the Old.

To be faithful to the divine authorship of his message, the ambassador prefers forms of speech that will say more than they seem to say, that will therefore call for imaginative activity on the part of the listener. Often there is an intentional double meaning to an act or teaching. A proverb, a stanza of poetry, a parable — these utilize simple images that represent meanings transcending the words. The listener is encouraged to hear the overtones that stem from a voice other than the messenger's. In an obvious truth, simple and elemental, he is led to detect a hidden clue to God's purpose. Frequent use of paradox also reflects this motivation: in what from man's standpoint sounds contradictory, the mind is prodded and tantalized into pondering the contrasts between man's ways and God's.

Still another means for accenting the divine origin of the word is the preference for direct discourse in which God speaks directly to the listener. The form of statement, " There is a God," does not communicate the same meaning as the form, " I am the Lord thy God." The former relates the listener to the human speaker and raises immediately the question of evidence dealing with a third-personal or impersonal object. The second does not assume the independent authority of the man speaking, but relates the listener to God as the object of God's address. The second stresses what God says rather than what is said about him. The second focuses attention upon the present moment, and calls for each hearer to respond directly to God now.[4]

These considerations apply to the prevalence in the Gospels of statements beginning with, " I am," and, " I say unto you." The tradition about Jesus was preserved in forms conducive to the crystallization and repetition of the I-Thou dialogue between the risen Lord and his servants. The nuggets of oral tradition that articulate this living spiritual conversation create a response far different from the editorial transitions which are cast in third-person narration and impersonal retrospect (cf. Matt. 7:24–27 with vs. 28, 29). The more frequent forms in early tradition preserve the direct speech: e.g., paradigms, controversies, poetry, commands, threats and promises, parables, in addition to the I-sayings already mentioned.

" I am not come to call the righteous but sinners to repentance " (Luke 5:32).

" Come unto me, all ye that labor and are heavy laden, and I will give you rest " (Matt. 11:28).

[4] Sören Kierkegaard gives a very instructive parable concerning the way in which a king's edict was subjected to scholarly casuistry and objective analysis by all his servants so that as a result " no one read the royal command with a view to acting in accordance with it." Cf. *For Self-examination*, trans. by W. L. Lowrie, p. 58. 1941. The Biblical spokesmen did their best to prevent such a transmutation of their message.

It should also be noted that memories remain more intimate and personal than books. A saying like the above, when preserved in memory, when uttered orally, produces an impact on the heart more intense than it does when read in a document. It is not strange, then, that early Christians long preferred the spoken word, and resisted the innovation of written scrolls or codices. The impression made by the spoken word of the Lord differs greatly from that of the same word when written. The former is more likely to provoke the moment of crisis, with its possibility of repentance and return to God.

Recalling what has been said above about the contrasts between accumulative and nonaccumulative knowledge, it may be noted here that these forms of direct speech are better adapted to the latter than to the former. When man seeks to share his store of conceptual knowledge, he commonly uses other forms: careful philosophical definition; precise, prosaic propositions; logical syllogism; orderly analysis of moral virtues and vices; chronologically arranged biography. But these forms of discourse are conspicuous by their rarity in Scripture. Is not this scarcity due in part to the fact that these forms seldom succeed in producing nonaccumulative knowledge or in precipitating existential consciousness? The abstract discussion of theoretical truths, or the objective narration of historical data, does not yield consciousness of God, conviction of sin, and experience of forgiveness. The faith of which the Bible speaks is not produced by gaining intellectual assent to propositions capable of logical demonstration. The apostle is commissioned to speak the word in such a way that it will prompt the response of faith. He therefore recognizes the incongruity of using these alien forms in fulfilling his task. He knows how inappropriate they sound in the context of worship, hymns, liturgy, personal conversation, and letters; when they are used in such contexts they mark an unimaginative pedant. The prophet and apostle found them equally incongruous as means of witness to God's speaking and acting. In modern practice, it is difficult to discover any basic contrast in form between the sermon and the politician's address, the philosopher's argument, the historian's research, or the moralist's reasoning. When this is true, the word of the Lord is muffled.

SPEAKING TO DEAF MEN

One condition laid upon the apostle, as upon his prophetic predecessors, is the necessity of adapting the message to men who have been deafened by sin and by trust in their own wisdom. The writings of Paul provide the clearest examples of the effect of this situation upon forms of discourse. Constrained to proclaim the word of the cross, he knows how foolish it appears to them that perish. Pride in its wisdom blinds the world to knowledge of God: Jews look for signs that will authenticate revelation, while the disputers of this world measure all wisdom in terms of their secular criteria. To those enslaved by conventional patterns of judgment, God manifests his power in such impotent and foolish guise that they are led to stumble. For this reason, he who utters the word of the cross is enjoined from utilizing customary appeals to worldly logic. He cannot depend upon " excellency of speech " or " wisdom." He must adapt " spiritual words " to " spiritual things " if he would communicate the mystery of a wisdom that is hidden from the " rulers of this world." The Spirit alone can carry conviction. He who receives the Spirit receives the mind of Christ, and henceforth judges all things in the light of that " mind." He cannot submit its validity to the tests of worldly wisdom, " lest the cross of Christ should be made void " (see I Cor. 1:17 to 2:16).

It is often assumed that the sharpness with which Paul distinguishes forms appropriate to the unconverted from forms appropriate to converts is not typical of the New Testament as a whole. One reason for this assumption is the fact that the New Testament is composed largely of materials addressed to converts, of didactic rather than evangelistic messages.[5] There are so few direct reports of sermons to nonbelievers that it is easy to conclude that the apostles addressed the world in the same terms in which they addressed the brotherhood. But a close study of the tradition destroys this conclusion. It is a commonplace of Synoptic criticism, for example, that the form used by apostles differ from those used by teachers. One notes in the Fourth Gospel that the style and structure of Jesus' conversations with the sons " of your father the devil " are in sharp contrast to his discourses with the sons of God.

Likewise, the sermons to the unconverted, as reported in Acts, contain notable stylistic and formal traits. The structure of these sermons

---

[5] Cf. C. H. Dodd, *The Apostolic Preaching*, pp. 1 f. 1937.

has been ably analyzed by Professor Dodd in a book that has become recognized as standard.[6] Looking more closely at these sermons, we find that they take their point of departure from a striking phenomenon in immediate experience, in some mighty work done in the midst of the spectators. Recognizing the ambiguous character of this sign, the apostle proceeds to expound its true implications which otherwise would be missed by the onlookers. He accomplishes this end by proclaiming an inner connection between this appparently isolated event and the other eschatological events that have preceded it, notably the death and exaltation of the Messiah. The meaning of this whole cycle of fateful events is illuminated by appeal to that history in which both the apostle and the listeners stand. For Jews, this involves reference to the living memories of Israel, the Law and the Prophets. This tradition provides a common background, but not a common point of standing with respect to the redemptive activity of God in the cross. The tradition must therefore be reinterpreted so as " to wound from behind." It has been fulfilled, but in such a manner as to convict them all of sin. The kerygma proclaims final judgment upon the present sin of the listeners. Unwittingly they participate in the rejection of the Messiah, and fall under God's drastic condemnation of sin. " This Jesus whom ye crucified," this stone which ye rejected, this Pioneer of life whom ye killed — he has been made Lord and Messiah. " Ye do always resist the Holy Spirit." Like your fathers, who spurned God-sent deliverers, ye are " uncircumcised in heart and ears." Ye are a " crooked generation," so blinded by rebellion that in ignorance " ye delivered up, and denied " Him who was sent to save you from your sin. The road forks here: repent and be saved; refuse and be damned.

First comes the appeal to Scripture, the reference to a common history, the citation of God's promise; then comes the vigorous denunciation that reminds one of John the Baptist ("Ye offspring of vipers") and the woes of Jesus (Matt. 11:20–24). You have seen and judged an event — you must now re-view your judgments; you have trusted your own righteousness — you must now re-turn to God's righteousness; you have resisted the Holy Spirit — you must now be reconciled to God.

It is a sad commentary on current preaching that modern historians so readily assume that the primary motive of the apostle was to conciliate men, and that to accomplish this end he adopted those forms which

[6] *Op. cit.,* Chapter 1.

would be most congenial to his listeners, modifying the message to conform to the opinions and prejudices of the unconverted. But the apostle was called and sent to proclaim divine *re*conciliation. And that reconciliation required a complete reversal in the opinions and prejudgments of the unconverted. The word of the cross required radical consciousness of sin, radical renunciation, a dying to the world and to the self. Ministers of such a message were prevented from becoming groveling salesmen who use every device "to make friends and influence people." To be sure, they could override ordinary distinctions among men; they could "become all things to all men"; but all accommodation of method must be subordinated to the mission of preaching the Gospel. The primary demands of that Gospel must be respected: its stark condemnation of all men, its sweeping judgment of all institutions, its stern requirement that death is the road to life. In preaching, nothing could be allowed that would cheapen the price of salvation. To see the truth in such a message, men must first be made aware of their own blindness. The message exerted a control over method.

It may be that the condemnatory tone of sermons preached to Jews was influenced by rising anti-Semitism; such sharp accusations of sin may reflect the bitter resentments of men who have been ejected from the synagogue. But the tradition of sermons preached to Gentiles substantiates our position. In addressing Gentiles, the apostles seem to have begun by establishing common ground, appealing to the religiousness of the Gentiles (as in Acts, ch. 17) or to the knowledge of God already accessible to them (as in Rom., ch. 1). In any colloquy a mutual basis of understanding must be established. But the apostle rapidly moves from this common ground to the forthright announcement of sin and judgment, and to the demand that the Gentile forsake his idols and turn to the living God. And this demand, to the Gentile, was no light thing. It challenged his whole existence — his loyalties, his wisdom, his securities, his righteousness. There is no evidence that the apostles, in order to win adherents, minimized the obnoxious elements in their message. The proclamation of the coming Day, of final Judgment, of resurrection, of a crucified Messiah — these remained as obnoxious to Gentiles as they were essential to apostles.

The requirement that the prophet, in addressing the multitude, must use forms of communication appropriate to their ears is recognized in the report on Jesus' teaching in Mark, ch. 4. We note five things in this report: (1) The primary purpose of the parable is to communicate the mystery of the Kingdom. (2) The form of communication must be adapted to the responsiveness of the hearer: " Who hath ears to hear, let him hear " (see vs. 9, 23). (3) The meaning is supposedly transparent to those with ears but remains opaque to the others. This double response is both anticipated and realized. (4) The twofold result is attributed at once to the intention of the speaker and the choice of the listener (vs. 10–12); this coincidence of two purposes in a single response is akin to the Biblical attitude toward God's participation in every human decision. In fact, Jesus quotes a passage from Isaiah to explain the outcome in terms of such coincidences. (5) Mark reiterates the point that it is for this very reason that Jesus used parables (v. 34), to separate listening ears from deaf ones, so that subsequent instruction may be given to the former group alone. Jesus counts on those who comprehend this parable to be responsive to all the parables (vs. 13, 25). Failure to " transfer training " leads to the special rebuke: " Having ears, hear ye not? " Like his mission as a whole, his parables bring " not . . . peace, but a sword," dividing men into two groups.

It is not affirmed that Jesus did not use parables for other purposes too, as, for example, the subsequent training of those with ears; but it is affirmed that in public address he constantly followed this pattern of baffling ambivalence, and that such a practice was required both by the character of the mystery and by the blindness of men. The whole body of Jesus' teaching might be scanned for other examples of his address to "outsiders," but this is perhaps sufficient to illustrate early Christian understanding of this particular form. The analysis of the synagogue sermon with which Luke keynotes the ministry is fruitful in this connection (Luke 4:16–30). The analysis of the motifs of the healing stories is also rewarding. It is no accident that the cures of deaf ears and blind eyes are so prominent in the tradition.[7] Nor is it accidental that many of these healing stories are almost indistinguishable in motif and structure from paradigms and parables. Used in apostolic sermons, all three forms confront the listener with an occasion for faith or unbelief. Like the Old Testament prophets and New Testament apostles, Jesus seems to have made much use of hard sayings — riddles, conundrums, stinging woes, and vigorous threats — to awaken a sleeping generation.

[7] A. Richardson, *The Miracle-Stories of the Gospels*, pp. 10 ff. N.d.

The distinction between faith and unbelief is the most radical distinction among men; consequently the distinction between forms of communication adapted to blindness and those adapted to vision is a radical one. Mediators of God's word, however, were forced to reckon with other distinctions when they addressed " believers." In the New Testament this is pungently expressed in the contrast between infants and adults, between those who must be fed milk and those who are ready for meat. In his letters, the apostle must contend with those " of little faith." The dependence on human wisdom, the existence of faction and jealousy, the misinterpretation of the new freedom — these are marks that the " new " men are still infants. Paul finds it an arduous task to adjust his message to their capacity to comprehend. He must make clear to them their status, restate the foundations of faith, underscore the responsibilities and implications of life in Christ, and point them anew to the coming day when all hidden things will be revealed. Until the Messiah comes, the steward of his mystery must remain faithful to his stewardship, though that may on occasion require him to be a fool for Christ's sake (cf. II Cor., chs. 10 to 13; I Cor., chs. 3; 4).

This distinction is carried, too, through other New Testament writings. Perhaps it is sufficient to cite Hebrews, the Fourth Gospel, and the Synoptics. In Hebrews the method of approach to those who have not advanced beyond the " first principles " is admittedly different from the speech used for those more advanced (Heb. 4:1–13; 5:11 to 6:12). The good news has not profited the outsiders " because it was not united by faith with them that heard " (ch. 4:2), but the danger of " an evil heart of unbelief " remains a constant threat to the disciple. Even the soil that at first receives the seed may produce " thorns and thistles " to choke it (ch. 6:6–8). The teacher must therefore return to the elementary postulates and demands of the Gospel if these tendencies are to be conquered.

In the Fourth Gospel, Jesus often distinguishes two kinds of disciples: those who are disciples because of the signs, and those who are disciples indeed (John 6:26, 60–71; 8:31–43). Consequently the form of discourses during the last evening is different from the forms used elsewhere in the Gospel. The locus of these materials in the life of the developing Church is correspondingly different. The farewell discourses are most appropriately "placed" in connection with the Church's eucharistic worship; the polemic discourses fit more naturally into the debates with false teachers. But each has its *Sitz im Glauben* as well as a *Sitz im Leben,* and both situations affect the form of communication.

In the Synoptics the same boundary is drawn between disciples who comprehend and disciples who are caused to stumble by worldly patterns of expectation and evaluation. No disciple is immune to this stumbling. Some of the parables which should be clear are misunderstood, leading to the protest, "Having ears, hear ye not?" At times disciples construe the signs according to the leaven of the scribes and Pharisees. They cannot grasp, for example, the meaning of the loaves or the significance of the transfiguration. Their nascent faith leads them into temptation, where they are sifted like wheat by Satan. Only the fresh impact of divine revelation can preserve them from falling; only the continuing presence of the Revealer can assure them of continuing understanding. Undoubtedly, these elements of the tradition reflect a recurrent and typical faith-situation in the Early Church; undoubtedly they left their imprint on the forms of tradition. To recover these traces, a more careful and detailed study is required than can be pursued here. What has been said may be sufficient to support the conviction that the communication of the word, in both its manner and its matter, required recognition of the hiddenness of God, the mystery of the Kingdom, and the blindness of men.

THE USE OF PARABLES

The requirements laid upon the prophet with regard to the form of his communication may be illustrated by a single group of forms — the parables. It is necessary to say "a group of forms" because the term parable is used with great flexibility in the Bible. Without attempting to be exhaustive, we may list the following types:

A popular saying (I Sam. 24:13).
A taunt (Ezek. 16:44).
A taunt-song (Isa. 14:4).
An aphorism of the wise man, arranged in couplet (Prov. 10:1).
A riddle (Prov. 5:15).
A prediction in allegorical form (Ezek. 17:2 ff.).
A fable (Judg. 9:7 ff.).

Illustrative story — parable proper (II Sam. 12:1 ff.).
An oracle of the future (Num. 23:7).
An apocalyptic vision (I Enoch 1:2, 3).
A simile (Luke 12:36).
A metaphor (Luke 12:35).
A beatitude (Luke 12:37, 38).
A similitude (Luke 13:6–9).
An allegory (Luke 20:9–18).
An example-story (Luke 10:30–37).[8]

There are, of course, many reasons for the popularity of these forms of narration. Examples of most of them may be found in non-Biblical cultures. Wherever oral tradition is the dominant method of social intercourse, these forms demonstrate their survival value. Yet there are special reasons why the prophet should employ them, reasons which emerge from the character of his message and from the situation in which he stands. It is not argued that every parable illustrates these motifs, or that any single parable illustrates them all. But to a very high degree the form is adaptable to the prophet's function.

Note, for example, some characteristics of the well-known parable of the Prodigal Son.[9] Notice how the story preserves the concreteness of an original situation that happened once upon a time and at the same time uses that situation to reflect the inner meaning of all situations. It becomes timeless without becoming separated from time; it does not diminish the historical uniqueness of either the prodigal son's dilemma or that of his contemporary counterpart. It is a story which is or can be repeated in every situation in which the listener may stand. Within the context of this situation it focuses attention upon decision, and this decision is represented in either-or terms. There is no interest in graded levels of obedience or in qualifications or modifications of the simple, rigorous alternatives. The decision, repentance-and-return, is an act that presupposes a leap of faith and a radical reorientation of personal relationships rather than a mere transference of ideas. Moreover, this decision is intelligible only in terms of memory and anticipation: a particular past has reached a moment of judgment; a particular future becomes real through a venture of expectation. The story conserves every man's involvement in his own past and future. In a real

[8] Cf. B. T. D. Smith, *The Parables of the Synoptic Gospels*, Chapters 1, 2. 1937.
[9] Cf. S. Kierkegaard, *For Self-examination*, pp. 62–66. 1941.

sense, it includes every major emphasis in the message of the Old Testament prophets: a story of the past, an assurance of imminent change, forthright command, threat against continued rebellion, promise of forgiveness. In a sense, it is an epitome of history and its rhythm of rebellion-and-return.[10]

What does the parable say about its author? Nothing. Its authority does not rest with the authority of the man speaking; he effaces himself completely. The listener is not prompted to consider his personal relation to any human teacher, but he can hardly escape confrontation by the divine Father. The listener becomes involved as a participant, though in the beginning he was only a spectator. And this change in status is not the result of a shift in ideas, nor of the persuasive power of a new proposition. He is led, quite unsuspecting, to a new point from which to view himself.

"The salutary application lies in ambush deep enough to take the listener by surprise." [11]

As his spirit shifts from passive listening to creative alertness, he receives new knowledge of God and new knowledge of himself. The speaker of the parable does not force the listener to faith, does not try to transfer to him his own ideas or demands. Rather, the listener is startled to find himself at the point where he must give an answer to the parable in terms of his own choice. He senses in the parable an indicative, "God loves me," and an imperative, "Come home," the two in closest interdependence.

The story reveals the paradox of the human situation: He who makes one aware of sin assures one of forgiveness. Judgment and mercy inhere in man's situation and not simply in the parable. The form of the parable helps to prevent these realities from being distilled into mere abstractions and at the same time from being exhausted in a specific moral act.

The implication of this parable is clear, even though it points to the invisible constituents of experience. It is safe to conjecture that it belongs in a context in which the hearers are either disciples or men who have been made hospitable to the good news by awareness of sin and despair over it. The penitent sinner hears the word with a thrill of joy.

[10] Cf. H. Thielicke, *Geschichte und Existenz,* pp. 362 f. 1935.
[11] W. A. Curtis, *Jesus Christ the Teacher,* p. 84. Oxford University Press, 1943.

In the context of argument within which Luke sets it, the pivot of the story shifts to the attitude of the elder son. The Pharisees are rebuked for their hostility to the forgiveness of sinners. For them the parable ends with a thrust of judgment. But even in this situation, there is no enigma to be deciphered.

Many of the parables in the Bible, however, spring from a different provenance, from a situation of bitter hostility or of stubborn skepticism. In such a situation the parable may become a " woe," as in Hab. 2:6, a curse on unrepentant cities, a prediction that wings forth to blight the false hopes of the wicked. Thus, a parable is " spoken against " the recalcitrant Pharisees by Jesus: "What . . . will the lord of the vineyard do unto them? " (see Luke 20:15 ff.). Or the parable may be acted: e.g., the disciples are commanded to shake the dust off their sandals as a testimony against inhospitable towns.

Where the people addressed include both hostile and hospitable listeners, a different tone is called for. Now the parable becomes a test of their hearing. It may be cast into the form of an enigma which attracts and repels, a story the point of which is not obvious to everyone. Hearers must " take heed what ye hear," for the hearing is the test of their response both to God and to the speaker. To him who has understanding much shall be given, but he who is deaf will lose what understanding he has (Mark 4:25). " What was said in order to enlighten and save becomes in fact an instrument of judgment." [12] The editor of Mark evidently thought that the parable of the Sower belonged in this category. And perhaps he was justified in this assumption. To those who did not know the mystery of the Kingdom, there was nothing in this parable to make it clear. How would the skeptical Pharisees know precisely what the seed was and how it was maturing silently? They required definite signs, hence there was taken from them whatever understanding of the Kingdom they might have possessed.

A slightly different situation and function is predicated by the apocalyptic parables of Ezekiel, I Enoch, Revelation, and the Gospels. Perhaps these should not be grouped together, inasmuch as the situations were not entirely analogous. In Revelation the apocalyptic visions are clear to the Christians but intentionally hidden from their enemies. In Enoch, the authority of the seer is accepted by a group of the faithful (no one knows how large) but the significance of the parables must

[12] W. A. Curtis, op. cit., p. 84.

have been opaque to all those who did not ardently long for the vindication of God's justice. The baffling character of the "Little Apocalypse" (Mark, ch. 13) attributed to Jesus must be due in part to the varying situations in which the separate predictions took their rise and later circulated.

It is by no means as certain as some scholars have maintained that Jesus used no allegories to describe impending events. Undoubtedly, some of his parables were transformed into allegories during their circulation in the Early Church. But it is clear that for the unbelieving he used many ambiguous teachings, hiding his authority and the exact import of the message. It is clear that he used baffling enigmas and that he often forced his adversaries to answer their own questions: "The baptism of John, was it from heaven, or from men?" (Mark 11:30). It is clear that he cautiously avoided any outright claim to Messiahship, leaving that to the faith of those who had eyes to see. It is clear that he used woes, taunts, laments, and predictive sayings which were certain to tantalize his adversaries rather than to clarify his position for them. It is antecedently probable, therefore, that some of his parables were couched in a form that would hide their meaning from the unrepentant, as long as they remained confident of their own wisdom. The new wine could not be kept in old wineskins; a message so different from current expectations could not be cast in the same forms as Pharisaic teaching. Like his predecessors among prophets and apocalyptists, Jesus was forced to adapt his style of communication to various listeners: some were disciples who had left all; some were disciples who looked back; some were casual spectators; some were argumentative scribes; some were bitterly hostile. And he found in the various kinds of parables appropriate means for sowing the word of the Kingdom of God.

An added note may be addressed, not to the general reader, but to the technical scholar who is engaged in the study of the forms in Biblical tradition. The problem is this: What was the basis and process of selection by which the prophet eschewed certain current forms of communication, and adopted others? In using those which he borrowed from contiguous cultures, how did he alter them to fit his particular point of view and his mission? When he used a well-known proverb, for example, did he provide a context for it which gave to it a peculiar accent and mood? What happened structurally to the tale or legend when it appeared as one of the forms embodied within Gospel tradition?[13]

Such questions as these, if they are to receive adequate answers, call for an extension and revision of the goals and techniques of Form Criticism. This type of analysis has registered marked success in its effort to reconstruct the history of oral traditions preserved in both Testaments. It has demonstrated the importance of the life-situations in which the traditions circulated, and the creative influences of motivation and function in shaping forms. In achieving these results, Form Criticism has been forced to stress the similarities between Biblical and non-Biblical traditions, has been forced to seek the laws governing the growth of oral tradition in every milieu. Quite naturally, therefore, it has not concerned itself primarily with the unique situations, motifs, and functions which pertain only to the oral communication of *revelation*. But these distinctive factors now call for closer attention. Having underscored the influence of sociological factors in the *Sitz im Leben,* we are now required to extend the analysis to the theological factors, i.e., to the *Sitz im Glauben.*

In the case of the Lucan beatitudes and woes (Luke 6:20 ff.), for example, it has been helpful to place the tradition in the context of the impoverished Jerusalem community and to note the different environmental conditions reflected by the Matthaean parallels (Matt. 5:3 ff.). Yet it should be clear that other influences were basic determinants of form: the prophetic situations created by the word of the Kingdom, the authority of the Messiah, the address to a community that had made a radical break with the world. In hearing these proclamations of blessedness, Christians heard more than the echo of their own class interests.[14]

As another example, consider the paradigms or pronouncement stories. In this case, critics rightly anchor the form in the preaching activity of the Church and search for parallels among non-Christian preachers. But the search for parallels is fruitless because Christian evangelists

---

[13] Cf. L. J. McGinley, *Form-Criticism of the Synoptic Healing Narratives,* Chs. 5–7. 1944; A. Richardson, *The Miracle-Stories of the Gospels,* pp. 34 f. N.d.; W. Manson, *Jesus the Messiah,* pp. 45 f. 1943.
[14] Cf. W. Manson, *op. cit.,* pp. 57–71.

had a vocation and motivation different from the itinerant peddlers of Hellenistic cults. To be sure, they employed cultic, etiological, and pedagogical motifs common to propagandists of every religion. But they also had other conditions to fulfill than simply the making of converts. Their faith, being unique, produced a new orientation toward every situation, and a distinctive mission called for distinctive methods.

11

SIGNS WITNESS TO THE WORD

A T THE juncture where God acts and man comprehends his act
there is found a sign. The sign is the visible happening or object
which communicates God's invisible purpose. It is the event
wherein God provides the occasion for faith or stumbling. It is that incident in the range of observable history which the prophet interprets to
his community, or which the prophet enacts for his community. The
more important signs are those that accompany the covenants in their inauguration, repetition, or fulfillment. But no sign is unimportant, for it
communicates the word of the Lord to a particular creature, and it is
by this word that the creature lives. Hence no study of the Biblical channels of revelation is complete if it ignores the utilization of signs.

"The Bible is always interested in characteristic actions and gestures. . . .
Each of them imparts to the narrative a peculiar *tone* which is not audible
save to the ear which can detect the genuine *Biblical* ring." [1]

Yet nothing is more repugnant to modern thought than frequent
appeal to "signs and wonders and mighty works." When we discuss
the theological topic "revelation," we seldom include these items in the
agenda. In our idiom, a parable as a medium of communication is quite
dissociated from any dramatic public gesture. To insist that signs are as
important as parables is objectionable; to speak of a sign as an enacted
parable is unintelligible. But that association is tacitly assumed in the
Biblical milieu. There it is quite possible to refer to actions by the declaration, " He says," and, conversely, to refer to a spoken parable by the
words, " He does." Because the wall between the two worlds of dis-

---

[1] A. Richardson, *The Miracle-Stories of the Gospels*, p. 52. Harper & Brothers, n.d.

course is so high at this point, the analysis of signs is both more difficult and more necessary.

We have chosen in this chapter to take up first the basic interrelatedness of speech and event at the point where God confronts man. Then the discussion turns to three major types of signs: those persons who serve as signs for their generation; those signs that are intended for the prophet's eyes alone; those incidents in the common life that the prophet elucidates for his people, whether it be to attract their attention, to confound their wisdom, or to accredit his message. Attention is then directed to the baffling problem of discerning true signs from false. Finally, it is noted that the prophet solves this problem by his expectation of a future confirmation of the true signs.

<h3 style="text-align:center">DEED AND WORD</h3>

First, we may inquire why speech and action are so nearly interchangeable in the Biblical vocabulary. A step in this direction is to recall what has been said about the initial attitude toward history as the sphere of personal meeting, and when we give due centrality to the purposes of the creative agents. We stressed earlier the observation that a person's purpose is manifested outwardly by his word and his deed, and that the integrity of the two marks the fidelity and power of the person. Perfect integrity is found only in God's faithfulness and sovereignty. God's speech and action are indissoluble, both expressing a single purpose. His word is his deed; his deed is his word. An experience of his word is in itself an experience of his power, as it shapes events; any understanding of his deeds includes a hearing of the message implied therein. "He spoke" and "it came to pass," "he speaks" and "it will come to pass," are practically equivalent ways of describing his active will. In him, authority and power are inseparable.

God speaks and acts; the prophet hears and sees; in turn, he is constrained to speak and to act. In accordance with the hiddenness of God's word, the prophet speaks in parable; in accordance with the hiddenness of God's deed, the prophet acts in signs. The commission of the revealer to proclaim the word is at the same moment a commission for him to work signs. This observation applies equally to the Old Testament prophet (e.g., Ezekiel), the prophetic Messiah (in apocalyptic expectation and in Jesus' vocation), and the disciples and apostles to whom

Jesus mediated the divine call.[2] As an expression of the hidden but sovereign will of God, both the word and the deed bear inherent power to produce their own fulfillment.

" The prophet says that Yahweh has commanded him to perform some symbolic action, and as he does it, or after he has done it, he uses the acted sign as an example and a proof that a certain action will take place, or a certain happening will befall the people against whom the sign is directed. The symbolic act was conceived as initiating the event of which it was a symbol." [3]

Professor Guillaume even goes so far as to say that " no man could hope to speak in the name of God unless he could show a sign." [4]

As in the case of spoken parables, some signs are directed against the rebellious, while some are intended to reassure the faithful. Some serve as the touchstone of faith, to cull out the seeing eyes from the blind. As in the case of parables, the rejection of a sign, or blindness toward it, is tantamount to rejection of God's call.[5] Just as the prophet uses a riddle or a parable to hide his message from the stiff-necked or to confuse the thoughts of the self-wise, so also he uses a sign to conceal or to baffle. Sometimes he may refuse to use a sign at all " because of their unbelief "; or he may use a sign that one group alone will understand.

Throughout the Bible it is assumed that to God alone belong the authority and power at work within every *sign*ificant event. He it is who places *sign*posts that point to the hidden purpose. And he is under no limitation in choosing the forms or media which he will use. They may be seen in the heavens: the orderly movements of sun and moon, or more portentous visions of the heavens rent asunder, of the moon turning to blood, of angels ascending and descending, of lightning and thunder. Or they may take place on earth: plagues and earthquakes, the turning back of the Red Sea, or the destruction of an army. Little distinction is drawn between wonders in nature and those in history. If one traces the character of the signs from the earliest Biblical narrative to the latest, he will of course discover great variation and development. Some of the epiphanies in the early legends (the floating axhead) are not repeated in the later accounts. These changes are defi-

[2] Cf. A. Richardson, *op. cit.,* p. 41 f.

[3] A. Guillaume, *Prophecy and Divination,* pp. 170 f. Harper & Brothers, 1939; H. H. Rowley, in *Harvard Theological Review,* 1945, Vol. XXXVIII, pp. 28 f.

[4] *Op. cit.,* p. 103.

[5] Cf. A. Richardson, *op. cit.,* p. 43.

nitely related to prevailing cultural patterns, but the modification in the character of the signs does not imply diminution in their importance. To Elijah, the "still small voice" was more significant than thunder and earthquake; nine centuries later, the destruction of Jerusalem was understood as a sign by suffering Christians and Jews.

But the wonders which God wrought in heaven and earth were not in themselves sufficient to make clear his purpose. They were happenings that required the elucidation of faith. As Alan Richardson points out, this is probably the reason why the Scriptures never mention wonders without referring in the same connection to signs.[6] There is no true communication of their meaning unless men share the purpose which they are designed to convey. They are set *between men and God,* and always serve that function. Thus, the Sabbath and circumcision, the Passover and tephillin, are the preservation in living, contemporaneous terms of the signs and wonders first manifested in historic events. Thus, also, the sacraments of the early Christians are signs which God wrought once, and once for all (Ex. 31:12–17; Deut. 6:8; 11:18; Ezek. 20:12–20; John 6:30–40; Rom. 4:11).[7]

THE PROPHET AS A SIGN

The relationship of the revealer to the divine sign possesses imaginative complexity rather than systematic simplicity. In the first place, the prophet or apostle is himself a sign. His activity as a whole points to the ingress of divine energy. For example, Ezekiel is commanded to be the sign of coming exile. Blindfolded and dumb, he digs through the walls of his house and moves out his household goods. When asked to give the reason for such behavior, he answers, according to instruction, "I am thy sign" (Ezek. 12:6 ff.; 24:24 ff.). Simeon predicts that the infant Jesus will become "a sign which is spoken against" (Luke 2:34). To those who seek signs, Jesus replies that, as Jonah was a sign to his generation, so also the Son of Man will be to his (Luke 11:30).[8] He also refers to John the Baptist as a sign to this generation (Matt. 11:7–19).

In many cases, the function of the revealer is to speak the word by a dramatic gesture. His act symbolizes the purpose hidden behind con-

---

[6] *Op. cit.,* p. 46.
[7] A. Guillaume, *op. cit.,* pp. 366 f.
[8] W. Manson, *op. cit.,* p. 49.

temporary events. Isaiah goes about naked (Isa. 20:2 f.). Micah rolls in the dust (Micah 1:10). Jeremiah wears and then buries a loincloth; he wears the yoke, first of wood and then of iron; he buys a field; he offers wine to the temperate Rechabites (Jer. 13:1–12; 27:1–15; 32:6–15; 35:1–17). Ezekiel, with tile and pan, predicts the siege of Jerusalem; the cooking of unclean food by measure portends famine; the shaving of his head and the burning of his hair symbolizes fire. Lying on his side, he mimics the iniquity of Israel. He refuses to mourn at his wife's death (Ezek. 4:1–12; 5:1–4; 24:15–24).[9] Hosea and Isaiah give their children significant names, or detect special import in the names. John the Baptist chooses appropriate garb and food. Many symbolic gestures are attributed to Jesus, among which may be mentioned the exorcism of demons, the entry into Jerusalem, the cleansing of the Temple, and the fateful movements at the Last Supper. The true apostle, according to both Acts and the Epistles, may be recognized by his works. Agabus the prophet predicts Paul's arrest in Jerusalem by binding himself with Paul's girdle. Speaking with tongues is a sign to unbelievers; prophesying is a sign to believers (I Cor. 14:22). In either case it is important that there be intelligible interpretation of the sign (I Cor. 14:6–25). Among the Christian gifts, Paul lists many signs, wonders, and powers (I Cor., ch. 12). One quickly reaches the point of satiety in trying to grasp in memory all these means of communicating the word.

The forms are so profuse that it is difficult to detect any common denominator among them. While no such denominator in form is apparent, in content an amazing continuity may be discovered. For example, one may take the five basic elements of the prophet's message as set forth by R. B. Y. Scott: historical declaration, reproach, exhortation, threat, promise.[10] Prophets convey all five of these in gestures as well as words.

The threat, "I will judge," is communicated through the actions as well as the words of the revealer. In fact, the enactment of a sign was often more startling than the proclamation of a woe. From the days of Amos' plumb line to the days of Jesus' clearing of the Temple court, the appearance of a sign could produce anger, terror, and bitter resistance. Other men than Jesus ignored Sabbath regulations with impunity, or refused to observe dietary restrictions, or spoke slightingly of

[9] Cf. H. H. Rowley, *op. cit.*, pp. 27 f.
[10] *Op. cit.*, p. 100.

the Temple. But as the gestures of a prophet, they were predictions of forthcoming abrogation of the Law, the Sabbath, the rules of purification, the Temple. Implicitly, they were threats which had as much power to work their own fulfillment as the explicit, " I will destroy this temple." As Guillaume writes:

> " The preaching of the word of Yahweh might only enrage: the presence of a sign could terrify." [11]

Conversely, of course, the sign had power to speak comfort and reassurance to exiled and ostracized believers. Hosea's faithfulness to his adulterous wife, Jeremiah's purchase of land, Jesus' healing of the lame and leprous, are expressions of God's promise, " I will forgive." [12]

THE SIGN FOR THE PROPHET

A slightly different context for the signs is provided by the accounts of visions and auditions of the prophet himself. The moment of his call is frequently marked by signs intended for him alone. These are not " staged " by him, but for him. They may take the form of a vision: Amos sees the basket of summer fruit; Jeremiah, the boiling cauldron; Isaiah, the Lord in the Temple; Ezekiel, the valley of dry bones; Daniel, the Son of Man on the clouds; Jesus, the Spirit descending or Satan fallen as lightning; John, the woman clothed with the sun. They may take the form of a quite trivial incident in daily life, in which the prophet sees ultimate significance. Expectantly watching the small happenings, he discovers ominous or propitious news in the flight of sparrows or the grazing of sheep. [13]

The prophet does not pause to distinguish between physical and psychical stimuli, between the relative objectivity or subjectivity of the phenomenon. He often does not treat the phenomenon as capable of demonstration to others, nor does he try to establish its validity by epistemological or experimental methods. The import of the vision is established in a sense that no degree of objective actuality could convey and no degree of subjective doubtfulness could shake. He may be aware that the vision is simply a vision; or he may be confident of the concrete actuality of the thing seen. The authority and source of the message

[11] *Op. cit.,* p. 150; cf. also H. H. Rowley, *op. cit.,* pp. 28 f.
[12] W. Manson, *op. cit.,* pp. 42 f.
[13] A. Guillaume, *op. cit.,* Chs. 3–5.

does not depend upon the substantiality of the signal or the form of its expression. His witness to the vision may be excited and ecstatic, or quiet and sober. He may speak of angels and seraphim, fire and cloud, aerial ladders and transfigured bodies; or, on the other hand, he may speak of a potter at his wheel and the fig tree in blossom. In either case, the epiphanous touches do not serve the function of mystification or compulsion; rather, they serve to mediate vocation, direction, power, and help. Signs viewed by a prophet yield a clearer understanding of the glory and will of God than carefully defined, prosaic, logically formulated propositions. Thus, as Professor Manson observes, for Jesus the developing apprehensions of the Kingdom and the work of the Messiah were conditioned by what Jesus saw God doing.

" Jesus in his characteristic words about the Kingdom of God reasons from present events and experiences to the coming of that Kingdom, not vice versa. His gospel of the End rests on the certainty of the power of God which is with him in the present." [14]

Inasmuch as the ears of the prophet are as important as his eyes, the media of communication are often auditory phenomena. He is granted an audition of divine secrets. He may hear a voice, but see no image. And when he hears, it may be such things as it is not lawful for a man to hear, or it may be a natural sound which no hearer would take to be extraordinary. It may be the voice of the Holy One whom the prophet is worshiping at the altar, or the voice of the Messiah to one who is persecuting Him. It may come in a moment of spiritual ecstasy, in prayer, or in the routine of daily business. It may be heard in dreams or when one is most fully awake, when one is expectant or unsuspecting. The immediate manner of audition is peripheral; the burden of the message is central.

THE INTERPRETATION OF SIGNS

A primary function of the prophet is to interpret signs to his people. Signs, so interpreted, may be past, present, or future, with regard to the moment of elucidation. The marvelous deliverance from Egypt, with all the attendant wonders which God wrought, becomes the object of later appeal, an event in the past in which the prophet finds great meanings (Ex. 10:1, 2; Deut. 4:32 f.; Ps. 105). The institutions of the Law,

14 W. Manson, *Jesus the Messiah*, p. 50. Hodder & Stoughton, 1943.

circumcision, and the Sabbath are perennial reminders of creation and redemption. At times, the past event is an incident in the life of the prophet himself, which at the time of happening seemed to have no significance, but which later became an object lesson of wide ramifications. The signs of earlier prophets were subject to reinterpretation by later ones, as they discerned in the traditional predictions a sign of approaching dawn. Thus Matthew finds in Jesus the fulfillment of Isaiah's sign (cf. Isa. 7:14 and Matt. 1:22 f.), and the fourth Evangelist discerns deeper meanings in the Synoptic healing narratives. Usually, however, the decisive sign which leads to reinterpretation of earlier signs is a contemporaneous event. The prophet notes a phenomenon in his immediate environment, or he himself makes a symbolic gesture; in either case, his function is the same — to understand and to interpret the message of God. His methods may approach those of other diviners and seers, using quasi-magical means in the interpretation of dreams or omens.[15] The character of his message, however, makes him aware of quite distinctive authority.[16]

Signs that happen in the present or are anticipated in the immediate future may be appealed to as credentials for his message. In the early historical narratives, this sign is usually a spectacular, objective miracle that supports the claim of divine commission. When Moses is diffident about undertaking his vocation, God overcomes his reticence by turning a rod into a serpent and by making his hand leprous (Ex., ch. 4). And God equips him to work similar wonders for gaining the allegiance of his people. The prediction that Jeroboam's Baal worship is about to be destroyed is verified by a withered arm and a broken altar (I Kings, ch. 13). Ahijah accurately announces the death of a child when its mother steps across the threshold (I Kings, ch. 14). Isaiah successfully begs God to cause the sundial to run backward (II Kings, ch. 20). Samuel predicts that Saul will find the lost asses, will meet with three men, and will be overtaken by a prophetic frenzy (I Sam., ch. 10). (These signs are reported to us in highly developed tradition, in which legendary accretion has expanded the spectacular touches. One cannot separate the original from the secondary elements in the narratives, but for our purpose such a task is irrelevant.) The announcement of coming redemption is often associated with the message, "This shall be a

[15] A. Guillaume, *op. cit.,* pp. 109 f.
[16] W. Manson, *op. cit.,* p. 43.

sign unto you." This confirmatory event in Isaiah (Isa. 7:14) is the birth of Immanuel, and in Luke (Luke 2:12) is the discovery of a Babe in the manger. In apocalyptic visions, much attention is frequently given to signs of the end, portents of the time when all promises will be fulfilled. Both Jesus and Paul point to signs as evidence of their mission (Luke 7:18–23; II Cor. 12:2). When apostles proclaim Jesus as Messiah, they give special prominence to those acts by which God has accredited him, those outward and visible wonders which confirm his mission as Deliverer. Jesus' deeds are signs by which God gives witness to his intention (Acts 2:22; 10:38). Professor Manson points out that this accent takes precedence over the appeal to the divine truth of Jesus' teaching or to the transcendent greatness of his Person.[17] The writer of Hebrews summarizes a typical early Christian attitude:

" How shall we escape, if we neglect so great a salvation? which having at the first been spoken through the Lord, was confirmed unto us by them that heard; God also bearing witness with them, both *by signs and wonders,* and *by manifold powers,* and *by gifts of the Holy Spirit,* according to his own will " (Heb. 2:3, 4).

This appeal to signs as having evidential force, however, was qualified and restricted by the prophet's message and commission. The above quotation indicates some of these conditions. The sign retains a secondary place, i.e., to confirm a word which has been spoken, to buttress a purpose which is already manifest. The sign is subject to the authority of God, and has import only as an indication of his will. When there are false expectations, God refuses to work a sign or hides the meaning of the enacted parable. In most cases the nature of the sign depends upon the character of the message revealed, rather than the reverse. Signs by themselves are never conclusive, are never clear in themselves, and seldom serve to compel faith. When they have served their purpose, they cease to hold the focus of attention.

They provoke the same range of faith and unbelief as the spoken parable. To those who have eyes to see, the sign is not necessary to create faith. Rather, it receives its meaning from prior faith. To those who are blinded, no sign can suffice to force open their eyes. The Egyptians and the stubborn Israelites did not perceive the message communicated at the Red Sea. Nor did the Romans or Sadducees perceive the signs at-

[17] *Op. cit.,* pp. 33, 34.

tendant upon the resurrection of Jesus. As a Pharisee, Paul interpreted "the gifts of the Holy Spirit" in a fashion far different from his attitudes after he became an apostle. This realistic awareness of the ambiguity of signs receives classic statement in the parable of Dives and Lazarus: "They will not believe even if one were to return from the dead" (Luke 16:31). In the Fourth Gospel one notes a wide range in the responses to Jesus' signs: some persons are antagonized by them; some are very dull of hearing; some are attracted to them and partially understand them; some fully appropriate the meaning which they symbolize. And in both Old and New Testaments, this variety of response is understood to be anticipated by Him whose purpose is both revealed and hidden:

"Who maketh a man dumb, or deaf, or seeing, or blind? is it not I, Jahveh?" (Ex. 4:11).

"I thank thee, O Father, Lord of heaven and earth, that thou didst hide these things from the wise and understanding, and didst reveal them unto babes" (Matt. 11:25).

TRUE SIGNS AND FALSE

Further evidence of the ambivalent and inconclusive nature of signs is provided by the fact that the appearance of a true sign may coincide with the appearance of a false sign which, on objective grounds, is just as persuasive. Competition in gestures between true and false prophets accompanies competition in words. Pre-exilic prophets openly recognize this competition; they admit that in terms of method there is nothing to distinguish them from their opponents. When Jeremiah gives a sign of approaching captivity by wearing a yoke on his shoulders, Hananiah gives a sign of a more hopeful future by breaking Jeremiah's yoke. Their contemporaries are forced to take sides, to refer to other criteria of truth. In such a dilemma, Deuteronomy suggests this test: if the prophet says, "Let us go after other gods," the observer may know that his sign is intended to test their loyalty to God and not to justify the false prophet's apostasy (Deut. 13:1 f.).

Because of this confusion in signs, some prophets dissociated themselves from the practice of using external signs. Others vigorously attacked the false prophets as deceivers who sought to coerce God's support of their plans rather than to bend their human desires in the direc-

tion of God's plans. They spoke, " Peace, peace; when there is no peace ";
they trusted in their hereditary position as servants of the court; they
shaped their predictions to meet the hopes of the rulers; they jealously
guarded their " trade secrets " and formed a " closed shop " to preserve
their privileged position. In short, they substituted an earthly angle of
vision for the point of view which God's visitation demands.[18]

The same conflict appears in accentuated form in the accounts of
Jesus' ministry. Does he cast out demons by Beelzebub or by the finger
of God? Does not Satan himself confront Jesus with signs of his authority over the kingdoms of the earth? With eyes of faith disciples see
things which " many prophets and kings desired to see," but the eyes
of unbelief are drawn away by other signs which in themselves are more
convincing (cf. Matt., ch. 11). The Christian teacher is opposed by false
teachers, the Christian prophet is opposed by false prophets, the signs
of the Messiah are opposed by the signs of false Messiahs;[19] in fact, all
these are episodes in the history-long battle between God and Satan,
each of whom uses signs to attest his sovereignty over men. As the end-
time approaches, the signs of Satan and his servants become greater and
more impressive.

Ultimately, however, the Jewish prophet and Christian apostle attribute both true and false signs to the purposes of God. He it is who gives
lying words and deceptive signs to the false prophet; he it is who allots
to Satan his authority during the present age. Signs are chosen by him
to test the vision and faith, the hope and endurance, of men. And the
final appearance of Satan in all his power will be the final sign for
the victory of God through his Messiah. And for rightly discerning the
signs of that time, Israel remains dependent upon the true prophet.
Upon his living word depends the meaning of the sign.

The ubiquitous misinterpretation of contemporary signs, occasioned
by different degrees of blindness and by the activity of false revealers,
perennially perverts men's understanding of former signs. The true
prophet is always intensely alert to this danger. He, like his people,
reverenced the tradition and was confident that the word of God as acted
in previous wonders would be fulfilled. He drew inspiration and guidance from the stories of former glorious deeds. He pointed to the marvels
of creation and to the reminder of those marvels in the Sabbath. He

[18] Cf. A. Guillaume, pp. 109 f.; R. B. Y. Scott, *op. cit.*, pp. 93–99.
[19] A. E. J. Rawlinson, *Christ in the Gospels*, pp. 34 f. 1944.

knew that circumcision served to re-enact God's selection of Abraham and his descendants. He recognized the meaning of the deliverance from Egypt and saw in the Passover a contemporary repetition of that sign. After the establishment of the Law, the Temple, and the synagogue, he viewed these institutions as signs of God's purpose for Israel and the world. But none of these signs was immune to misinterpretation by unbelief.[20] Each of them was capable of hiding God's purpose as well as of revealing it. Each of them was " a stone of stumbling." In fact, such institutions were particularly conducive to misunderstanding. It was dangerously easy to substitute an I-It relation for an I-Thou relation, in which the " It " is an objective rite (circumcision), a codified Torah, a sanctified Temple. It is perhaps easier to view a past event in speculative, nonexistential terms than a present event. Loyalty to social memory may lead one to depend upon an inherited past rather than upon a living present. It is easy to deceive oneself into believing that present rebellion is actually faith, if authority for it can be found in objectified tradition. It is easy to test the validity of living prophets by the signs of dead prophets, as those signs are misinterpreted by living rebels.

The true prophet is thus placed in a difficult position vis-à-vis the tradition. He defends it as a valid word from God which is soon to be fulfilled; but he knows that it serves also as a resource for his enemy, for his hearers are led astray by false loyalty to ancestral institutions; he must therefore challenge their attitudes toward Law and Temple and Sabbath, and must supply the true understanding of those signs. In his eyes, the people who suppose themselves to be faithful are actually renegades; in their eyes he appears to be an iconoclast and an enemy of God. How can this clash be resolved? Both scribes and Jesus claim authority to interpret the Law, but they arrive at opposite conclusions. How is the issue to be settled? Again, the prophet and his hearer are forced to choose whether this authority be from heaven or from men. And the presence of conflicting signs and conflicting interpretations of signs makes the choice more difficult. But this greater difficulty makes the decision *his* decision, and makes him see it as an ultimate decision of faith.

In short, the presence of a sign does not solve the question of authority but raises it in new intensity. The function of the sign is to bring the acts of God within the range of vision of man, to crystallize the occasion

[20] G. Stählin, *Skandalon*, pp. 271 f. Gütersloh, 1930.

for faith or stumbling. The sign which purports to be a proof of God's authority is, at the same time and at the point of decision, a proof of man's faith. If man seeks to evade this issue by relying upon the objective evidence of circumcision, Law, or Temple, he employs those signs to defeat their original purpose.

THE FUTURE REFERENCE

The inherent and ineradicable contradiction between the signs of the true prophet and the signs of the false prophet is a contradiction which *in the present* can be resolved only by faith. This faith, however, rests upon God's faithfulness to the promises which he has revealed in these very signs. The contradiction, therefore, cannot be fully resolved except in the future. And to this future all the prophets point; it alone can provide objective ratification of their message, or, rather, of God's message, which they as ambassadors carry. And three things are certain about this future.

In the first place, it will mark the fulfillment of the inner meaning of all the signs that God has wrought in the past: the fulfillment of creation, and the Sabbath rest which is its sign; the fulfillment of the call of Abraham, and the circumcision which is its sign; the fulfillment of the Exodus, and the Passover which is its sign; the fulfillment of the revelation to Moses, and the Law which is its sign; the fulfillment of God's tabernacling with men, and the Temple which is its sign; and the fulfillment of all the prophecies and the signs of the prophets.

In the second place, the final salvation will take the form of a judgment upon all the false signs, and the false prophets who have used them to mislead the people, and Satan who through them has blinded men. And this judgment must, in the nature of the case, involve a condemnation of the false interpretations which have clustered around the pivotal institutions. It will indicate the true meaning of circumcision, the Sabbath, the Law, the Temple, and in so doing it will bring to nought the rebellion which has used these institutions as the cloak of hypocrisy. And those teachers who have been blinded, who have relied upon the institutions to guarantee their piety, will fall into the ditch along with their pupils.

In the third place, the final salvation will inaugurate perfect rapport between God and his creation, so that the need for signs will vanish. No longer will his word come to men through others; no longer will the prophet speak parables which baffle as well as clarify; no longer will he enact parables in the form of gestures that offend and attract; no longer will men need the memorials of past wonders. Then will men know as now, whether in faith or in unbelief, they are known. Then will the psalmist's lament be answered:

> " We see not our signs:
> There is no more any prophet;
> Neither is there among us any
> that knoweth how long "
> (Ps. 74:9).

Until that time signs will seem to be absent, or they will be intermittent, or they will continue to obscure as well as reveal. And when that time comes, the faithful interpreters of signs will be justified by their faith. Just because every true sign is a revelation of God's purpose, its meaning is ultimately inclusive of the meaning of all history. In fact, to the prophet who understands a single gesture of God there is communicated a saving trust in all God's acts. The whole vista of history is telescoped into this single scene. To the prophet's eye, all history becomes a sign, all history becomes a parable, all history becomes a miracle, all history becomes a test of man's eyes and ears, all history becomes the arena within which God's word precipitates the conflict between rebellion and return.

The prophet, therefore, finds himself standing at the boundary line between God's act and man's response. In him meet two competing histories: the false history which is seen through the eyes of human rebellion; and the genuine history, which is seen through the eyes of faith. To him " is given the mystery of the kingdom of God: but unto them that are without, all things are done in parables " (see Mark 4:10–12). He is forced to reckon with the gibes of those who trust in other standards of wisdom and power; he is himself subjected to the temptation of unbelief. He is as aware of the contradictions between the two histories as his bitterest opponents, and more aware of them than Israelites who assume that the contradictions can be met within the forms of conventional piety without much agony of spirit on their own part. He cannot evade the contradictions so easily as that, because he is minister plenipotentiary from God with a message *to the world*. He stands on the boundary, risking all his hopes on the revelation of God's will

which has been channeled through parables and signs and appropriated in faith. When he speaks as a prophet, he stands within the sequence of God's deeds and God's words. Every event in that history is
a sign of genuine creation and redemption, and the validity of this
history is inseparable from the validity of the signs by which its presence
is manifested to men. Standing within this genuine history, he must
address men who have been deceived by the illusions of human historical knowledge. To men enslaved by this false *kairos*, his mission, his
words, his deeds, are signs of God's *kairos* set forth to bring the planted
word to its harvest and to winnow the wheat from the chaff. It is in such
terms as these that early Christians described the mission of their Messiah. The final issue for them is the validity of the death-exaltation of
Jesus, as a sign of God's salvation. And they repeatedly give witness to
faith through the sign of the Eucharist, whereby they " proclaim the
Lord's death till he come." These two signs, united in Christian experience, define the boundaries between the old age and the new.[21]

[21] A. E. J. Rawlinson, *op. cit.*, pp. 38 f. A penetrating analysis of Jesus as a sign may
be found in S. Kierkegaard, *Training in Christianity*, pp. 124–144. 1941.

*THESE THREE WAYS of understanding time —
present-mindedness, retrospection, and foresight —
belong together, and combine to give the present
moment its absolute significance. The uniqueness of
a moment of history results from three factors — the
synthesis of ever varying contents, the appreciation of
their significance, and our reaction in the face of them.
In such a moment everything is placed in jeopardy;
everything can be lost and ruined " in a moment."*
— Fritz Kaufmann, in *Philosophy and Phenomenological
Research,* March, 1944, Vol. IV, p. 299.

12

ISRAEL FORGETS AND REMEMBERS

THE BIBLICAL point of view has been set forth with respect to the angle of vision of the man of faith, and to the event in the foreground which God uses to precipitate that faith. The experience of seeing God's deed or of hearing his word opens up new horizons which provide the context necessary if the experience is to have ultimate significance. The delineation of these horizons is now our major concern. The peculiar structure of prophetic retrospect is the subject of the present chapter; the next chapter will direct attention to the pattern of prophetic prospect.

To introduce the problem, it is well to recapitulate the basic axioms of thought which condition attitudes toward the panorama of history.

1. It is from within the present moment that man senses the unity of his history and appropriates its significance. His active will creates a particular *kairos* which unites retrospect and prospect at the point of immediate decision. The past and the future are extensions of the present, the past entering it as preparation and the future as anticipation. Purpose serves to define the temporal horizons, the relationship of the tenses, and the sense of duration.

2. Within this same *now,* within the observable process of his experience, man is involved in an incident that purports to disclose another purpose than his own, a will with greater endurance and power. And this purpose stems from a Person who claims to be Creator and Lord. As such, this purpose lays absolute claim to man's allegiance. And this purpose creates a *kairos* of its own that incorporates the past and future deeds of God.

3. Within this *now,* man is made aware of sharp conflict between these two purposes, and between their corresponding histories. In set-

ting up and following his own purpose, man has distorted his whole understanding of his history, has corrupted his memory and made futile his hope. And the sign which discloses God's will discloses at the same moment the whole vista of genuine history. The act of disclosure is not an isolated phenomenon, but one event in a dynamic sequence moving from creation to fulfillment.

4. He who is led in faith to affirm his dependence on God's history perceives the vanity of his own history apart from God's word and Spirit, perceives that " the whole relative world of visible and audible things is in itself of no account." [1] Yet that same world is found to have great dignity when seen through new eyes. Observable history

" witnesses, indeed, ' beyond history,' beyond itself, yet not away from itself to some second world running parallel with it but at no point touching it; not to some wholly other reality the discovery of which empties the observable world of final significance. The observable world witnesses in such a way that it *is* what it signifies as seen by God and apprehended by men." [2]

By itself, however, the course of man's fortunes does not have the power to communicate its true origin or end. The man who is confident of his power to read the scroll of destiny is enslaved and deluded by a spurious history. Only a word initiated by God and received in faith can free him from the fatal consequences of this delusion.

5. When by repentance man leaves his detour and returns to God's highway, he appropriates the beginning and end of this new road. The false retrospect and prospect in which he has trusted are abandoned; a new memory and hope are now determinative of decision. Different events now mark the milestones in the movement toward the future. Some events which earlier seemed ordinary will now be described as strategic turning points. And because the touch of God's hand on history comes from a point beyond man's experience, the revelation of his purpose will disclose meanings hidden from ordinary observation. The story of his acts will therefore retain the quality of parables that require faith to be understood.

" The Old Testament is continually wrestling with the non-historical, ultimate problem of the relation of each and every point of history to God. The Old Testament writers, be they historians, prophets, psalmists, or wise men, see each situation confronted by the Word of God. They are driven to do so,

[1] E. C. Hoskyns, *The Fourth Gospel,* Vol. I, p. 6. Faber and Faber, 1940.
[2] N. Davey, in Hoskyns, *op. cit.,* Vol. I, p. xxiii.

of course, by history — the history behind them which illuminates their own experience, and their own history which unveils to them the meaning of the experience behind them — but what is always of primary importance to them is the analysis of history, not in terms of itself, but in terms of the truth of God, to which, so they believe, it bears witness, and which dignifies it as a revelation of God." [3]

THE GRAIN OF MEMORY

The forms in which they render an account to themselves of their past are primarily determined by this unique consciousness of the present. Each form has a definite anchorage in faith; each form is determined primarily by motivation stemming from this faith. Their recollection of previous happenings is never described as the conducting of innumerable post-mortems, as " the rolling up of the carpet after the procession has passed." Rather, this recollection remains a constituent of the living present; it illuminates and enforces the demands of the present for decision and action; it suggests and supports the confidence in coming fulfillment. The Hebrew-Christian tradition, so permeated by the sense of the dynamic meaning of the past, produces many histories, first oral and then written. They deserve to be called histories, if the term " history " be defined as " the intellectual form in which a civilization renders account to itself of its past." [4] Friedrich Nietzsche's dictum applies to the Biblical outlook: " The verdict of the past is always an oracle: only as architects of the future, as knowers of the present, will you understand it." In order to be applicable to the Bible, however, both of these quotations must be qualified by the conviction that the prime agent in the past is the power of God. This orientation, of course, excludes Biblical writers from serious consideration by so-called objective or scientific historians. J. W. Thompson, for example, complains that ecclesiastical history has been " violently distorted " from the beginning,

" first by the adoption of ancient Jewish history as pre-Christian history; secondly by its association of revelation and history; thirdly by the vicious distinction made between ' sacred ' and ' profane,' or secular, history." [5]

[3] N. Davey, in Hoskyns, *op. cit.*, Vol. I, p. xxxi.
[4] J. Huizinga, in R. Klibansky and H. J. Paton, *Philosophy and History*, p. 9. Oxford University Press, 1936.
[5] *A History of Historical Writing*, Vol. I, p. 125. The Macmillan Company, 1942.

This conclusion is inevitable if one grants the premises of the scientific historian! But the purpose of Biblical reminiscence excludes the desirability and possibility of producing objective data of the sort which the modern historian desires. Such data may be found in the Bible, but they do not constitute the major concern of prophet or apostle. He is concerned with the enhancement of existential, nonaccumulative knowledge of God, not with the piling up of facts about the past, separated from the crucial issues of present decision. He would agree with Croce's thrust: "Knowledge for the sake of knowledge would be an idiotic pastime for idiots." Only because what God has done is intrinsically related to that which he is doing does the prophet become a historian.

The reading and interpretation of the written histories profusely scattered through the Bible requires these preliminary questions: *What* were the authors trying to say to their auditors? How did they feel impelled to say it? Under what limitations did they place themselves? To whom were they speaking? How did they desire these listeners to relate themselves to the narrative, or to God through the narrative?

In evaluating the initial impact of these narratives upon their first listeners, it must be remembered that we are dealing in the first instance with oral traditions rather than with written documents. Biblical histories were spoken before they were written, were heard with the ear and preserved in the mind rather than read with the eyes and preserved in the library. And historical tradition that is memorized creates a mood and response quite different from the same tradition when it is deposited in a document. Oral transference of common memories is more productive of creative listening and active imagination. It facilitates a more complete fusion of tradition with the total apperceptive mass of the individual. It provides greater flexibility in the adaptation of tradition to the immediate purpose of the narrator and the immediate concerns of the listener. It encourages the application of retrospect to a greater number and variety of situations. Finally, it is more conducive to the sense of contemporaneity and vitality, of gratitude and obligation and solidarity. Rote memorization of dates and names can dull historical consciousness, but creative and imaginative use of oral tradition can intensify that consciousness. In the Biblical period, the latter far outweighs the former.

To be sure, oral history is beset with many dangers. Like any recollection of the past, it may lead to ancestor worship or, as Voltaire remarked, to playing ribald jokes in the cemetery of one's forebears. It may be simply a worm's way of gaining self-confidence by snubbing the dead. It may attract the historian "from an office where one is afraid of a sergeant major into an office where one can intimidate generals." It may provide a dreamland for "tight little faces from Oxford, fish-shaped faces from Cambridge," a place devoid of all dangers where "one can meet with perfect ease not only kings, but people who are even rarer on one's visiting list (courtesans)." [6] The historical narratives in the Bible, however, are remarkably free from these eccentricities. In fact, their tone and mood is quite the opposite. They confront listeners with ancestors who are very much alive; they confound the complacency of current historians; they condemn the cowardice of listeners and call them into the path of dangerous decision; they increase the tensions and suffering of the present toward the end of return and rebirth.

It must, of course, be granted that many of the anecdotes do not directly enhance or revivify the historical consciousness of the present. In some, etiological motifs predominate, i.e., the desire to explain the origin of a name, a person, or a practice. Simple curiosity may weave fanciful tales of why the leopard has spots or a rainbow appears in a storm, how Beth-el received its name, and why the carpenter's son was called Jesus. People crave to know how some sacred ceremony originated: the Sabbath, baptism, or fasting. Anecdotes arise to satisfy this craving. In the Bible one may also find legends embroidering the portraits of noted saints or notorious sinners. When a character has won a permanent place in the epic of salvation, imagination begins to weave around his head the halo of sanctity or the curse of treachery. For example, we may cite the New Testament accounts of the death of John the Baptist, of Herod, of Judas. One finds also genealogies that seem to represent only the "squirrel instinct" or the megalomania of elite or effete families; and there are court annals designed to exalt the prestige of a particular dynasty, to preserve for later generations the obituaries of illustrious rulers. Historical narratives thus motivated differ but little from similar narratives in non-Biblical environments. But this is not true of the narratives that are intrinsic to the revelation of God's word

---

[6] E. M. Forster, "Consolations of History," in *Abinger Harvest*, pp. 167, 168. Harcourt Brace and Co., 1936.

and deed. And it is this revelation which provides the context for most of the historical accounts, and for those accounts which are most vital.

For an example, we may turn first to Ezekiel, with special reference to ch. 16. The prophet looks backward because he is so instructed of God; the story of the past becomes a parable and a sign of God's continuing purpose. He assumes that his listeners share his acquaintance with the events of the past, but they misinterpret the present implications of those events. Certain motifs, therefore, dominate his narrative. First of all, God requires the sacred city to recognize her abominations, her trust in her beauty, her countless and recurrent whoredoms. She must realize her complete dependence upon God. Before he adopted her, she was abhorrent rather than beautiful; bloody, helpless, naked, and hungry. Time and again, after she had become beautiful and powerful, God had been provoked to anger and had diminished her food supply and frustrated her insatiable lust. The sinful woman, however, had not learned obedience from these previous judgments, but had turned from one rebellion to a greater one. Moreover, she kept deceiving herself by pointing to fancied superiority over more wicked harlots, Sodom and Samaria. The prophet must destroy this invidious comparison, must make Jerusalem aware that her sins are the greater because of this very condemnation of her sisters (v. 52). He must warn her of an approaching judgment more devastating than all the earlier ones. He must revive her gratitude to God even in the midst of that punishment. He must assure her that the punishment is a means to an end, the original design which God has revealed in every generation — to establish the covenant. He must make clear that this redemptive purpose will be realized only if the memory of her shame and of unmerited forgiveness remains alive. Her own salvation and reconciliation with her sisters depend upon continuing repetition of this recognition of sin and dependence on God's mercy. In short, the recital of history reveals (1) that every good gift has come from the Creator, (2) that every evil has been a punishment for rebellion, but intended for good, (3) that now is the time for repentance and the fulfillment of the promise, and (4) that return requires the remembering of what has been forgotten.

A slightly different pattern of narration appears in the Second Isaiah, due to an altered situation. In Ezekiel, the problem faced by the prophet is the sin of *defiance,* supported by proud self-confidence in the past and future. In the Second Isaiah, the prophet confronts the sin of *despair,* supported by doleful memories and fearful expectations. A people in exile is oppressed by a retrospect that seems to show nothing but the failure of God's purpose, and by a prospect that seems to hold no hope for his covenant. References to historical tradition, therefore, reflect a different motif and mood.

The present moment is seen as a moment of preparation and fulfillment. Iniquity has been punished and pardoned (Isa. 40:1, 2). To people conscious of their impotence (vs. 6, 7), it is now time to proclaim, "Prepare ye," and to shout glad tidings of coming glory (see vs. 3–5, 9–11). But this hope can be nourished only by the confidence that "the word of our God shall stand forever." And this confidence can come only from a new conviction of his power. Jahveh is Creator, calling all things into being through his word. He sits above the world and all the nations are as nothing before him. He gives all men life and food, and calls the seed of Abraham and forms Israel. He makes the work of men vain and reduces the idols to "wind and confusion." He destroys the power of princes, and raises up deliverers even among alien peoples. The very captivity of Israel signifies his power (ch. 42:24). All that has happened has been due to his plan, and nothing can happen contrary to his design (ch. 43:13). Those who despair of his justice (ch. 40:27) are blind to the present, hidden working of his righteousness (ch. 42:18). They need to forget the "former things" that have led them to doubt his power, and expectantly to await the "new thing" which will vindicate that power (ch. 43:19). They have been formed to set forth his praise. Assured of his mercy, they must forget their guilt and fear. God has blotted out their transgressions for his own sake. He will reverse all the doleful signs and predictions of men who detect in the baleful present no portent of coming restoration (ch. 44:24 f.).

The prophet defies the evidence of the recent past and the disastrous present. He challenges the opinions of wise men, though they seem to be supported by objective indications of historical events. Without evidence to justify his optimism, he reinterprets the destiny of his people wholly in terms of the covenant promises and the inner intimations of God's Spirit. Retrospect continues to include a long sequence of catastrophes, but the significance of these catastrophes is now revealed as marking God's power and offering ground for hope. Hindsight is used to correct foresight, but, first, hindsight must be corrected by insight. Present awareness of God's sovereignty must enable Israel to forget what should be forgotten and remember what should be remembered. Otherwise the blindness due to sin will cause them to remember what should be forgotten and to forget what should be remembered (cf. Josh., ch. 24; Neh., ch. 9).

It is significant that the Genesis stories of creation are permeated with the same motifs as the prophetic witness, and are designed to produce the same response on the part of the listeners. The creation epic clothes in narrative form the basic affirmations of Isa., ch. 45: " I am Jahveh, and there is none else "; " I form the light, and create darkness "; " I have made the earth, and created man upon it "; " I . . . have stretched out the heavens; and all their host have I commanded "; " I make peace, and create evil." The power of the word, the goodness of creation, the multitude of God's gifts, the rebellion of man, the frustration of man's hopes, the curse as an act of punishment and mercy — these are central to both prophet and historian. (The analysis of the stories of the first Hebrew kings discloses that the motifs of the Genesis account of Adam provide the recurrent pattern for the memories of the monarchy.[7])

A similar use of retrospect motivates the liturgical materials. Psalm 78 is a typical example. The memories of the community are " dark sayings " which are preserved from generation to generation as witness to the praises of Jahveh, as record of his wondrous works. The purpose is frankly stated:

> " That they might set their hope in God [future],
> And not forget the works of God [past],
> But keep his commandments [present],
> And might not be as their fathers [past],
> A stubborn and rebellious generation,
> A generation that set not their heart aright,
> And whose spirit was not stedfast with God."

History is the story of successive signs of God's activity, a narrative punctuated by the stumbling of the people. They forget his doings; they tempt God by seeking their own desires; they do not trust him for salvation; they flatter him with their lips, but do not live by his covenant. The rhythm runs from creation, through forgetfulness and rebellion,

[7] Cf. K. C. Evans, in *Christendom*, Vol. VIII, pp. 362 f. 1943.

then through punishment and recollection, to return and a new creation. The pivotal points of *divine* action are the signs that embody his justice and mercy. The pivotal points of human response are the transitions from (1) remembering to forgetting, which constitutes the rebellion, and from (2) forgetting to remembering, which constitutes return. Historical narratives center in the events that manifest these transitions, transitions in which the divine actions produce the human responses.

The axioms presupposed by the Deuteronomic law follow this same configuration, for the law always appears within the context of retrospective narrative. As in the case of the histories, the motif of the law is "lest ye forget" (see Deut. 4:23; 6:12). The law is itself a means by which the sign of the Exodus deliverance is to be repeated in full contemporaneity (see ch. 6:20–25). And the burden of the law is not so much the itemization of all duties as the preservation and renewal of the life-giving relationship of creature to Creator, of the elect community to its God (ch. 5). To be sure, many details of cultic and moral observance may be detached from this context; their origin may be traced to other sources than prophetic revelation; emphasis upon them reflects the centrifugal pull away from the perspective center in the direction of objective fixation of the demand of God. But this tendency to transform revelation into legalism is countered by the centripetal power of a living God whose demand remains the same: the circumcision of the heart in continued repentance (ch. 10:16). The enunciation of a law code, fixing in terms of external behavior the content of divine demand, may encourage the substitution of accumulative knowledge and merit for nonaccumulative repentance and its fruits, the stepping down of the high voltage of prophetic revelation to a current manageable by the prophet's successors. Yet the recollection that the law originates in an act of God constitutes an ever-present stimulus to reenact the history of that original meeting. In its Deuteronomic setting, the law conduces to this initial historical consciousness more than to an objective historical knowledge that can be transferred on grounds of empirical evidence to those outside the covenant community.

RETROSPECT IN THE NEW TESTAMENT

As we have noted, the Hebrew pattern of retrospect is adopted with eagerness by the early Christians. Their references to the past are the testimonies of believers to believers, designed to renew, correct, and extend the initial faith and hope. As a first example, one may cite the book of Revelation. Though this prophet does not indulge in extensive narratives of past events, he takes for granted the accepted fund of memory. This memory of definitive events constitutes the ground of identity between speaker and listener, and contributes to the existential authority for his message (Rev. 1:5, 6, 9). The command to remember implements the charge of sin, the call to repent, the demand for " first works," and the promise of imminent fulfillment (ch. 2:4–7). The priority of heavenly over earthly history is everywhere taken for granted. In heaven originated the saving events which have now served as signs to draw men into the Church. In heaven has now been terminated the conflict between Christ and Satan, a conflict still being waged on earth. What has happened on earth and what has now happened in heaven — these events — place disciples in a situation of final decision and judgment. Salvation depends upon obeying the authority which the God of all power has given to " the Lamb that hath been slain." Loyalty to him has plunged believers into mortal danger and into the temptation to deny him. This crisis is, in fact, the earthly field in which Christ battles the Antichrist. Only the act of faithfulness, supported by his power, can manifest their heavenly citizenship and his triumph. Participating in his sufferings, they participate also in his victory. He confronts them anew, summoning them to this destiny with the words: " I am," " I have," " Thou hast," " Remember," " Repent," " I will come," " I will judge," " I will bless." Tempted by the external course of events to shift their angle of vision, this new disclosure of the source of events calls them back to the perspective of faith.

As another example, consider the First Epistle of John. Here too the initial concern is to establish the common field of vision; the author recalls to mind " that which we have heard, that which we have seen . . . concerning the Word of life " (I John 1:1). These signs constitute the only foundation for fellowship and joy (vs. 3, 4). The teacher who ignores or denies these signs of God's activity in the flesh and blood of Jesus is a false teacher, a servant of the Antichrist, who enslaves men with spurious interpretations of history. To deny that the Son of God has come in the flesh is to empty the good news of saving significance by setting up human wisdom as the measure of truth and power. The advent of the Messiah, viewed as a redemptive work of God (though hidden from the world and rejected by it), must constitute at every moment the ground of existence of all sons of God. Recollection of this Advent convicts men of sin, so that he who says, " I have no sin," is a liar, dead while he lives. But the sign which convicts of sin also is the warrant of forgiveness and life, through the Light which was and is in Christ. To repeat the sign of the Passion is to re-enact in full, contemporaneous actuality the memory, the repentance, the return. Thus alone is broken fellowship between God and men restored in Christ. Thus alone is joy renewed and hope established. Here is no objective historical record, but witness to that historical act whereby God re-creates man's history from within. The disclosure of his purpose in Christ is a single Word which incorporates the whole of genuine history, past present, and future.

THE PASSION STORY

This same pattern of retrospect dominates the Passion story as told by the Synoptists. Its true *Sitz im Leben* is the sermon, the witness of the apostles to the world. Its true *Sitz im Glauben* is the existential relation of the believer to God, as that relationship has been, and continues to be, defined by God's love in Christ. As a story, it presents the formal characteristics of indirect communication. The human speaker is unimportant; the divine authority is all-important. And the focus of attention centers, not on what is said *about* God, but on what he says in and through this event. The story preserves the distinctness and concreteness of a single series of happenings ("he was crucified under Pontius Pilate"), but it is so told as to involve the listener in that same drama and to plunge him into a sharp either-or dilemma, faith or unbelief. Though the events are firmly rooted in acted history, the narrative form shares many characteristics of parable. In form it also bears the marks of a sign, a gesture of God described in such a way as to reveal what is hidden and to hide what is revealed. It communicates divine wisdom in a word which underscores the irreconcilable antithesis between heavenly and earthly wisdoms. It is a word that requires the hearing ears and produces those ears among both Jews and Gentiles: " Truly this was the Son of God." To the community of believers, the story is a witness to the contemporaneous re-enactment of God's saving deed: " This *do* in remembrance of me." And as a living memory, the repetition of the event in the Eucharist has power to convict of sin and to assure of forgiveness. It " finds " the disciple in a situation of betrayal (Judas) or denial (Peter) or doubt (Thomas) or blindness (Mary) or misunderstanding (the Emmaus disciples). It calls him to new repentance and faith. It calls him to share now the sufferings of the Messiah and so to anticipate the restored fellowship in the Kingdom, showing forth the Lord's death " until he come." Genuine history is here constituted by an act of God which reveals what he has done, is doing, and is about to do. Here in a single all-inclusive word is true creation, judgment, and redemption. God visits man with his call to remember, repent, believe, and hope. Those who enter this new relationship receive a new point of standing within God's history which enables them to understand the source and structure of all history. And the forms with which they now describe their past are shaped by this understanding.

It is not surprising, therefore, that the interpretation of the Passion story becomes the crux of debate between Christian and non-Christian historians, between objective and subjective historical methodologies. (This is an issue which is involved in the interpretation of every pivotal event of Biblical history. For the Jew, the crux of the problem is found in the evaluation of the election of Israel in the divine deliverance from Egypt.) The rationalist and objectivist historian may agree with the Christian historian in accepting the authenticity of certain happenings, e.g., that a man named Jesus was crucified under Pilate. But his objectivist point of view, his methods, and the character of the data available, will force him to deny, or at least to take a neutral attitude toward, the evaluation that early Christians gave to that event. And, like Charles Guignebert,[8] he may conclude that the faith of the apostles was produced by the hallucinations of seeing the risen Lord. He may then attribute the subjectivist elements in the Passion story to the bias produced by this faith. As historian, then, he must attempt to separate the dependable data from this subjective interpretation. And the resultant deposit of " pure " happenings will be small indeed.[9]

The Passion story itself preserves the recognition by the apostles that observable evidence was quite insufficient to establish their deductions. They testify that they themselves had been caused to stumble by the

[8] *Jesus*, pp. 515 ff. 1935.
[9] An excellent treatment of this topic may be found in A. M. Ramsey, *The Resurrection of Christ*. 1945.

offense of the cross. The true character of Jesus' Messiahship had been hidden from their eyes, and is still hidden from the eyes of most of their contemporaries. Nowhere do they claim that empirical evidence is sufficient to prove to the casual or interested onlooker what God is in fact doing through Jesus. Each step in the fateful drama had been and continued to be a mystery, a miracle, a sign, a parable; each step revealed the depths of man's blindness and sin at the same time that it manifested the powerful love of God. Only through faith was the meaning of any step communicated to men.

The apostles found that radical revision was necessary, not only in judgments regarding the cross, but also in judgments regarding the purport of prophetic predictions. Their reinterpretation of the Law and the Prophets was occasioned, not simply by the desire to find proof texts to support the new faith, but by the new illumination which the anointing of Jesus threw upon every item of memory.[10]

> "The stone which the builders rejected
> Is become the head of the corner."

But though the apostle knew from bitter experience how confusing the objective evidence could be, he could never agree that his interpretation of previous events was a concoction of his own imagination, a creation of his subconscious desires. He knew with complete inner certainty that he had not created his own faith. His prejudices had been overridden, his attitudes had been turned topsy-turvy, his sins had been revealed and judged, his complacencies and securities had been shattered, his reasoning, wishes, and fears had been condemned and submerged by a voice not his own. And that voice had spoken to him, not in some timeless, rarefied medium, but through these very events of the past. God had raised Jesus, and thus had manifested the meaning of these disturbing events, and of all the events of history. If faith had come to him dissociated from those events, it would have been sufficient for him to have described in nonhistorical terms the moment of vision when he saw the exalted Messiah. But since faith had come through those events, the witness requires the form of historical narrative. To be true to his faith, the apostle must recognize that only by " placarding " the death of Jesus can he speak the word that produces faith among unbelievers and renews faith among believers. That story, and not his subjective

[10] Cf. A. G. Hebert, *Throne of David*, Chapters 5, 10. 1941.

experience, must be the spearhead of preaching, the central sign of the community's worship, the ultimate reference of its ethic, and the principle of its organization. From this memory the Church could free itself only by ceasing to be the Church. To be sure, this memory is continually contradicted by the evidence of observable history; but the true believer is not disturbed by this contradiction, for the memory itself points to events in which the contradiction reached its maximum. The memory was born in contradiction, is maintained in the midst of contradiction, and foresees the continuing intensification of this contradiction until the end of history. The Passion story must, therefore, until the end retain its character as a mystery, a parable, and a sign.

STRATEGIC EVENTS

Having considered the grain of memory that characterizes Scripture, let us note four types of events on which that memory focuses. The first of these may be called covenant-making events. The shared memory of prophet and people gives central place to these moments of new beginnings. The initial covenant was sealed with creation as a whole when God first spoke and acted.

> " To him that by understanding made the heavens; . . .
> To him that spread forth the earth above the waters; . . .
> To him that made great lights; . . .
> The sun to rule by day; . . .
> The moon and the stars to rule by night "
>
> (Ps. 136:5–9).

This covenant makes of existence a single road, its beginning and end defined by the single purpose of God. His word is the source, which retains sovereign power and ordains for creation its all-inclusive *kairos*. This is a covenant which man cannot break.

" If ye can break my covenant of the day, and my covenant of the night, so that there shall not be day and night in their season; then may also my covenant be broken with David my servant " (see Jer. 33:19–26).

Within the time and space continuum of this covenant, God makes another with man, when he creates him and breathes into him the spirit of life. For him is ordained a distinctive purpose and *kairos*. Special obligations are imposed and special promises are invoked. The significance of this covenant is expressed, not in detailed descriptions of *how* man is created or *when,* but in staccato proclamation of *why* he was created and *what this implies* as to his present relationship to his Maker.

Looking backward, many writers focus attention upon the covenant with " the fathers," with Abraham, Isaac, Jacob, and the twelve tribes which constitute their seed. In this covenant, or series of covenants, God creates a separate race to share a distinctive duty and destiny. Abraham becomes a unique bearer of history, and circumcision becomes the sign by which this covenant is remembered and repeated. The people may forget, but God never forgets. In his act of salvation, he visits his people anew:

> " To show mercy towards our fathers,
>   And to remember his holy covenant;
>   The oath which he sware unto Abraham our father "
>   (Luke 1:72, 73).

The next great pivotal covenant is made with Moses and the tribes delivered from Egypt:

> " To him that smote Egypt in their first-born; . . .
>   And brought out Israel from among them; . . .
>   With a strong hand, and with an outstretched arm; . . .
>   To him that divided the Red Sea in sunder; . . .
>   And made Israel to pass through the midst of it; . . .
>   But overthrew Pharaoh and his host in the Red Sea "
>   (Ps. 136:10–15).

Israel becomes a chosen instrument and a holy possession, receiving a distinctive role in the human drama. Again, the covenant is marked by God's powerful acts, by a special purpose and *kairos,* by appropriate demands and promises, and by signs which accompany the perennially re-enacted Passover. In its purpose, this covenant preserves close continuity with earlier ones and maintains constant pressure upon human choices in the later generations. " Obey my voice, . . . so shall ye be my people, and I will be your God " (see Jer. 11:3–8). Deliverance from Egypt is the basis of the primal demand, and also the prototype of coming emancipation (ch. 16:14, 15).

Still later appears the covenant with the wandering tribes as they cross the Jordan to inherit the Promised Land. As heirs of the promise made to the patriarchs, Joshua and his people ratify a new covenant that covers their historical existence in the new land. (Josh., ch. 24; Ps. 136: 16–22). Later still, after the establishment of a kingdom under the Davidic dynasty, a covenant is made to express the unique obligations and potentialities of this new creation.

The second major type of strategic event in the retrospective panorama is that turning point when a particular covenant community breaks its covenant. Forgetful and self-willed, men disobey the commandments and forfeit the promise. Attributing false reality and power to an idol, they make with the idol a contrary covenant, which involves the acceptance of another purpose and another *kairos*. They commit their fortunes to following another road. The revealer confronts his people on this detour and calls, " Let the wicked forsake his way." With respect to the making of the covenant, his memory agrees with theirs. But with respect to the defection from that covenant, his understanding is the reverse of theirs. Moreover, he knows that his understanding is not his alone but God's. His understanding stems, not from a more extensive or trustworthy fund of historical data, made available to him by the annalists of his day. Rather, it stems from his own grappling with contemporary sin. He therefore accents those events in retrospect which illustrate and corroborate God's current controversy with his people.

The people eulogized the covenant as an assurance of privilege; the same covenant caused the prophets to tremble at the popular violation. Because of the covenant, the people claimed to be superior to other nations; because of the same covenant, the prophets detected in Israel a more heinous sin. The people trusted that external and formal observance of their obligations was sufficient; the prophets realized that lip service covered an inner defiance. Revelling in the glories of their past, the people beheld a glorious future of peace, security, and joy. But in the same situation, the prophets saw the anger of a Master who has been defrauded: " I will meet them as a bear that is bereaved of her whelps." Consequently, the prophet was impelled to trace the tragic history of rebellion back to the point where it started. And that event he narrated in terms calculated to produce conviction of guilt and eagerness to repent. In effect, he told and retold Nathan's parable, but addressed it to the people and drew the materials from their memories.

Jeremiah, for example, traces the detour to events transpiring after the settlement in Canaàn. From the day that it was built, the city of Jerusalem has been a " provocation of mine anger . . . even unto this day " (Jer. 32:31). The primary agents of evil have been " their kings, their princes, their priests, and their prophets, and the men of Judah, and the inhabitants of Jerusalem " (ch. 32:32). The primary form of apostasy included: abominations in the Temple, encouragement of Baal worship, dependence upon foreign nations, and trust in self-guided political wisdom. The chief defiance has been directed against the covenant *with David*. It is natural, therefore, that Jeremiah's vision of the future should center in national disaster and exile; in the nation's return, after repentance, to the homeland; and in the re-establishment of a purified Davidic kingdom.

The retrospect of the Deuteronomic literature is different at a number of points. Whereas Jeremiah locates the beginning of the detour at the point of defection from the Davidic covenant, the writer of Deuteronomy carries it back earlier to the defection from the Mosaic covenant in the wilderness. To Jeremiah the wilderness period had been one of holiness and loyalty to the Mosaic covenant; to the Deuteronomist it exemplified the initial case of backsliding, which all later history had accentuated (cf. Jer. 2:2, 3 with Deut., chs. 1 to 3). In the latter's case, the sin of the present seemed epitomized in disloyalty to the commandments of God: idolatry, laxity in Sabbath observance, neglect of racial separatism, national complacency and pride, approval of decentralized worship in the high places. The defiance was directed against the covenant *with Moses* rather than that with David.

Whether the wilderness wanderings actually represented a period of ideal piety or a period of ceaseless rebellion is a question we can hardly answer. Nor is it important that we should. Undoubtedly, there were many reasons why Amos, Hosea, and Jeremiah viewed the time as a Golden Age, while Isaiah, Ezekiel, the J and E histories, and Deuteronomy viewed it as the beginning of sin.[11] It is doubtful whether this variation in retrospect would have disturbed these men, or whether it destroys an essential agreement in the *form* of their testimony. For they were primarily concerned with contemporaneous rebellion. They did not consult the tradition in order to establish the exact date of the period of sin or the precise responsibility of the various guilty parties. They were more concerned to relate men to the tradition in such a fashion as to remove the disrelationship now existing between men and God's cove-

[11] Cf. A. Guillaume, *op. cit.,* pp. 83 ff.

nant. They used the tradition to confront men with the fact of estrangement, to isolate and identify the sin, and in so doing to point the way
to reconciliation. One prophet was troubled by the political defection
from the Davidic covenant, another by the popular disregard for the
Mosaic covenant. Each viewed the past from his angle of vision, and
his choice of Golden Age and of the Age of Revolt depended in part on
this standpoint. But it is significant that the idealization of a Golden
Age did not eventuate in an archaistic imitation of all the institutions
and practices of that age, a forcing of the external forms of national life
into the patterns of an obsolete society. The reference to ancient glories
was motivated rather by the desire to renew a covenant relationship
with God, to accept again the demands for obedience, and to enter into
the promises made with the fathers. In the metaphor of a journey, the
prophet called the people to return, not to the starting point, but to the
right road, the road which begins with the covenant and ends with its
fulfillment, rather than to remain on the deceptive bypath that begins
with rebellion and ends in futility. The prophet stood as a signpost on
the false road, pointing to the true highway of destiny by reference to
the map of God's purpose. And on that map, he concentrated first on the
events which marked new starting points (covenants) and then on the
events which marked the false turnings of the human pilgrims.

In addition to covenant-making and covenant-breaking, covenant-
restoring and covenant-fulfilling were the object of prophetic sight. The
third type of strategic event in historical narration, that of covenant
restoration, consists of the response of the people to the prophet's message, to " return unto the Lord "; the fourth type consists of the divine
approval of this return. The prophet stands at the juncture of present
decision. From his perspective these events are still impending in the
future. But this perspective causes him to select, from the retrospective
panorama, prototypes of human obedience and of divine salvation. He
foresees and predicts the repetition of these events wherein man's repentance is fulfilled by God's reward. Because the memory of these two
types of events is woven so closely into the prophet's prospect, the consideration of them belongs in the following chapter.

Here it should be observed finally that the motives which occasioned
the formation of oral histories also conditioned their preservation in
written form. They are preserved because God has spoken through them.
He uses the memories of what he has done in previous generations as a

witness for the contemporary generation. Ever and again, through them he utters his call and renews his covenant: " I am," " I have," " Thou shalt," " Thou hast," " I will." This living relationship of memory to decision explains many things about the Bible as a whole. It explains the spontaneity and flexibility with which each generation reinterprets its past without destroying its fidelity to the covenants. It explains the absence of attempts to adopt a single expurgated objective description of what happened in the past, and the absence of any sense of dismay at the variant interpretations by different prophets of the same historic event. It explains why conflicting narratives (such as J, E, D, and P) could be welded together into a single document without thoroughgoing efforts at harmonization. It explains why conflicting prophecies and conflicting reinterpretations of prophecies could all be cherished as true manifestations of the divine will. It explains the resistance of a covenantal religion to a literalistic legalism. It explains the vitality of oral tradition even after the appearance of sacred documents. It explains why the heirs of the covenants attributed to the same historical tradition radical continuity and radical discontinuity, relativity and finality, complexity and simplicity. It explains why, through all the changing landscapes of vision, a single angle of vision could be maintained. Each man, in meeting God, saw a single situation in the light of its total context, and saw the total context in the light of that single situation. And it was God who provided the man of faith with the light by which he saw all things in a Moment.

13

ISRAEL DESPAIRS AND HOPES

E SCHATOLOGY is indigenous to the Biblical point of view. He who created will also redeem. He is Omega as well as Alpha. He always manifests himself as One who "is to come." Sovereign over his elect community, he establishes this sovereignty by determining destinies. The covenant always rests on a promise: "Therefore as I live, I will . . ." (Zeph. 2:9). His will is the ultimate ground of man's life, but *will* by its nature is future-regarding, future-seeking, future-creating. It is his purpose that gives to every present its particular future, and gives to every future its particular present. A purpose lives in hope and by hope.

Biblical eschatology, however, is alien to modern thought patterns. It is probably less difficult for us to share imaginatively in the retrospect of Isaiah or Peter than to share their prospect. Their interpretation of past events may be acceptable, but how can we accept their expectations with regard to the future? Were not their predictions proved by events themselves to be illusory? Is not an exploded hope as impossible to reconstruct as a child's soap bubble?

In this area, a translation of mere words is wholly inadequate; there must be a translation of meanings. A translation of meanings requires an understanding of more than the prophet's vocabulary, grammar, and syntax. Comprehension of the linguistic structure of his *life* must supersede the analysis of the linguistic structure of his *speech*. His predictions were *literally true* to the vocabulary of his life, although that truth ceases to be literal when we transfer his predictions to the vocabulary of our thought. We destroy the literalness of the truth for him when we isolate his predictions from the entire structure of actual relationships within which they had meaning for the prophet himself. His existence was defined by his personal relation to God; consequently, his hopes for the future must everywhere be subsumed under that basic category. His predictions must be grasped within the context of the actual, intimate filiations of his existence under God. When we separate the speculative *content* of his hopes from their existential *context,* it becomes impossible to harmonize our expectations with his.

Each man finds himself *en route.* Each step is energized and directed by an expectation. Each step brings to fulfillment the past and anticipates the future. Only by knowing the future can he take the right direction; but he does not know (although he thinks he does) what the next step may bring. To the prophet en route comes the disclosure that he and his people are following a mirage: " We have turned every one to his own way." The prophet proclaims, " Return." He foretells what lies ahead on each of the two roads — futility or fruition. The experience serves to alter his retrospect; now he sees in the past the beginning of the detour; now he remembers how other travelers had in earlier times been brought back to the main road. He faces a new sign-post and, looking back, sees that it is one of a long series which God has erected to guide his people.

" As Jonah became a sign unto the Ninevites, so shall also the Son of man be to this generation " (Luke 11:30).

Inasmuch as he himself is now impelled by the signal to make a choice, to turn back or to push ahead, and inasmuch as he knows that the results of either decision will be fateful, he reinterprets the past, noting the sequence of decisions and their respective outcomes. With the strategic human decisions he associates the strategic divine acts of salvation and punishment. Each sign provokes faith or rebellion; each decision in turn leads to judgment or mercy. And this retrospect corresponds exactly with his prospect. The contemporary sign makes a choice of roads inevitable. And the choice determines the destination.

" As it came to pass in the days of Noah, even so shall it be also in the days of the Son of man " (Luke 17:26).

Does the retrospect shape the prospect, or does the prospect shape the retrospect? It is impossible to separate the two, for they interpenetrate the consciousness of man as he takes each step. Which of us can assess within the continuum of his own personal consciousness the effects of the present on the past, and the past on the present? Should we find that a deceptive memory has caused us to stumble, our discovery does not thereby absolve us from relying upon memory; should we discover that a present urgency has warped our memory to serve an immediate purpose, we cannot thereby escape the necessity of taking the next step under the same hazards. To separate past and present by objective analysis may distort one's sense of duty more than to act in repentance, subjectively unifying past and present so that each is conditioned by the other. Perhaps it is only in present decision that vital unity can ever be realized. At any rate, the prophet stands at the center of such a continuum. And standing there, his " forthtelling " must include both " retelling " and " foretelling." And none of the three can be separated from the other two; none of the three is capable of final proof by objective measurement, because in each case the prophet is concerned not with relating one segment of man's story to another, but with relating the purpose-charged *kairos* of man to the purpose-charged *kairos* of God.

THE GRAIN OF ANTICIPATION

In his visions concerning the future, what, then, does the prophet see? How does God disclose the invisible writing within the scroll of destiny? What does God say to him, and through him to the community? What sort of communication takes place? Always by his word and his act, God is calling his people to re-enact and renew the covenant, by providing again the threat and promise which define their existence as his people. Prophetic predictions, therefore, are always an assurance of the imminent fulfillment of a prior covenant. The coming event is not the impulsive or capricious act of a tyrant, playing a sadistic game, but the sovereign act of a righteous King who is faithful to his pledge. The scope of the covenant may vary: it may be one that relates an individual person to God, or one that binds a communal entity to him, such as the covenant with David, with Moses, with Abraham, with Adam. In any case the broken covenant can be restored only by a divine initiative that cuts fruitless branches from the tree and grafts in other branches.

But the fulfillment of a covenant, in Biblical thought, calls for more than the restoration of the *status quo ante*. It calls for the ratification of a more perfect covenant, a new relationship between creation and Cre-

ator. God will do a new thing in these days. He will change the leaden
heart of man and heal his deafness. Because man's relation to God will
be purified, man's very existence will be changed. Because this forthcoming change takes place primarily at the junction of divine and human purposes, the character of the coming era is envisaged in terms of
perfected *relationships* rather than in terms of perfected *arrangements*.
The root of Messianism lies in *hope* rather than in *speculation*. As Lev
Gillet writes, Messianism consists in the Messianic *attitude,* " the experience of expectancy." [1] It is designed to provide, not a detailed chart of an
unexplored land, but the set of the sails for pilgrims en route.

Let us draw from the teaching of Jesus some examples that illustrate
Jewish as well as Christian attitudes. To the speculative, conceptual
question concerning how many are to be saved, he replies with an existential thrust: " Strive to enter in by the narrow door " (see Luke 13:23,
24). He refuses to answer queries concerning the precise time of the
Kingdom's coming, or he gives at most a riddle to be solved (Luke
17:20–30). But he allows little ambiguity in his commands concerning
the saving *attitude* toward the Kingdom: " In an hour that ye think
not "; " At midnight "; " Suddenly in your midst "; " Except ye repent,
ye shall all likewise perish." Men ask for signs of a tangible evidential
character, but he refuses except to point to ambiguous manifestations of
power which force them to answer their own question. Concerning the
future they must " believe in order to know." Over and over again
Pharisees and halfway disciples query Jesus about the Kingdom. Over
and over again their queries seek for objective speculative knowledge
about the Kingdom; but Jesus refuses to answer such queries. His message springs from subjective existential knowledge *of* the Kingdom. Before answering their queries he must change the perspective of the ques-
tioner and the form of his questions. The coming sovereignty of God
cannot be made intelligible except to those who in repentance and faith
have taken upon themselves the yoke of the Kingdom. Neither Jesus
nor the prophets claimed to produce external guarantees that would give
men control over the future. Rather, their work was designed to create
a new mood, a new striving, a new commitment. Their predictions can
only be understood when it is seen that they produced resignation rather
than fatalism, enthusiasm rather than prescience, humility rather than
pride, dependence upon God rather than superiority over other men,

[1] *Communion in the Messiah,* pp. 103 ff. 1942.

trust in God rather than in earthly treasures, joy when others are mourning, mourning when others are rejoicing, and commitment of all energies and possessions. Such predictions are bits of defiance hurled in the face of adversity; songs of joy when the night is darkest; marching orders for those whose steps are failing; orders to stand for those inclined to retreat. They bespeak the alertness and endurance of an athlete, stretching forward to the goal. Men seeking the Kingdom press on like wild ducks, winging on through the storm toward a winter haven.[2]

It is significant that the prophets locate and condemn false predictions by discerning the false *attitudes* which produce them and are produced by them. It is complacency and pride that encourage men to predict, "Peace, peace," and their predictions confirm their blind self-centeredness. Or, in bleak despair, men may predict the end of the world, but their prediction is expression of their nihilism, and will therefore engender nothing but passive waiting for dread fate to accomplish its predestined task. Quite the reverse is the patience of those whose expectation nerves them to face the bitter curses of the world:

" Be patient therefore, brethren, until the coming of the Lord. Behold, the husbandman waiteth for the precious fruit of the earth, being patient over it, until it receive the early and latter rain. Be ye also patient; establish your hearts: for the coming of the Lord is at hand " (James 5:7-8).

The true prophets rejected the cry of those who said, " The vision that he seeth is for many days to come." And this postponement is not repudiated on grounds simply of more accurate data. Estimating the interim, the scoffer may be as accurate as the prophet, but the scoffer is calculating the length of a *different* interim. And the scoffer's attitude toward God, as revealed by his prediction, is seen by the prophet as a prime instance of rebellion. His heart is far from God, his purpose is quite content with its fruits, he does not see his security as in jeopardy. In Jesus' day, the religious leaders had many a dispute over the problems which God would face in the Kingdom. What about a woman who had had seven husbands? Whose wife would she be? Such disputes revealed a false attitude toward the future, which could not be removed with exact information about the status of men and women in heaven. It indicated that a new relationship must be established between the questioners and God before any prediction concerning the future

---

[2] Cf. W. Manson, *op. cit.,* pp. 61-63.

would have meaning. " He is . . . God of the . . . living." In reading
this incident, we may question the exegetical methods attributed to
Jesus, but in doing so, we should not overlook the actual difference between his assumptions regarding the future and those of his adversaries
(Mark 12:18–27). He judged falsity and truth of prospect by the existential attitudes which produce them and are produced by them. For example, Jesus condemns the process of *calculation* by which those who
accept the promise of the Kingdom seek to reserve special seats of honor
in that new age (Mark 10:35–40); and, on the other hand, he himself
promises that those who humble themselves will be exalted, knowing
that true repentance altogether eliminates the process of calculation:
" We are unprofitable servants " (see Luke 17:7–10).

It is clear, then, that predictions are always grounded in the situation
that obtains between men and God. It is in an act of decision that man
gains his knowledge of the future, and, conversely, it is through God's
self-disclosure of the bent of his purpose that he confronts man with
the necessity of decision.[3] Through his promise for the future, God precipitates in man the response by which this promise is appropriated as
defining man's striving. Through the assurance of his mercy, God
creates in man the mercy through which man comes to know God as
merciful. The predictions of the future are not, therefore,

" glimpses of a predetermined future which is shortly to come to pass through
the present moment into the past, like a motion-picture film passing the lens of
the projector." [4]

A predicted calamity may be turned aside by repentance, and a predicted redemption may be negated by stubborn despair (The Book of
Jonah; Amos 4:10–12; Isa. 7:4, 7). The vision of the time to come does
not, therefore, represent the prophet's guess at the more probable con-
tingency among the countless potentialities which the present moment
holds — each potentiality unreal until it happens. Nor does his vision
betoken an unusual mantic power to read tomorrow's newspaper today. His vision stems from his double involvement in the *kairos* of man
and the *kairos* of God's purpose.

[3] E. Brunner, *The Divine-Human Encounter,* pp. 50 f. 1943.
[4] R. B. Y. Scott, *The Relevance of the Prophets,* p. 10. The Macmillan Company, 1944.

THE PRESENTNESS OF HOPE

There are many ways in which he articulates the vision of a future that is *real in the present*. In the first place, he describes the future as that which is now hidden, which will soon be made manifest. The future is now at work secretly, as a germinating seed, or spreading leaven, or ripening harvest. As such, it is as actually present as the external, tangible phenomena which men see and hear. In the second place, the vision communicates an event that has already happened in heaven. Final authority belongs there. Thence comes every impulse of power and life. Satan's fall from heaven is prelude to his defeat on earth. God's will is done in heaven, adequate warranty that it will be done on earth. From heaven comes his word, with power to bless and curse. It does not return without fulfilling its mission. To him who hears this word, assurance is given of its imminent fulfillment, as when a person receives a letter from a trusted friend saying that a package has been dispatched and is on the way.

In the third place, the promise is present in the signpost which brings the future within the range of visibility. In the person and work of the prophet himself, the voice of the future is now heard. His spirit-propelled words and gestures are signs of the times that require men to change their actions, just as weather forecasts alter men's plans for the morrow. The fourth way in which the future manifests itself, almost indistinguishable from this third, may be described in the words of Rudolf Bultmann:

" The kingdom of God is a power which, although it is entirely future, wholly determines the present. It determines the present because it now compels man to decision; he is determined thereby either in this direction or that, as chosen or as rejected, in his entire present existence." [5]

When man reaches a fork in the road, the end of the alternate paths is actually represented by his steps. In the fifth place, the community which lives by the sign itself becomes a sign to the world of the present efficacy of future promises. The future is present in the continuing empowerment of the people by their God, the life within the new covenant, the " fruit of the Spirit." In their expectancy and patience, in the conflict into which they are plunged, in the love which edifies the

[5] *Jesus and the Word*, p. 51. Charles Scribner's Sons, 1934.

brotherhood, the powers of the future are known to be operating. The first fruits of the final harvest are being gathered. For them, the temporal boundaries have shifted. The children of the Day give witness to the presence of the Day.[6]

It is thus clear that in the Bible an idle or isolated guess concerning some future happening that conceivably may come to pass is worlds removed from the prophet's "word of the Lord." The former has no theological significance, except that it betrays the gullible and superstitious into misguided actions. Only the latter has significance as a promise by which God now confronts man.[7]

THE FUTURITY OF HOPE

We must not, however, be induced by these considerations to underestimate the future character of God's promise and of the prophet's hope. Old and New Testament alike are studded with predictions of coming events that will mark radical changes throughout the whole range of objective phenomena. He who sees the finger of God in contemporary events sees it pointing to new things about to happen. In what sense, then, are these future predictions to be taken? How is this future separated from the present? Why do Biblical writers so stubbornly insist upon this futurist reference?

In the first place, a future reference is necessary to distinguish the age of sin from the age of salvation. A relative end can be fully realized in the present, but must not an absolute end be sharply distinguished from all relative ends, since in relationship to God, "the whole of time and existence should be the period of striving"? If one were not related to God's promise in terms of "becoming," would he not erroneously conceive of the possibility of "realizing a union in existence in terms of rest"?[8] Does the Christian anticipate a human situation in which the prayer for the Kingdom has become obsolete? God's will is not now done on earth as it is in heaven. The word precipitates conflict, bringing "not . . . peace, but a sword." Yet this same word creates the confidence in God's victory over all his adversaries. The faith in the nearness of a future age stems from this conviction that there must be a

---

[6] Cf. T. H. Croxall, in *Expository Times*, August, 1945, p. 294.
[7] Cf. N. Davey, in E. C. Hoskyns, *The Fourth Gospel*, Vol. I, p. xxxix. 1940.
[8] Cf. S. Kierkegaard, *Concluding Unscientific Postscript*, pp. 355 f. 1941.

terminus to the tension between the two ages. The interim character of the struggle underscores the necessity of speedy intervention by God.[9]

In the second place, and correlated to the first, a future is required to provide for the open manifestation of that which is now hidden. The powers of the future are now operating, beginning in the commission of the prophet himself. But the world in its wisdom does not know God, the eyes of flesh do not see his saving deeds. The time will come when what is spoken in the ear will be shouted from the housetops. Until that time the faithful look forward to the " appearing " of God's salvation. There is thus, implicit in revelation, a future terminus. There must come that " future revelation of the truth that already *is* because it is the truth of God " — not yet, but soon.[10]

A third way of stating this is to say that God purposes the redemption of the whole creation. Only in a small segment of creation is his sovereignty now re-established. He must reign until he has put all enemies under his feet, but the faithful do not yet see all enemies subjected. The future remains future, in order that the witness may be given and that men may repent. This is one reason that impending events are seen to tarry as well as to hurry. In God's mercy, he is giving the enemies opportunity to respond to his ultimatum of surrender. But the intransigency of creation, while it may delay the future, cannot succeed in evading inexorable judgment. The *kairos* of the world must be judged. Travelers along that road will come to a dead end. Assurance of this outcome can be expressed only in prediction of judgment.

EXPECTATION OF JUDGMENT

Predictions of judgment are thus implicit in the existing situation, and such predictions are always definite, specific, unexpected, and undesired. Judgment is inevitable, not because of observations of man's inhumanity to man, but because God will avenge himself of man's faithlessness to him. The prediction stems, not from empirical rationalization after the event, but from awareness of divine displeasure within the event. And the primary purpose of judgment is not to vindicate man's sense of justice or his claim to reward but to vindicate God's purpose in the face of human transgression. The end of rebellion may

[9] Cf. A. E. J. Rawlinson, *op. cit.,* p. 51.
[10] Cf. N. Davey, in Hoskyns, *op. cit.,* Vol. I, p. xxxv. 1940.

be indeterminate in terms of *chronos,* but it is certain. Evil has its appointed time, but that time is limited.

The prediction appropriate to the situation will be specific and concrete, because the sin has taken the form of tangible social and religious policies and the hopes that must be frustrated are directed toward mundane ends. The predicted judgment will surprise its victims, because their sin is compounded of false expectations. It will be more ruthless than they have supposed, because their sin is made up of complacency and confidence in their immunity. When they assume that judgment will fall on other nations alone, the prophet proclaims a heavier one on their own nation. When they assume it will fall on other groups within Israel, the prophet proclaims the imminent reversal of fortunes within Israel. God judges, but not as sinners expect. From their standpoint, therefore, the judgments of God will seem unmerited vengeance. But to the prophet, those same judgments will be seen as necessary expressions of God's love. He delays the time in order to permit repentance; forced to punish, he refuses to destroy utterly; he seeks in the punishment itself to "humble thee, and . . . prove thee, to do thee good at thy latter end" (Deut. 8:16). He sends famine in order to invite men to return (Amos 4:6); He wounds in order that he may heal. (Hos., ch. 2). He blocks their self-chosen road in order that they may find the only road that has no dead end. And with each catastrophe he sends a prophet to interpret its true meaning.

Every moment of judgment, therefore, is a moment wherein the promise is reiterated. Judgment is not the terminus of God's *kairos,* though it may be the terminus of the tangential *kairos* of men. This is the fourth reason why the prophetic future always includes a prediction of coming events. God ever confronts men in terms of "becoming"; he ever condemns those who imitate Lot's wife; he ever calls disciples to "leave the dead to bury their own dead." Even at the moment of judgment, he opens to men a road to the future, and gives to them the freedom to choose.

"He is . . . God of the future, because he gives man freedom for the present instant of decision, and sets before him as the future which is opened to him by his decision, condemnation or mercy. . . . He never relinquishes His claim on the sinner and opens to him by forgiveness a new future for new obedience."[11]

[11] R. Bultmann, *Jesus and the Word,* p. 221; also see p. 50. Charles Scribner's Sons, 1934.

In judgment, man's time is brought to an end; but through repentance that end marks a new beginning. To this new future, man is called to yield himself by selling all that he has, by hurrying forward in alert expectancy and trust.

It is in order to express this relationship that the future is always seen *as future, but as an impending event*. To know God is " to follow on to know him." The nearness of God becomes articulated as the nearness of his coming act. And this nearness marks the victory of realism over illusion, the victory of freedom over finality, the victory of God's living purpose over man's partial and futile desires, and the liberation of man from slavery to chronological time to the life of a freed servant of God's *kairos*. It is only by relating himself to God's *kairos* that man's future is assured: " Seek ye me, and ye shall live." Man's future is destroyed if he depends upon human calculations of past, present, and future, for those calculations are built on illusions and sin. But his future is assured if he grounds his whole existence (past, present, and future) upon God's promise as manifested in the covenant.

Future predictions thus articulate the miraculous potentialities of man's present plight. Apparent actualities are never as final as they seem. The covenant community may carelessly forfeit its inheritance, but it does not thereby obliterate its mission. When other nations hold them in bondage, God cries, " Let my people go." When his people rebel, he cries, " Away with them to exile." But even in exile he does not let them go. When they become despondent, when no help appears on the horizon, he sends a word that restores their self-confidence by a vision of the future. He snatches a bone or two from the mouth of the lion. He unveils to his prophet a vision of life returning to the valley of dry bones. When Israel is at the point of death, he makes it clear that it is " Israel, in whom I will be glorified " (see Isa. 49:3, 6; 56:9).

" For why will ye die, O house of Israel? For I have no pleasure in the death of him that dieth, saith the Lord " (see Ezek. 18:31, 32; 33:11 f.).

The prediction of the prophet always underscores the fact that the impossible is possible with God, that the inherited guilt does not require aeons of expiation but that a new heart and a new spirit is now possible. The command to return is always relevant, always within reach of man. When man thinks that he is farthest from God's road, he discovers that he needs but to turn himself. The prediction of imminent events thus destroys all quantitative measurements by which human complacency or despair are confirmed. Confrontation with God's mercy in the form of a prophet's prediction makes it immediately possible for the blind to see, for the hopeless to hope, for the poor to rejoice, for the lame to walk, for the sinner to repent, for the nation or individual to be reborn. Such transitions would be impossible if human expectancy were defined by the observable forces that appear at any moment to be shaping the future. Faith in God produces new faith in self, by way of a prediction of what God is about to do. This last qualification saves the new self-confidence from destroying itself in pride, for the new faith rests upon a self that has been reconstituted by a word not its own.

JUDGMENT OF EXPECTATION

The profusion of specific predictions has created many difficulties, both in the Biblical period and in our own. A man's hopes reveal his neuroses. The prophet's stinging curse may be attributed to his petulant vindictiveness against his personal adversaries. The boy who has been bested in a street fight will shout loudly about what his father will do. Those whose political counsel has been rejected by their nation may cry, "Wait and see who is right." Dreams of bliss may serve as compensation for the man who is not appreciated by his fellows. Beggars dream of horses on which they may ride. Those who lose the struggle for power dream of unlimited power placed at their disposal. Those for whom history is filled with too much " blood, sweat, and tears " escape to a never-never land of fancy. Some of them end in institutions; others are merely labeled religious fanatics. But the road to lunacy is paved with such escapes.

These objections were not, however, taken very seriously by the Biblical prophets. Their predictions did not spring simply from their wounded egos, from their desire for self-vindication. They sprang from their faith in God. Upon their wills was laid a constraint stronger than themselves. They were surprised, chagrined, and repelled by the word of doom and dawn which they must perforce proclaim. The vision they saw of coming events proclaimed judgment upon themselves and upon their own community, to which they were bound by ties of strong affection and loyalty. That vision seldom coincided with policies of expediency or popularity or accommodation. Seldom was it supported by the analyses of expert news commentators or historical scholars. The prophets were ambassadors of a king whose authority was everywhere defied by men relying upon empirical evidence. And they were not self-appointed to that mission. They realized with poignant sensitivity that their friends thought them mad. Their call plunged them into a situation rather more difficult than more simple. Their visions provoked the maximum of derision, abuse, ostracism, and fear, but they could not evade the demand to speak. To contemporaries normally adjusted to the environment, they must have seemed highly abnormal in the gestures and words by which they heralded coming events. But their own testimonies to spiritual struggle hardly justify the charge of their being neurotic.

They were constantly faced with a more severe test, however, and one which they could not take lightly. Their predictions were not vindicated by events themselves. One's interpretation of the past cannot be disproved to the same degree as can his predictions regarding the future. Final, objective knowledge of the past is forever made impossible by the irreversible sequence of time. But it is different with proclamation of coming events. The spectator preserves the words, and is forced to conclude, "Things just don't happen that way." Even the prophet's own experience confronts him with the failure of his own hope, and the resulting frustration he cannot ignore.

There is, to be sure, one consideration that must be kept in mind in judging future expectations. It is absolutely impossible for man in his successive decisions to jettison completely all thought of the future. Every purposive choice involves a hope of some sort. As we have seen, it is an unreal alternative to suppose that man can choose between serving some God and not serving any god; either man serves the true God or he serves a no-god. So it is an unreal alternative to suppose that he can choose between seeking a specific future and not seeking any future. His purpose commits him irrevocably at every step into seeking either his true future or a false future. His destiny depends upon the *telos* which he actually chooses. Therefore, the spectator, in judging the prophetic hope to be mistaken, is not thereby absolved from responsibility to envisage an alternate hope. And his experience surely teaches him how ephemeral and misguided and disappointing are most, if not all, of the expectations by which he determines his course. Frequently he may find that an accurate prediction has betrayed him, while an inaccurate prediction may open up the truer attitudes toward the unknown and unknowable future. At least, this consideration may well cause us to hesitate to affix a final and arbitrary verdict to the prophetic hope.

Even in objective historical terms, we may detect the fact that the problem of unfulfilled expectations is not the same for him who stands within the perspective of faith as it is for the outsider. It may not be *less* troublesome, but it provokes a different kind of crisis. Even when the falsity of a former prediction has become apparent, the prophet finds his *new present* to be dependent on his God-relationship. However bitterly he may protest that God has made him ridiculous, he feels again " a fire burning in his bones, that could not be contained, and he had to burst forth into prophecy again." Such was the discovery of Jeremiah as he found his own forecast to be mistaken.[12] The problem, therefore, is not primarily one of the logical consistency and exact correspondence of event to former prediction, but rather of the immediate significance of this new situation; it is a question not so much of the apparent collapse of specific predictions as of the vindication of man's hope and of God's promise. The prophet cannot separate, as can the spectator, the content of his prediction (now proved erroneous) from the hidden purpose of a living God who wills to guide men's destinies.

For this reason, the mere failure of a specific prediction seems to trouble the prophet less than it troubles his contemporaries. The prophet knows that the prediction is an expression of God's purpose toward men rather than the fortunetelling of a mantic oracle. He knows that the real end of the prediction is to produce repentance, to articulate the actual though hidden state of the covenant. For the same reason, he is not disturbed greatly by the fact that different prophets are given different words to utter or that the message varies for different generations. He knows that the truth of the communication lies, not simply in the accuracy of detail, but rather in what God's word accomplishes in the heart and affairs of men. The predictions, as a matter of fact, are often vague in detail regarding the *what* of coming events because they are more concerned with the *how* of man's relationship to destiny. Thus is the historical scholar more confused than the prophet by bewildering inconsistencies in Messianic speculation: Son of David, Son of Man, one

[12] Cf. H. H. Rowley, *The Relevance of the Bible*, pp. 38, 39. The Macmillan Company, 1944.

" like unto Moses," " a high priest after the order of Melchizedek." Often the prophet weaves new predictions out of conflicting older predictions without being aware of logical difficulties. Perhaps this shows great historical ignorance and naïveté; it may also reflect the fact that, to prophetic faith, these predictions speak of deep-seated hopes more than of sharply defined prognostications.

Another contrast between the prophet and the spectator is thus apparent in their attitudes toward unfulfilled predictions. The spectator is usually unconcerned about the challenge to *hope* which the delay in the promise produces, whereas the prophet is tremendously concerned. Why have not the justice and mercy of God been enforced? Why does the covenant still suffer disuse and misinterpretation? Why has the word of God simply provoked greater alienation from his will? Why are people so blind to his deeds? When will God move to restore and fulfill the broken covenant?

The prediction, which had been born in faith, received with abuse, and denied by events, thus provokes a greater crisis of faith on the part of the prophet. And this crisis cannot be resolved save by another word from the King. How long will he defer his promised judgment? When will he take his power and reign? How is he at work even now to prepare men for that fulfillment? If he has deceived us, *why* has he deceived us? How has our sin prevented us from understanding his message? Such questions as these remain in the forefront of the prophet's encounter with God. Only in faith does he expect to find the answer to the seeming failure of his hope.

It is this problem in a thousand different forms in a thousand situations that torments the soul of Israel during the Biblical period. The ultimate question raised by the whole Bible is this: Does God fulfill his covenanted pledge?

14

PROPHETS LOOK BEYOND HISTORY

FOR the man of faith, the primary reality is encompassed in the *now*. It is here that the demand of God for obedience meets man's resistance. It is here that the covenant which God has made in the past is contradicted by the historical situation of the elect community. It is here, also, that God's dynamic purpose is frustrated, his promise delayed. And the parable or sign which God utters through the prophet locates the core of rebellion and discloses the implicit but hidden threat and promise. This element of contradiction is present, therefore, in Biblical experience in every situation in which God shows his hand. But the degree to which men are made aware of the contradiction is capable of infinite intensification. The sequence of tragic frustrations, from the Babylonian exile through the two destructions of Jerusalem by the Romans, served to strain to its very limits Jewish faith in the covenants. During this period, the external course of events appeared more and more completely to defy the inner logic of the covenant relation.

Our concern here is to trace the impact of these challenges on Jewish thought and faith. This necessitates the effort to interpret the inner meaning of apocalyptic and its connections with earlier prophetism. A threefold conviction underlies this interpretation: (1) The development of apocalypticism is explicable only as a response to the problems which the prophetic outlook produced. (2) Apocalypticism, in its valid forms, maintained an essential continuity with the perspective of the Old Testament. (3) The hope of the Kingdom of God, as proclaimed in the apocalypses, clarifies in sharpest terms the ultimate issues confronting the men of the Old Testament.

It is well, before essaying this task, to say a word about method. In the first place, the study is limited to the formal or structural patterns underlying apocalyptic thought. It is impossible here to review in detail the conceptual content of the different visions. In the literature of Messianism there is an endless heterogeneity of materials. The vocabulary is drawn from diverse sources and is loaded with poetic, symbolic, typological connotations. And if one tries to construct a composite portrait by drawing from all the documents, the result is a baffling hodgepodge. In each separate writing, such as I Enoch or the Testaments of the XII Patriarchs, the picture of the Messiah and of the Kingdom is nebulous. Taking each concept in terms of its content, no intelligible unity is discernible. We are concerned with *how* the prophet orients his position vis-à-vis the future, rather than with *what* he says about that future. Is there an inner rationale of apocalyptic thought which permeates the highly diverse predictions?

Since we are interested in structural aspects, the study does not require a strictly chronological order of treatment. It is as yet quite impossible to be confident of the exact dates of the apocalypses, due perhaps to their semi-independence of calendar measurement and to the fact that their original locus in fluid oral tradition made them subject to many revisions. Nor will we pause to reconstruct the particular milieu of each writing, the political, economic, and cultural factors which provoked its original appearance. There are, of course, wide variations in the occasions which prompted the writings and it is unsafe to ignore them. But for such data we must here be content with referring the reader to other studies.[1]

Much valuable research has been addressed to recovering the cultural history of the concepts that formed the stock in trade of apocalyptic writings. Undoubtedly the Jewish writers borrowed many terms and connotations from neighboring cultures and from the vast mythological reservoir of the ancient Orient. However, we are not primarily concerned with such origins, but with the distinctive meanings of the concepts for the Jewish borrowers. Why were they adopted? How were they fitted into the Biblical perspective? How were they changed in their new context? We must be ever alert to the fact that the primary problem for the Jewish prophet was the problem of decision and suffering, rather than the problem of thought and speculation. A philosopher who adopts a concept for his system of ideas must carefully examine

---

[1] Cf. the books by W. O. E. Oesterley, R. H. Charles, H. H. Rowley, and F. C. Porter, and the articles by Leslie E. Fuller in *The Abingdon Bible Commentary*.

the precise connotations of that concept; a prophet who adopts a poetic image to express an aspect of his struggle for faith will do so as the result of a different " screening " process. For him the *Sitz im Glauben* will be determinative.

Perhaps a comment is needed to account for the inclusion of apocalypses in the study of Biblical perspective. In the first place, the Old Testament itself includes prophecies that must be classed with the apocalypses in form and function. Moreover, as the attempt to draw up a list of apocalypses will show, it is ultimately impossible to draw a sharp line between prophecy and apocalyptic. Furthermore, as we have noted, the apocalypses reflect a logic implicit in prophetic faith; they indicate the most vulnerable and the most stubborn axioms in that faith and thus serve to clarify its character. Finally, a consideration of this literature is essential if we are to understand the connections between the two Testaments. Apart from this bridge, it is difficult to understand the continuity between the Testaments or to define the points in which the New Covenant gives a new answer to the problems of human experience.

The opening paragraph of this chapter sets forth the basic problem which confronted both canonical and inter-Testamental writers. It is the problem of human destiny, the problem of the fulfillment of God's *kairos,* the problem of an elect community frustrated in its vocation, the problem of human history as a whole, when that history is seen in proper focus as the conflict between genuine history (as God's creation) and spurious history (as man's rebellion). In both Old Testamental and inter-Testamental periods, the contradictions of the present are resolved by hope in the fulfillment of God's promises, by the existential orientation toward judgment and mercy. In both it is precisely this hope which is jeopardized by historical observation. The hope which resolves the contradictions thus becomes the focal point of intensified contradiction. How certain is God's sovereignty? How soon will he awake? Through what means will he overcome the fateful contradictions of the present? What must we do to be saved? The fact of revelation precipitates the problem of destiny; the problem of destiny raises the question of the validity of revelation to its most intense form; and the validity of revelation is inseparable from the problem of the future. The problem of revelation thus becomes the problem of eschatology. The whole structure of faith stands or falls with the fulfillment of the promises in the *end-time*. But because it is faith which creates the ultimate problem, it is within the context of faith alone that it can be solved. And its solution rests not upon an effort of thought so much as upon the concrete decision of man in the existing moment. The problem created *by* the interim can thus be solved only *within* the interim by the man of faith.

THE PRESENT AS A PARENTHESIS

The changes in the attitude toward this interim are, therefore, the crucial changes in the whole outlook upon history. The angle of vision and the focusing of vision upon events in the foreground condition man's view of the horizons. So we begin our study of apocalypticism with an analysis of changes in the attitude toward the interim. And the crucial changes in this area stem from man's awareness of *the length, depth, and power of the contradictions,* and the inability of man to surmount them. Stated in other terms, the decisive factor is the deepening awareness of sin. In still other terms, the decisive factor is the degree of divergence between man's spurious history and God's genuine history. The more man is enslaved to this spurious history, the more completely is he alienated from God's creative design.

In different writings, this crisis is precipitated by different objective factors. In some cases, it is the *suffering of the nation* which thwarts God's covenant with David. The promises of national independence, peace, prosperity, and righteousness are contradicted by the Babylonian exile, or by the weakness of the repatriated Jews, or by the violent measures of Antiochus Epiphanes, or by the successive triumphs of the Romans. Each successive national disaster aggravates the strain placed upon the faith of the loyalists (cf. the Books of Daniel, Zephaniah, Malachi, I Enoch). In some cases, the agony of the righteous stems from *economic and social discrimination* within the nation. Wicked Jews flourish in proportion to their oppression of the righteous; apostates consolidate their political and economic power at the expense of servants of God. This conflict continues throughout the centuries, from the return of Babylonian exiles to the final destruction of Jerusalem. But it reaches a climax during the waves of oppression under Alexander Jannaeus and the Herods (cf. the later psalms, Job, I Enoch 37–71, 91–108; Assumption of Moses, Testaments of the XII Patriarchs). In some cases, the crux of the conflict is provided by the *martyrdom of loyalists*. Those who trust God's promise are literally forced to renounce all else; those who seek his Kingdom must surrender all their goods in this age. When martyrdom is due to political tyranny, it indicates the failure of God's covenant with David. When martyrdom is the price of faithfulness to the law, it places under question his covenant with Moses. When martyrdom stems from the hatred of Gentile for Jew, it seems to disprove the covenant with Abraham. Usually the conflict embraces several of these areas of revelation, and involves the whole series of divine covenants. But whether the crisis places in jeopardy one or many covenants, the question of God's faithfulness cannot be evaded.

Because the structure of the problem was the same in all these various situations, we can pass over the varieties of expression and try to generalize concerning attitudes expressed by many different apocalypses.

For all of them, the interim is characterized by the apparent omnipresence and omnipotence of evil. This encourages the elaboration of a demonology, which imaginatively articulates this historical struggle. This age, this world, belongs to Satan. His authority is inescapable, but temporary, and limited, because it is allotted to him by God. Satan operates through a hierarchy of messengers: agents with power delegated to them torment men in every area of their experience. Heathen rulers, Jewish tyrants, the wealthy oppressors, the cowardly apostates, the burdens of sickness and poverty and temptation carried by the faithful — all are due to his power, and signs of his authority.

Sin and death are but alternate ways of describing the same tyranny. Sin is as universal as is the sway of the devil. It entangles all men in its net and invades every corner of their existence. Men are powerless to escape its baleful results. They are bound together in a body of sin and in a body of death. Although apocalyptists stubbornly relate sin to the free decisions of responsible men, they are forced to reckon with its corporate power and its objective status.

A correlate of this attitude is the effective restriction of the areas within which God's immediate demand for obedience is applicable to the individual. Man has lost the opportunity of effective action within the realm of determining political policies, economic organization, social and cultural institutions. Tendencies toward quietism, a religious quietism expressed as resignation, become more pronounced. In fact, the inclination to chafe under oppression is condemned as rebellion against

God, and the free acceptance of one's lot is praised as a duty required by obedience to God.

But if the areas open to independent moral decision are increasingly limited, those areas become invested with increasing importance. The absolute demand of God becomes concentrated at the point where the individual remains wholly responsible. For the poor, it calls for the renunciation of the world, for complete trust, for a spirit of utter dependence upon God. For the potential martyr, the demand is focused upon a single "Yes" to be uttered when the judge calls for him to say "No." Even the most impotent slave always has open an alternative choice where he is free and responsible, and upon this choice the absolute authority of God brings to bear an absolute imperative. With the narrowing of the "space" within which God's *kairos* and man's destiny coincide, the transcendental importance of that particular space is seen more clearly. Thus is quietism linked to an intensified activism, and the tendency toward irresponsibility for this age is offset by the consciousness of absolute responsibility toward God.

An interim ideology, consequently, is characterized by certain changes of emphasis with regard to the activity of God. The qualitative distance between his purpose and man's rebellion tends to approach infinity. He and his Kingdom are viewed in wholly other, supertemporal terms. The vocabulary for describing his reality and power becomes more explicitly mythological in tone and temper. His activity within the scope of man's experience now appears more and more intermittent, more and more variable. The fulfillment of his will is suspended rather than realized. Man's consciousness of the difference in temporal duration between human affairs and God's *kairos* is heightened. God's measurement of time is wholly inexplicable from the human standpoint. In his sight a thousand years of man's struggle may be but an instant.

The basic attitudes toward God's method of communication with men show corresponding changes. He continues to reveal his word and his power to the faithful; otherwise they could not endure. But because of ubiquitous evil in the present age, the sign which sets the immediate human decision in the perspective of the coming age becomes more other-worldly in *form* without becoming less-worldly in *relevance*. The message which it communicates becomes more contrary to the wisdom of this age, and therefore more extraordinary and unexpected.[2]

[2] Cf. G. Stählin, *Skandalon*, pp. 274 f. Gütersloh, 1930.

Because its reception demands the seeing eye in an age when blindness is endemic, the sign appears in more esoteric guise. Because of the assumption that prophecy has ceased, the visions are usually assigned to some ancient prophet or revealer. Because of the assumption that God's activity in this age is suspended, the sign of his purpose becomes unearthly and supernal. To modern readers, as to the exilic prophets, the journeys of Enoch and the dreams of Daniel can hardly appear to be other than fantastic. Yet they were intended, in the first instance, to produce the consciousness of impelling immediacy sufficiently powerful to motivate greatest loyalty in the midst of greatest agony. And this objective was all the more difficult of accomplishment because contemporaries took it for granted that God's Spirit had departed from Israel. The revelation, therefore, that breaks through such a shell of resistance must be anchored in the periods before and after the interim. It must emanate from the seventh heaven (often requiring the mediation of angels), must transcend the law, and must represent the threat-promise of the coming age (often requiring the reference to a transcendental Messiah).

The struggle with forces that dominate the interim thus affects profoundly both the retrospect and the prospect. Looking backward, the interim seems longer than it did to earlier prophets; looking forward, the interim seems shorter. Man stands in the present very near the end of the interim. In temporal terms, the word seems to say, " It is later than you think." But the sign which communicates this Messianic expectancy is a sign that intensifies the present conflict. In fact, controversy centers around the problem of the sign. " By what sign? " is a question that confronts every messenger.

The interim in which the prophet stands differs sharply from that sense of duration which characterizes the unbeliever, whose frame of reference is the present age. The latter has a very short memory and a very long prospect. He lives by the expectation of an unlimited future devoted to the expansion of present securities. In effect, he says to the prophet, " It is not so late as you think." And the sign of his complacence with regard to the future is the *absence* of any final conflict in current choices.

THE BEGINNING OF THE PARENTHESIS

In tracing the retrospects of the apocalyptic writers, one detects a more or less common pattern. And this pattern reflects in almost every particular the tensions in current experience. We have already noted the elongation of the detour backward to express the qualitative distinction between God's will and present revolt. The same existential consciousness underlies the elaboration of a *Paradise Lost* motif. As the sinful interim becomes more and more inclusive, the chasm widens between existence now and existence as it was originally intended. Attention focuses upon fewer, earlier, and more spectacular events. This is partly conditioned by the fact that present signs are also rare and spectacular. It is also conditioned by the prevalent skepticism concerning the validity of earlier signs, and doubt concerning the manifest destiny of Israel. Under conditions of anarchy, the community's memory is disrupted and loses the power of common conviction. Therefore, in appealing to that memory, the prophet must concentrate attention upon the earlier and more fundamental covenants on which consensus of agreement is still maintained.

As we have already noted, the prophet who is most distressed by the failure of the national hope seeks to revive the memory of God's covenant with David. The prophet who is much more concerned with the failure of the law, seeks to revive the Mosaic covenant. Consciousness of even deeper roots of historical rebellion both undermines and underscores the validity of the promises to Abraham. As realization of the solidarity of sin approaches its maximum, the dependability of God's covenant with Adam becomes a dominant concern. Finally, awareness of the cosmic ramifications of sin places in question God's covenant with all creation.

Prophetic experience thus leads to an existential interest in the initial creative act and in the mythological description of that act. And this same interest demands that the "myth" shall articulate both the primal goodness of creation itself and the primal source of sin. In creating the world, God made a covenant with it. In creation, God's word and Spirit are fully expressed, to a degree made impossible by subsequent rebellion. In creation, his power and his goodness are manifested as ultimate. To him alone belong the Kingdom, the power, and the glory. He is Sovereign over all times. And as surely as night follows the day, his purpose will be done. *"Heaven and earth shall pass away,"* but his word remains the final arbiter of all existence.

But the same myth that stresses the ultimacy of his purpose must, for the same reason, stress the depth of creation's fall. Creation is the true beginning of God's *kairos;* but sin is the beginning of Satan's *kairos.* The real beginning of man's detour is thus traced back to the first free response of creation to its Creator. Some of the apocalyptic myths stress the fall of Adam and Eve from their lost paradise; some describe the fall of the angels from their heavenly paradise. In some cases, the myth has developed into empty and fantastic speculation that simply feeds the appetite for the bizarre and grotesque; but in other cases, the myth gives existential witness to the consciousness that " before God, man is always in the wrong." As objective explanations of precisely how sin entered into the world, these tales are patently inadequate. As expression of the consciousness that sin *has* entered, that it actually infects *all* creation, that sin enters *only by sin,* and that it can be overcome *only by God's act* — these myths had profound meaning in their original settings.

The retrospect of these latter-day prophets also is conditioned by their agonized awareness of the chasm that separates the false Israel from the true Israel. The suffering of their day has taught them that the latter is extremely small in numbers. Political, economic, cultural oppression has produced the conviction that only a few belong to the elect. Only a remnant still lives by inspired memory and hope. The way to the Kingdom is narrow, and few indeed are those who find it. This colors their view of the sacred traditions, and leads them to select those strategic instances when only a valiant minority have been saved. Not only does memory focus upon the earlier and more fundamental covenants, but it recalls with vivid emphasis the more decisive judgments, when God reversed a long interim of rebellion with a spectacular intervention. Only two of the twelve spies were preserved to enter the Promised Land, and there were very few exceptions to the apostasies of the tribes in the wilderness. The Noachic flood and the devastation of Sodom become favorite pivots of history. The punishments meted out to Cain, to Lot, and to the fallen angels likewise become subjects for edifying reflection. We have noted the recurrence of this pattern in the retrospect of the canonical prophets; the apocalyptists simply etch the pattern more deeply.

In this area too the tendency to vain, parasitic elaboration grows apace. These earlier judgments all too easily become the milestones of a deterministic and foreordained series of weeks, which cut history into equal segments and enable the curious to arrive mathematically at dependable, objective knowledge of the future. In each segment the pattern of the present interim is repeated in detail — from one judgment and repentance, through a long epoch when the righteous suffer and the wicked flourish, to the next unexpected, cataclysmic purgation. The affirmations that spring from the subjective passion of the faithful are thus transformed into an arbitrary schema that provides the fortunate knower with an objective control over history. Nonaccumulative knowledge of God that springs from authentic passion turns into its opposite, an accumulative knowledge that falsely dispenses with the need for authentic passion. To study the wide contrast in the two, a contrast that is obscured by similar vocabularies, one may consult the Psalms of Solomon and the Book of Jubilees.

There is one other aspect of the apocalyptic retrospect that calls for attention: the idea of pre-existence, which is increasingly prominent in apocalyptic and even in rabbinic thought. To conform to the Biblical perspective the term " pre-existence " should be understood in the sense of pre-rebellion. As usually considered, the term pre-existence arouses a false connotation in modern minds. " Pre " connotes temporal priority; existence is equated with time; and this time is considered as *chronos,* as a single all-inclusive frame of being. From such a standpoint, pre-existence is nonsense, a contradiction in logic that cannot be resolved. But in the Bible, existence is defined as relation to God; existence *now* is defined as rebellion against God. Consequently, the prophet's reference to the time before this rebellion is communicated by means of historical narrative, but the source of the communication is the living God who now speaks to man's faith. " Pre-rebellion " thus includes both a temporal and a nontemporal meaning. As time is defined by the duration of purpose, whether man's or God's, so pre-existence refers primarily to the period before the misdirection of man's destiny begins. For one prophet pre-rebellion may be equivalent to pre-David; to another, pre-Joshua; to another, pre-Moses. In each case it refers to God's initiation of a covenant prior to the false *kairos* in which the covenant community now stands. And as apocalypses extend this false *kairos* back to Adam and to the " fall " even of angels and of creation itself, the con-

cept of pre-existence "moves backward" until it becomes equivalent
to pre-creation. Thus the rabbis were inclined to stress the pre-existence
of the Torah with God before the foundation of the world. Apocalyptists who sensed the imperfection of the Torah, on the other hand, were
inclined to accent the pre-existence of the Word, of the Spirit, of repentance, and of the Messiah.

To say of the Messiah that he is pre-existent articulates the same motif,
the same retrospective meaning, as to say of him that he is a Second
Adam, a *New* Man, *the* New Man. It is to say that in him God is re-
enacting in purer form his initial covenant with all creation, restoring
it to that end for which it was originally intended. To say of the Messiah that he is a second David, or Jonah, or Moses, or Elijah, is less radical and a less inclusive description of his function in human history, in
turning the hearts of the children back toward their fathers. This type
of thought articulates the Messiah's transcendence over the powers of
evil and at the same time his absolute claim upon present devotion.
In authentic apocalypses, the development of the myth concerning the
pre-existent heavenly Son of Man never provides a sentimental, dishon-
est, or cowardly escape by way of intoxication with hallucinations, but
rather intensifies the conflict between good and evil in which the man
of faith is now immersed. He does not find the yoke of the Messiah an
easy burden, that is, if he measures its weight by the anguish in his
relation to the world.

THE END OF THE PARENTHESIS

We turn now to an analysis of the modifications in the *prospect* of
the apocalyptist. We have already noted how the crescendo of internal
and external tragedies beat upon the Jewish heart, and in so doing
placed in sharpest contrast the present age and the coming age. The
more sustained and aggravated the tragedy, the greater the qualitative
difference between the ages. In this context, when God utters his "I
will judge," he places in jeopardy the *entire* present age. Correspondingly, the prophet accentuates the suddenness and unexpected character
of this assize. In form, the coming judgment is envisaged as the most
cataclysmic upheaval imaginable, inasmuch as God must subdue all
the forces of rebellion that now pervade his creation. His intervention
involves a stupendous miracle, the moving of mountains. Because jus-

tice is so completely ignored in this age, the scope of final judgment is extended to include all men, living or dead, and all the times, past as well as present.

But God also says, " I will redeem," and this promise is as inseparable from the threat of judgment as in the case of the earlier prophets. In the delineation of the coming forgiveness, the prophetic pattern is followed. Though the picture of heavenly glories utilizes highly figurative and other-worldly images, the center of hope lies in the purification of the relationship between God and his creation, in events which restore and fulfill the covenant. In the elaborate dreams of *Paradise Regained,* understatement is naturally as foreign as in the claims of the most enthusiastic Texan. An economy of plenty will replace the economy of scarcity; the whole earth will be renovated. But the dominant motif in most predictions deals with the new knowledge of God, the new heart of obedience, the new life as sons of God, upon whom the Spirit has been poured out. This motif, however, is subject to multiple expression: the fulfillment of the covenants, the banishment of Satan, the destruction of idols, the annihilation of sin and death, the planting of the tree of life, the springing forth of the river of life, the coming of a new heaven, a new earth. In the most thoroughgoing apocalypses, there is a resurrection of all the dead to correspond to the realization that neither the righteous nor the wicked receive justice in this age.

These visions, because they are more completely freed from the sober practicalities of the present interim, tend to proliferate in a wild tangle of supertemporal myths. The coming age, as wholly other, wholly new, and wholly divine, defies description in terms of the realities of this age, yet analogies must perforce be drawn from experience in this age. Some apocalypses therefore revel in dreams of heavenly vineyards and banquets, while others use more rarefied and abstract images. And in the same writing, one finds a baffling alternation between highly spiritual and crassly physical pictures. But however inadequate these prognostications of coming glories may be, apocalypses in their original context were entirely adequate to communicate God's assurance of justice and mercy.

We should perhaps note that only in the apocalypses do we find a view of human history that arrives at a final unity including all men and all times. The earlier prophets were unconcerned about including in their field of vision the destiny of all races and nations. But to the later apocalyptists, the horizons of history become all-inclusive. The coming age is a final age, which will bring fulfillment to the whole creative process. But it is significant that the apocalyptists arrived at this universal perspective by consciousness of the misdirection, from its source, of human history as a whole. They arrive at a "philosophy of history," not by viewing the entire past objectively as a historian or sociologist, but by sensing in their own present struggle their solidarity in sin with the whole creative process.

" The Kingdom of God is the dynamic fulfilment of the ultimate meaning of existence against the contradictions of existence." [3]

What has been said makes immediately intelligible the expectations of the Messiah who is to usher in the great change. The reason should be obvious why few apocalyptists felt that help in the form of a human leader would be sufficient. The Messiah must have power adequate to defeat every adversary; he must bring healing for all the sickness of creation; he must be One who will reveal the true knowledge of God to a world of blinded men; and he must be able to communicate his heavenly powers to the elect. Hidden from the foundation of the world, he will appear at the final summing up, " coming on the clouds of heaven." He shares the creative power of God, and his judging and redemptive power as well. It is inevitable that there should be a profusion of portraits of the Messiah, with little agreement in the details of appearance, but with large consensus on his functions. Some apocalyptists, to be sure, did not envisage any Messiah but God himself. But, in their case, God fulfills the functions which other writers assign to the Messiah. The existential content of expectation is much the same, whether God or his " Elect One " presides at the Judgment.

This is indicated by the fact that all authentic apocalypses stress the nearness of the end. The days have been shortened, for the sake of the elect. The period of preparation is about to give way to the period of fulfillment. Already the fig tree is putting forth its shoots. " The axe lieth at the root of the trees." Nevertheless, though judgment is at hand, things will get worse before they get better. Satan's last fling will be his worst; the final conflict will be most intense.

[3] Cf. P. Tillich, *The Kingdom of God and History,* ed. by H. G. Wood, p. 119. Willett, Clark & Company, 1938. H. D. Wendland, *Geschichtanschauung und Geschichtsbewusstsein im Neuen Testament,* pp. 16 f. 1938.

This urgency intensifies the demand placed upon the faithful. Their vocation becomes more strenuous. In repentance they must cut all the ties which bind them to the dying order. Their dependence and trust must be placed upon God alone, as he alone can bring in the new age. It is he who says, "Come ye out . . . , and be ye separate." Their response must be, "Let goods and kindred go, this mortal life also." In faith, they renounce all other securities except that life which is hid with God. In faith, they accept the evils of the present age in active resignation. In faith, their patience and endurance are welded together with eager expectancy and watchfulness. In faith, they suffer the loss of all things in the hope of gaining all things. In faith, they give witness to the signs of the times and call their fellows to flee from the coming wrath. The new community of the coming age takes over the historic mission of Israel. And with ardent longing they pray for the coming of the Messiah.

THE SYMMETRY OF HORIZON

In the case of the prophets, a marked symmetry between their forward and backward looks has been pointed out: the future and the past are extensions of the present, and this present remains the effective center that alone creates a unity of perspective. This unity and symmetry become even more marked in the apocalypses. The apocalyptist stands in an interim, a parenthesis. The beginning of the parenthesis corresponds with its ending; the breaking of a particular covenant is matched by its coming restoration. An all-inclusive rebellion determines and demands an all-inclusive judgment. The story of creation is balanced by the promise of a new creation. *Paradise Lost* provides an analogy for *Paradise Regained*. The pre-existence of the Messiah is matched by his postexistence. The myth of the end is woven with threads from the myth of the beginning: the tree of life, the Sabbath rest, circumcision in heart, the baleful activity of the serpent.

There is an even more significant type of symmetry to be detected in this pattern. That is the correspondence between God's activity and human response. In the historic initiation of the covenant, God's word prompts human faith, as in the case of Abraham and Moses. In the historic breaking of the covenant, man's sin draws with it God's penalty in the vanity and miscarriage of human history. In the present moment, the sign is comprehended only by those with eyes of faith. The proclamation of the future fuses man's continued rebellion with God's judgment, man's repentance with God's forgiveness. The historical landscape corresponds to the spiritual inscape. "There exists in the world of the spirit a situation which does not obtain in the world of finite ends and values, namely, a one-one correspondence between object and subjective attitude." [4]

These considerations may indicate the relevance of the phrase "beyond history," a term widely used by modern theologians but one that does not appear in the Bible. It is a dangerous term because of the ambiguity of the word "history," which likewise does not appear in the Bible. Yet the phrase may with caution be used, if by history one refers to the *kairos* of sin, the parenthesis characterized by rebellion-frustration, the detour in which man walks ever farther from God's road. Used in this sense, for some Biblical writers the phrase "beyond history" would denote the period before the destruction of the Davidic kingdom and after its expected restoration; for others it would denote the period before the repudiation of the Mosaic covenant and after its revival; for some apocalyptists it would refer to the period before the fall of the angels and after the final triumph over "the principalities and the powers." But we should remember that this horizontal, temporal reference always stemmed from the consciousness of vertical, qualitative distinctions between present sin and divine purpose. With reference to the process of revelation, "beyond history" connotes the source and ground of present existential reality, pointing to the divine *kairos* as it is mediated through a word, which cannot be heard by men who are blinded by the measurable, objective standards of this age. As such, that which is "beyond history" actually constitutes the only genuine history, while that which is "within history" actually constitutes a pseudo history to which men are enslaved. In other words, to say that the Kingdom of God lies "beyond history" is equivalent to saying that a particular age of rebellion lies within the span of God's overarching purpose.

The symmetrical pattern of prophecy and authentic apocalypse just outlined may be of service in identifying spurious aberrations of apocalypse. Ultimately the false apocalyptist is a false prophet, as judged by the standards of a Jeremiah or Isaiah. And there were as many false

---

[4] D. F. Swenson, *Something About Kierkegaard,* Revised Edition, p. 126. Augsburg Publishing House, 1945.

prophets in the first century as in the seventh century B.C. These aberrations included the following:

The substitution of speculative for existential interest.
The development of mechanical devices for measuring quantitatively the sequence of ages.
The use of predictions to foster self-righteousness and to support complacency.
The vain calculation of astrological signs and portents, to provide chronological accuracy.
Premature efforts to force the issue, to bring in the Kingdom by human efforts.
Arbitrary schematization of external history into a fatalistic determinism without respect for subjective response.
Too facile an identification of the Kingdom with a change in external earthly arrangements more desired by self-seeking men.
Exact computation of merits which God must enforce in the judgment, merits which can be measured by men in terms of external behavior.

It will be seen that each of these violates the inner character of prophetic faith; each reveals an " angle of vision " radically different from that created by God's visitation with man. And because the angle of vision is altered, the view of both foreground and background is falsified.

But other apocalypses preserve the genuine orientation of Biblical experience. And they do this during a period when the absolute *telos* meets an absolute contradiction, when God's promise meets its greatest denial, when the validity of the covenants is most severely tested. Faith must meet its own opposite; it must answer the contradictions which it has itself created; and it can answer these contradictions only by a more strenuous commitment to God's faithfulness.

" The absolute telos exists for the individual only when he yields it an absolute devotion." [5]

Each successive challenge to faith can be met only by a deeper level of faith; the successive deaths of hopes can be surmounted only by a hope that refuses to remain dead. Such faith and such hope can spring anew only from a sign that God is now acting to restore the covenant, and to bring it to the long-intended but long-delayed consummation.

It is thus that the apocalypses disclose to the discerning reader the essential axioms of Biblical thought, the points of greatest vulnerability,

[5] S. Kierkegaard, *Concluding Unscientific Postscript,* trans. by D. F. Swenson, p. 355. Princeton University Press, 1941.

the aberrations which ensue when faith breaks, the infinite agony of men who remain loyal, and the absolute necessity of God's intervention to manifest his faithfulness to his promise. New Testament Christianity refused to dispense with the apocalyptic perspective, but insisted upon it as a gateway into the Kingdom of Christ.

"The late-Jewish Messianic world-view is the crater from which burst forth the flame of the eternal religion of love." [6]

[6] A. Schweitzer, *Out of My Life and Thought*, p. 18. Henry Holt & Company, 1933.

THE NEW TESTAMENT recognizes the end not only as a future, but also as a completed event. This event is the sending of Jesus Christ. . . . He is the End. . . . Eschatology becomes history and creates history. . . . This Jesus of Nazareth, the New Man, the World Savior, the Slave of God and His Elect, the Messiah . . . is the revolution of inherited and traditional concepts. This historical once-for-allness of his mission and person are decisive for the New Testament consciousness of history.

—H. D. Wendland, *Geschichtsanschauung und Geschichtsbewusstsein im Neuen Testament,* p. 22. Göttingen, 1938.

15

THE MESSIAH COMES

A T THE outset, four things must be kept in mind as axiomatic within the early Christian orientation to history. The first axiom is the validity of God's former covenants, the events by which those covenants had been made and restored, and the faith by which men had appropriated them. The apostolic message presupposes the angle of vision of the prophets, and the history of revelation by which that perspective had been produced. It would be a repudiation of the new covenant to attempt to exalt the superiority of Christian morality and institutions at the expense of the old covenant. Such an attempt destroys the existential dimensions of faith, and makes the new religion definitely inferior to the old, as Kierkegaard so conclusively shows.[1] It is doubtful if a person can appropriate the Christian Gospel without at the same time appropriating the *faith* of Israel, for apart from the presuppositions common to both Testaments the act of God in Jesus Christ is neither intelligible nor essential.

The second axiom is the affirmation of the Messianic hope and the eschatological horizons within which that hope alone has relevance. Eschatology, as we have seen, elucidates the loyalties and purposes which determine the direction of human activity. It articulates the particular end which now defines the *kairos* of human destiny. It enunciates God's promise, which marks out the beginning and end of his creation. His final judgment and mercy are revealed in signs that have power to produce faith and hope. By this response, man accepts his Creator's *kairos* as determinative of his " way " and directs his steps accordingly. Eschatology thus comprises the perspective of the man of faith, his sense of the meaning of today, of yesterday, and of tomorrow.

[1] *Concluding Unscientific Postscript*, pp. 494 ff. 1941.

Eschatology is an existence-communication that springs from the inner dynamics of the situation when God visits man. It therefore accents the conflict which is precipitated by that visitation, the conflict which appears at history's source and is resolved only at history's end. It evokes the sense of standing at the junction between the genuine history of God's deeds (viewed from faith's angle) and the spurious history of man (viewed from sin's angle). The Christian Gospel speaks to man at the point where he realizes that the eschatological crisis is inescapable — and insoluble apart from divine intervention. It speaks to the man who knows the vanity of self-generated, autonomous history, whose faith in God is subjected to the maximum strain by awareness of the power of sin and death. The Messianic hope is most intelligible to him for whom it is at once most necessary and most impossible, if the problem of his destiny is to be solved within the perspective of faith in God without jettisoning the realities of his own involvement in the entire creative work of God. Only by fulfilling this Messianic hope, does God's *agape* in Jesus Christ offer the final salvation to men. Apart from this context, the Christian experience of atonement and resurrection loses its ultimate significance. It is not strange that modern men who have not passed through the abyss of apocalyptic despair find the distinctive New Testament doctrines incongruous and unconvincing.

The third axiom underlying early Christian witness is the affirmation of a decisive change in God's dealings with men. He has spoken and acted in an event which constitutes a new parable and sign. In Jesus the Messiah his word and deed have initiated a new age, which men may enter by faith. The New Testament shouts this news from almost every page. All things have become new: a new age has dawned; a new Israel has been called; Satan has been vanquished; a new heaven has begun its descent to a new earth; the kingdoms of the world have met a superior Kingdom; the final conflict is joined; a new covenant has been sealed; men are being born again; slaves are ransomed, refugees resettled, enemies reconciled, sinners forgiven, diseased men healed, prisoners unchained, and the dead raised.

The apostle proclaims these events as fulfillments of prophetic hopes, and utilizes the idiom and vocabulary of the Old Testament; the structure of experience and expression maintains direct continuity with prophetic patterns. But the discontinuity is equally unmistakable. Now has transpired what prophets and kings had long hoped to see, but had *not* seen. Nor can this transformation be described simply in terms of the emergence of new ideas, new feelings, new moral codes, new institutions. There are changes, to be sure, in the content of knowledge and behavior; but the more significant revolution takes place in the heart of man. He is reborn. Not only does he see new things; he stands with new eyes at a new point from which to view God's activity; the light by which he sees is new. His vision undergoes revision. For him, to say, " The Kingdom has come," does not mean primarily an added idea or belief, but a changed personal orientation; nor does it mean that something " objective " has happened irrespective of his response, for there is a necessary correspondence between the coming of the Kingdom and the repentance and faith by which it is apprehended. To say, " Jesus comes," is to say, " Come, Lord Jesus."

This, of course, does not mean that to him the Kingdom is a purely subjective, individual creation of his own imagination. Such a change as has taken place can be understood only by the unconditioned grace of God. God takes the initiative. He alone can reveal his will, choose a community, ordain for it a *kairos,* and empower his creation to fulfill that *kairos.* Early Christians attribute every new element in their situation to the marvelous grace of God.

" Blessed be the God and Father of our Lord Jesus Christ, who according to his great mercy begat us again unto a living hope " (I Peter 1:3).

This, then, is the fourth axiom of the new covenant: early Christians assume that *every* new element in their situation is traceable to that historical event wherein God's mercy is manifested,

" who according to his great mercy begat us again unto a living hope *by the resurrection of Jesus Christ from the dead.*"

There are as many ways of describing the work of the Messiah as there are ways of describing the new situation in which his disciples stand because of his work. But all agree that in his total career a mission from God has been fulfilled which serves to draw his disciples within a new field of magnetic force. The Kingdom of God comes, has come, is coming; and the point at which it comes nearest to men is the death-resurrection of God's Anointed One. After that event, the *now* in which men stand is very different from the *now* in which they stood before that event. But again and again we must recognize that this new situation is apprehended only within faith, where the dying and rising of Jesus the Messiah is repeated in the dying and rising of those who are his. Conversion now presupposes the total renunciation of the old aeon and the total commitment of self to the new aeon. The *rebirth* of the Christian is a re-enactment of the sign of the resurrection of Jesus as Messiah.

This leads to the basic question: In what does rebirth consist? How does it affect the central structure of man's response to each situation? Exactly what difference does it make in the angle of vision of the individual? How does this *kairos* differ from all others? How does the coming of the Messiah transform the conditions of human living as a whole? We shall seek an answer to these questions, not by taking them up seriatim, but by studying in this chapter changes in attitudes toward the interim, and in the concluding chapter the modification in retrospect and prospect. Treatment must be extremely condensed; accordingly, the reader is urged to read slowly, and to make frequent references to parallel sections in Part III.

THE REVISION OF THE INTERIM

We have noted that the impact of God's visitation creates an acute sense of suspense. The *prophet* understands his *now* as an interim of rebellion which had begun with defection from the covenant, when man had forgotten what he should have remembered. He *re*tells the story of covenant-making and covenant-breaking events. By word and deed, God places the prophet before his contemporaries as a parable and a sign, reviving their memory and calling them to decision. He reveals the end of the interim in judgment, repentance, mercy. The prophet *fore*tells this imminent end, which will mark the restoration and fulfillment of the covenant. He defines existence by reference to this end.

The *apocalyptist* views his *now* as an age-long period of almost total rebellion, a period in which rebellion has passed into all men, enslaving them to its body of sin and death. Looking backward, he finds all history a long detour from God's road; he sees God's covenant broken, immediately following its inception. Looking forward, he anticipates the speedy termination of the detour in a final and universal act of judgment and mercy. The contrast between God's holiness and man's sin yields a black-and-white contrast between the *now* and the *then,* the *here* and the *there.* This contrast will be broken only when God's Anointed comes from heaven to restore and fulfill the covenant; consequently, the apocalyptist calls men to define their existence solely by reference to the Messiah who will come.

Within this interim of total rebellion, the *apostle* witnesses God's actual visitation in the person of the Messiah. His existence is defined by reference to this event, which restores and fulfills the covenant. He is confronted by a deed of God through which the *there* enters the *here.* Inconceivably miraculous, the Kingdom of the Messiah, in spite of its " wholly-otherness," breaks upon the kingdoms of the world with judgment and mercy. The *then* enters the *now;* the end comes before the end; within the interim, the interim is terminated.

" Between the sentences (1) God is the Lord of history, and (2) there comes the day of His salvation and judgment, the end of the world's time, there is inserted a third sentence which basically and completely changes this relationship: (3) God has taken possession of his Lordship. His kingdom has come." [2]

God speaks and acts; the apostle, seeing and hearing, is himself reconciled to God. To him is committed the word of reconciliation. He is sent as ambassador on behalf of Christ to entreat men: " Be ye reconciled to God. . . . Now is the day of salvation " (see II Cor. 5:20 to 6:12). He tells the story of a Man, Jesus of Nazareth, a carpenter, an unauthorized teacher, a troublemaker, a Jew who was killed as an enemy of the people. He shouts the claim that this man, long considered dead, is in fact alive, chosen by God to be his Messiah. He announces that the end of all the ages, the purpose of all creation, is realized in this crucified Galilean. As Son of God, he had died; as Messiah, he is now setting up his Kingdom. The listener repents and yields his life to the service of such a Messiah. What happens?

In the first place, man's relationship to the now is revolutionized by the *form* of the revelatory event. God's salvation appears in the form of a Servant who humbles himself! This form directly contradicts the expectations of both prophet and apocalyptist. Those who anticipated the coming of a Messiah had been forced to recognize an unbridged chasm between the present epoch of sin and the coming epoch of righteousness. They had been led to accept the prevailing skepticism concerning

---

[2] H. D. Wendland, *Geschichtsanschauung und Geschichtsbewusstsein im Neuen Testament,* p. 22. Göttingen, 1938.

the activity of the Spirit, postponing its revival to the last days, when the Prophet Elijah would again proclaim "the word of the Lord." Until that time, God could speak only through the pseudonymous visions of the fathers. The mode of his communication must be more and more indirect: angels, dreams, and the reinterpretation of Scripture. Against this background, the message that God has spoken directly and finally in the word-deed of Jesus comes as an astounding reversal.

This reversal becomes total when it is seen that the Messiah is one who carries his obedience so far as to die the death of the cross. He inaugurates his Kingdom at the point where the sin of the present age reaches its maximum. The Kingdom comes through a Messiah who comes incognito, and who dies impotent. The life of the Kingdom comes in death, its wisdom appears as folly, its righteousness is disguised as sin. The apocalyptist had assumed that the conflict between the sin of the world and the holiness of God was so universal that God was inhibited from acting directly within the interim of this age. Yet *the Messiah comes in the form of sin* to condemn sin; he mediates the righteousness of God *by taking upon himself* the sin of the world. He does not lessen the condemnation of sin, but makes that condemnation the final judgment; yet in and through that judgment he reveals the final mercy, thus delivering man from despair.

This event transforms man's relationship to both ages, for through the Messiah he participates in both ages *in the same way in which the Messiah* had shared both.[3] Since the Kingdom has come in the casting out of demons and the Messiah's aggression against Satan, it comes for the disciple when he through faith enters the same battle and is given the same powers. Henceforth, to exist means to stand with the Messiah at the spot where maximum conflict with sin is made possible by maximum help of God, the spot where the interim of rebellion is now being terminated by the love of God. Man stands in the interim, but in standing here he is conscious also of standing at the end of that interim, on the border between it and the coming age. He suffers the buffeting of Satan, but energy and joy stem from the fact that God sends the Spirit of his Son into his heart. He is immediately related to the Messiah, subject to his guidance, and recipient of his power. No longer can he

[3] Cf. R. Otto, *The Kingdom of God and Son of Man,* trans. by F. V. Filson and B. L. Woolf, pp. 47–57. N.d.

postpone to the future the needed manifestation of the divine purpose. No longer can he evade the infinite possibilities of the present moment. At the point of Satan's greatest strength, the Christian receives power over Satan by understanding how Satan blinds men, by what subterfuges he attacks the Messiah, with what weapons he resists the coming King-, dom, and how God through Christ triumphs over the rulers of this age. The Christian's expectancy is raised to the nth degree. Now it is possible to discern God's purpose and to return to God; now no situation is so evil as to be immune to the invasion of the Messiah. Because the Kingdom comes in the Messiah's death and resurrection, the primary tension set up within the believer's consciousness is not that between the present and future ages, but that between Satan's kingdom and Christ's, both of which are realities in the present. Now he is transferred from one of these kingdoms to the other, from slavery to the spurious history of vain rebellion to " slavery " to the genuine history of God's creation.[4]

Now are accessible two factors long denied to men because of their sin: adequate knowledge of God's purpose; adequate power to respond. These are accessible, not because man has become righteous through his own power, but because God has initiated a new movement of redemption, sending his Son to die for men. Man is justified by faith in this saving activity of God. It is God who sends the Messiah, and who through him establishes the Kingdom as full expression of his sovereignty. Man's relationship to Jesus as the Christ is therefore one of complete dependence and complete gratitude.

A Christian's eyes are opened to see everywhere the *marks of the Messiah's triumph*. What Rudolf Otto has written of Jesus may be applied to the disciple:

" He already lived in the miracle of the new age which was active even in the present; . . . he saw this as something already developing and growing around himself; . . . he knew himself to be supported by powers which . . . were already penetrating the world, and, supported and filled by these powers, he worked and preached." [5]

To live in the midst of this miracle meant for the Christian that he could now identify many signs of God to which he had earlier been

[4] Cf. N. Berdyaev, *Slavery and Freedom*, pp. 247–255. 1944.
[5] *The Kingdom of God and Son of Man*, trans. by F. V. Filson and B. L. Woolf, p. 155. Lutterworth Press, n.d.

blind and many signs of Satan by which he had been deceived. He is enabled to know the true character of sin and death, the real nature of the dominion of Satan; and this knowledge communicates power to escape his *slavery* to this tyrant. He need not wait, as did the apocalyptist, until that future when the Messiah should come. The Messiah has come, delivering him out of the night into the day. The Messiah has established a new *modus vivendi* with regard to both the night and the day.

In a succinct metaphor from the New Testament, the Christian, with his Master, dies to the kingdom of Satan. This means, in the first place, a radical repentance by which man realizes his implication in " the body of sin " that has imprisoned mankind. He is thus saved from hypocrisy. But this awareness of sin does not lead to a despairing sense of exclusion from God's Kingdom; rather it reveals his inclusion in the sphere of grace and forgiveness. He can thus recognize the depth of sin and at the same time experience victory. In seeing himself as worthy of death, and involuntarily accepting that death, he finds himself completely dependent upon God, and receives the gift of life. " If Christ is in you, the body is dead because of sin " (Rom. 8:10).

Dying to the world also means renunciation of those false securities and false hopes through which Satan gains control over man. He voluntarily surrenders wealth, occupation, home, family, and even his own life. He no longer has treasures that can be lost. His fears of what men may do are dwarfed by his fear of God. His anxieties concerning food and clothing are replaced by singlehearted quest for the Kingdom of God. He dies to the world by breaking all ties to it, so that he no longer defines his existence by reference to this age. " We who died to sin, how shall we any longer live therein " (Rom. 6:2).

Dying to the world means, finally, sharing the suffering which Satan's tyranny produces. It means voluntary acceptance of all the evil that enemies may work. It is a standing invitation for crucifixion from the same powers that crucified Jesus. It is an acceptance of judgment, the final judgment which rightfully begins with God's servants. It is the daily patience that endures the burden of the world's alienation from God. To die thus to the world is to live to God. " The death that he died, he died unto sin once: but the life that he liveth, he liveth unto God " (Rom. 6:10).

Standing beneath the cross, the Christian views the evils of this age with complete realism, having in the cross the sign of man's total bondage to sin and death. He understands that corruption has spread throughout creation, so that creation as a whole is in agony " until now " (see Rom. 8:20–23). By the revelation of God's righteousness in the cross, each individual is brought to see clearly his own solidarity with the sin of the age, to an extent unmatched in the earlier apocalypses. Yet this penetrating realism did not provide excuse for despair, for antinomianism, for passivity. For the apocalyptist, his *dream* is the only bulwark against despair. From such despair, the Christian is saved by his point of standing within the *kairos* of the risen Lord, which makes the resources of the Messiah accessible to him. In the Messiah God has provided both the End and the *Means,* both the Life and the *Way,* both the Sheepfold and the *Door.*

The Son of God wins his victory by dying to the world; the cross is the way to victory for his brothers. God shares his joy and peace with the Messiah, in the midst of his agony. And the Messiah shares his joy and peace with those who by faith step with him through the narrow door. Death to this age means life in God's Kingdom; the two are forever united, and the union verified by God's act in Jesus Christ. " If we have become united with him in the likeness of his death, we shall be also in the likeness of his resurrection " (Rom. 6:5). The present Kingdom thus terminates the present age of sin by an experience of resurrection into the coming age. This experience revolutionizes the pattern of one's attitudes toward the coming age. In the midst of sin the new Adam shares the Messiah's righteousness; in the midst of death he shares the Messiah's life. The mystery of redemption is thus revealed to the Christian. Whereas the apocalyptist lived by hope, the Christian lives by Christ, who *is* the hope of glory.

The experience of resurrection produces a drastic change in attitudes toward death and life. It makes absolute the qualitative difference between two kinds of death and two kinds of life. In this age Satan has blinded men by impressing on their minds entirely false conceptions: what passes for death in this evil age may actually hide a " dying life "; what passes for life may actually hide a " living death." True death is an event in the genuine history of encounters with God, that act of rebellion-punishment whereby God excludes man and his deceptive *kairos* from continuing qualitative relationship to Himself. This is the *second* death from which the faithful are saved. The death which consists of a quantitative termination of one's days, the *first* death, the death which came to Jesus and to his faithful witnesses — this death can never separate one from God's love in Christ (Rom., ch. 8). To those who are in Christ, this death is actually a sleep (see I Thess., ch. 4; I Cor., ch. 15; John, ch. 11). This death comes to all men. Though this death seems to prove estrangement from God, it is an estrangement which the crucified Messiah overcomes.

RESURRECTION TO LIFE

Conversely, the Messiah has revealed the character of that life which is true, eternal life in relationship to God. This too is wholly a gift of God, an event in his history, which communicates the Spirit and the mind of the Spirit. This life begins by a new birth that re-establishes the right relation of the creature to the Creator, i.e., a relation of absolute dependence, that of the clay to the potter. Through the Messiah, God introduces man into this new *kairos* wherein he realizes his total creatureliness and yields the glory and authority to God alone. It is God's Spirit within the new son which cries " Abba," it is God's Spirit which nerves all his willing and his doing; it is God's love which is shed abroad in his heart. Rebirth introduces him into the life of the coming age, making him a son and heir of God. The experience of this relationship is life indeed. Here at last is that true history, that new age, that restoration of the primal communion with God which had been broken by sin.

With the exaltation of Jesus and the communication of his life through the Spirit, the general resurrection has begun. Both apocalyptist and legalist had yearned for this consummation. But their hope had been constantly subject to self-righteousness or despair. Now that the Christian has been raised to the new life, his confidence rises to a pitch not expressed in earlier apocalypses. "There is therefore now no condemnation to them that are in Christ Jesus.". . . " If God is for us, who is against us? ". . . " We are more than conquerors " (see Rom., ch. 8). Hope has turned into something stronger than hope, into a passionate assurance that no external adversity may destroy. Yet this confidence does not encourage self-righteousness. Boasting is, in fact, excluded by the very means through which God has made redemption accessible through Christ Jesus (see Rom. 3:24–27). All men have been shut up under sin in order that God's grace might be manifested as a free gift to all.

Consciousness of adoption as citizen of the new age also gives to the new Adam an immediate sense of reconciliation with God. This mood of buoyant peace and joy, so characteristic of the New Testament, is quite rarely discovered in apocalyptic or legalistic writings. The cross communicates at once a knowledge of sin and a knowledge of forgiveness. To him who confesses his sin, it provides an Advocate with the Father and an Atonement. To him who confesses his blindness, it gives "the light of the knowledge of the glory of God" (II Cor. 4:6). This knowledge which shines "in the face of Jesus Christ" is sufficient for all the needs of his followers. It insures immediacy of access to the throne of God. It furnishes an eternal sacrifice in an eternal tabernacle, purifying man's conscience from dead sins and bringing him peace (see Heb., chs. 7 to 10). The relationship which God has inaugurated in Christ marks the perfecting of all the covenants between God and man, opening the way to adequate knowledge of God's will, adequate obedience after the pattern and in the power of Christ, and the adequate fulfillment of all the promises.

It is little wonder that life in the Messiah produced among Christians such a profusion of spiritual gifts, little wonder that each of these gifts was regarded as a sign of the end-time and as an expression of the Messiah's powers. This mood of expectant wonder, of ecstatic joy, of buoyant confidence, of enthusiastic acceptance of tribulations, can hardly be paralleled elsewhere in the Bible, or, for that matter, anywhere in the world's literature. Two more facets of this mood may be mentioned here.

FREEDOM AND FELLOWSHIP

The first is the spontaneous outburst of freedom that accompanies rebirth into the new age. By looking to Jesus, the disciple is freed from his fears of what men may do to him. He is freed from anxieties concerning the morrow, from the law of sin and death, from the condemnation which the Torah evoked, from the institutions of this age. Christ levels all the barriers erected by men in their effort to objectify moral and religious distinctions. He blesses the poor, the hungry, the meek, the oppressed. He destroys the power of the heavenly rulers of this age, emancipating men from the heavy thralldom of Satan and all his cohorts.

Here too there is a sharp contrast with prophet and apocalyptist. To be sure, they had stoutly affirmed and tacitly assumed that man is responsible, and that he is always free to fulfill God's demand at the moment. They too had been aware of the power of the divine imperative to override the authority of Antiochus or Caesar. And they had acted in full accordance with this freedom. But in the New Testament, the area in which freedom is experienced is enlarged to include all creation. In and through the act of faith in the redemptive work of Christ, man is freed from all the contaminating tyrannies that have tormented God's creatures from the beginning. Because of the total scope of this freedom, it is seen by Christians to be a final emancipation, decisive for all coming time. Moreover, this final and total freedom is not only a corollary of God's demand but a gift of his love. Through suffering the loss of all things, Christ brings freedom to men. " For freedom did Christ set us free " (Gal. 5:1). The early Christian mood, therefore, is one that links freedom to an infinite gratitude and to an inner responsiveness to the working of the Holy Spirit. This clearly represents a transformation of the earlier perspective.

The last aspect of the new life in the Messiah to be mentioned is this: through Christ God has created and is creating a new Israel. When man is adopted as son, he enters a family of brothers. He becomes a member of the Body of Christ, a priest in the new temple, an heir of the promises to Abraham. The cross serves to define Israel anew, so that men can now distinguish the true Israel and the Israel according to the flesh. One characteristic of the dying age is that men are led to judge the constituency of Israel by external evidences and by reference to the past: race, nation, circumcision, the law, the Temple. And men come to expect that the promises made to Abraham are intended for this Israel according to the flesh. At the end of its natural course of history, in space and time, will come a triumph that will be measured by the changed relationships between this empirical entity and other races and nations. But the coming of the new Israel in Christ reverses that line of logic. From the stones God raises up new children to Abraham. The true Israel is recognizable as these sons of God according to the Spirit, these who orient their lives by the present repetition of the promises. In Christ they perceive that God does not make promises to an already existing historical entity, Israel, but that he creates Israel ever anew *by* his promises. The Church appears as " a single divine-human organism reaching from heaven to earth." [6] And in Christ it becomes apparent that this new Israel is the final inheritor of the Kingdom (Rom., chs. 9 to 11).[7]

Thus the Christian experiences a decisive at-homeness, a fellowship with the saints in the life of the covenant community. Not only does this mean that the ties to this new household are stronger than all ties to institutions of this age; it also means that the character of his filiation with the brotherhood will have a different quality. Its distinguishing mark will be the love which God has manifested in the Messiah. This love is the dynamic motivation of the mission of Jesus to sinners; it is the grace which God communicates to penitent sinners through the risen Lord; it is the demand which that Lord makes upon those who belong to him; it is the innermost character of that community which now is created by the impact of final judgment and redemption.

Communion in this Messiah thus furnishes the commands by which the disciple orders his steps. He must walk appropriately to the new *kairos,* guided and empowered by the Spirit. The words of Jesus before Calvary become the Word of the Messiah after Calvary, clinched by his example and verified by God's signature. The Christian reads the Sermon on the Mount as if he were hearing the Messiah speak from his cross. The words, like the cross, become signs of the Kingdom, marking the boundary between the ages. They are events which, to the hearing ear, witness the ingress of final judgment and final mercy: repentance, forgiveness, sacrifice, trust, expectancy, obedience, love. Seeing the cross, the disciple knows the possibility, the reality, the contemporaneity of such events. Standing beneath the cross, he experiences the call to decision accentuated to its highest potency. No man, standing here, can serve two masters, or seek heavenly and earthly treasures, or have eyes directed toward a double goal. He either is or is not

---

[6] L. S. Thornton, *The Common Life in the Body of Christ,* p. 2. Dacre Press, 1942. This book is a penetrating and thorough study of the early Christian concept of the Church, and should be read with care.

[7] Cf. comments in Thielicke, *Geschichte und Existenz,* pp. 8–10. 1935.

within the magnetic field of the Messiah's dominion. He either is or is not transferred from the night into the day.

THE SIGN OF THE CROSS

So great a transformation in the human situation is effected by the Passion story of God's Anointed. Here is the parable and sign by which God restores his covenant and calls his elect to repentance. Here is the true miracle which serves as a clue to the meaning of all the miracles. Here is "the most significant recent event in human history," which illumines all events. With such ultimate claims, with such rigorous demands, it is little wonder that the cross has stood not only on the altar of Christian worship but at the forefront of the Church's witness to the world. And it is little wonder that it has occasioned not only unquenchable faith but also unceasing antagonism.

> "The stone which the builders rejected,
> The same was made the head of the corner "
> (Matt. 21:42).

Jews were the first to believe, and the first to stumble. From their number came the most enthusiastic apostles and the most bitter enemies — witnesses to both the fulfillment of the Law and the Prophets, and the radical revision required by faith in the cross. Even those who first believed found faith subject to all the doubts projected by the form of this revelation — God's Son hanging on a cross. Those who continued steadfast in tribulation, patient in hope, could do so only because the sign of the Messiah was repeated, in their inner life and their outward behavior, by the sign of the Eucharist:

"This is my body which is given for you: this do in remembrance of me. . . . This cup is the new covenant in my blood, . . . which is poured out for you" (Luke 22:19, 20); "As often as ye eat this bread, and drink the cup, ye proclaim the Lord's death till he come " (I Cor. 11:26).[8]

When repeated by the Christian, this sign marks not only the source of the strength by which the new Israel lives but also the high barrier between the new Israel and the world. The sign remains, in Biblical terms, an offense (σκάνδαλον).

The distinctive characteristics of the apostolic *now* are grounded in

[8] Cf. R. Otto, *op. cit.*, pp. 277–305.

the absolute importance of the cross. But the hallmark of this importance is its offensiveness to the world. Professor G. Stählin has exhaustively examined the history of this concept of the scandal. Some of his conclusions are pertinent here: (1) the concept is almost entirely absent from extra-Biblical literature. (2) It takes its rise in the prophetic literature of the Old Testament, but (3) finds its strongest pre-Christian expression in apocalyptic. (4) The largest importance is attached to it in the New Testament, particularly in the writings most firmly grounded in Jewish thought (Matthew, Paul, John, the traditional words of Jesus in Mark and Luke, I Peter). (5) In Jewish apocalypses and in the New Testament, it denotes "the occasion of inner ruin," "the obstacle to the life of faith." (6) In keeping with the sharp dualism of apocalyptic thought, those writers view the offense as a work of the devil, which the Messiah in his coming is expected to destroy. (7) In the New Testament, a very different accent emerges. In some cases, the devil acts through the offense to undermine faith. But the origin of the offense lies predominantly on the divine side. The tension between faith and offense which the dualistic world view stresses is caught up within the effective range of God's sovereignty. The tension retains an undiminished sharpness, but its point of emergence is the very intrusion of the coming age into the present age. God sets out to conquer the present age as territory subject to his exclusive sovereignty. Where he makes this claim most actively, i.e., in Jesus Christ, there is the acme of offense. Because God appears in flesh, in sin, in death, it is he who commands faith and at the same time occasions stumbling. This revelation is therefore in this age *always and inevitably a scandal.*[9]

[9] G. Stählin, *Skandalon,* pp. 271 f. Gütersloh, 1930.

16

THE CHRISTIAN SEES NEW HORIZONS

THE Messiah comes to bring to an end one history and to inaugurate another. Within one history, the word of the cross is an intolerable offense; within the other, it is the power and wisdom of God. The Passion story is the drama of the meeting of the two histories: "He came unto his own, and . . . his own received him not. But as many as received him, to them gave he the right to become children of God" (John 1:11, 12). The Messiah meets men enslaved to a false, illusory history, and reveals both their slavery and the road to freedom in the true history of God's love. When this Word meets the response of faith, false history ends and true history begins. Then and there the old Israel dies and the new Israel is born. Then and there man dies to himself and his world, and is born again. Then and there all things pass away and all things become new. The cross is the " still turning point " of the world. It does not recede into the past as a recollection that becomes fainter and fainter, but remains at every moment a sign of the beginning of a new *kairos* now.

THE KINGDOM AS A NEW TIME

One result of the Messiah's coming is therefore a new apprehension of the nature and structure of time itself. Since the end has come before the end, something has happened to measurements of duration, to the relationship of the tenses. This event demonstrates the incommensurability of the world's time and God's. The acts of creation, of decision, of incarnation, of resurrection — these events communicate the true time of the coming age. These events are once-for-all events that took place once-upon-a-time; they are completed in actual happenings, but they cannot be acclimated to the ordinary human treatment of history. In understanding them one arrives at an understanding of all true history, i.e., God's creation and redemption by the Word.

In creation, God communicates a primal sense of time, a time that is *finite* and determined by God's purpose. But in repudiating this covenant, man's sense of time is diseased. He constructs a sense of time that is *infinite,* impersonal, and *independent of God's purpose* — and he lives within the prison so constructed.[1] In Christ, God restores a true sense of time by drawing man within his Kingdom. The new world brings its own time, the dimensions of which are vastly different from the conceptions which man has exalted to tyrannous authority.[2] Thus the Kingdom destroys the this-worldliness of earth-bound idolatries without substituting an unearthly and abstract mythology of pure spirituality. Thus it destroys the idea of an unending cycle or chain of aeons without substituting a timeless medium of static and deadly finality. The Kingdom remains an age — different from all other ages — but still an age, with its beginning and end, its seed and its fruit.

REVISION OF MEMORY

When he steps into this *kairos,* the Christian for the first time receives a true retrospect and prospect. Taking first the grain of Christian memory, we note a bifocal view of the beginnings of the new age, to correspond to the dual character of its time-dimension. By reference to one dimension the new age begins with the mission of Jesus in Nazareth and Judea, the events under Pontius Pilate. " The law and the prophets were until John: from that time the gospel of the kingdom of God is preached " (Luke 16:16). The coming of Jesus effected as radical a transition in this chronologically ordered history as in the life of the individual at the time of his rebirth.

The Passion story, which narrates this beginning, must respect this involvement in man's *kairos.* It must remain a narrative of historical events, must present Jesus as fully subject to the limitations of all existence — its time, its law, its carnality and mortality. It must not minimize the offensive paradox, nor turn into abstraction the concrete character of Jesus' ministry to sinners, his conflict with demons, his ethical

---

[1] Cf. T. Spencer, *An Act of Life,* pp. 80 f. 1944.
[2] Cf. W. H. Auden, " For the Time Being," in *Collected Poetry.* 1945.

demands. The Christian views the entire period before the Advent as a period of preparation and expectation, of prophecies and hope. Only at the end of this period has God set forth his Son to be atonement for " sins done aforetime."

But there is a second way in which to describe the beginnings of the new age. The Kingdom is a *new kind* of time. It has been in heaven through all the times. The Messiah is its pre-existent head. " Before Abraham was born, I am." As creative Word, he *is* the beginning, the first and the last. One not only speaks of the time before and after Christ; one also speaks of the Christ before and after time. For this reason, the Passion story never becomes past history in the same sense that other events become past history, but in continued immediacy points to the repeated coming of the Messiah into the personal history of the disciple and the corporate history of the Church. The separate units of Gospel tradition, as well as the tradition as a whole, precipitate this immediate confrontation of the believer with Christ as the Son of God. Because Jesus the Messiah existed before creation as creation's Lord, and because he inaugurates a new kind of time, Christians see him as a contemporary of all earlier epochs.

Viewing the past in the light of the cross, the disciple found the cross prefigured in the ancient traditions. The sin revealed in the cross makes clear what actually constituted sin in all the previous ages; the love of God in the cross discloses the enduring will of Him who is Lord over all ages. The simultaneous experience of two ages, Satan's and Christ's, predisposed Christians to realize that the same duality had been true of earlier epochs. For the decisive distinction, then as now, is not the purely temporal distinction between *what is* and *what is to be,* but the existential distinction between the *kairos* of Satan and that of Christ. The real contrast is between those *inside* and those *outside* that *kairos,* and not between those *before* it and those *after* it.

One mark of this contrast is the double connotation of the term " generation " in the New Testament. Not all contemporaries belong to the same generation. Believers are saved from this " crooked generation " (Acts 2:40). They see the signs which Jesus refuses to show " unto this generation " (Mark 8:12 f.), and are introduced into the mystery which has been hidden from generations (Col. 1:26). Sons of this world have a different generation from the sons of light (Luke 16:8). Decisive importance inheres, not in the sequences of generations, quantitatively measured, but in their standing before God, qualitatively measured in terms of faithlessness, adultery, and sin (Mark 8:38; 9:19; 13:30; Heb. 3:10).

"The men of Nineveh shall stand up in the judgment with this generation, and shall condemn it: for they repented at the preaching of Jonah; and behold, a greater than Jonah is here" (Matt. 12:41).

The retrospective view of the beginning of the *kairos* of salvation thus includes both the contemporary and all preceding generations.

This dual view of the beginnings is also reflected in the attitude toward the prophets and apocalyptists. On the one hand, the historical career of Jesus is a fulfillment of the former prophecies. Those who see him as Messiah are, for the first time, enabled to see the true bearing of the hope of Israel (Heb. 11:39 to 12:2). On the other hand, since Jesus is the primal Word, the Alpha of true time, his disciples affirm the presence of his spirit in earlier epochs, testifying beforehand to "the sufferings of Christ, and the glories that should follow them" (I Peter 1:11). He is the fulfillment of the promise because all along he has been the author of the promise.

The dual view of beginnings also explains what seems to be a logical contradiction in descriptions of faith. On the one hand, the Christian knows that the cross of Jesus has created a new situation which makes faith in him as Messiah something *sui generis,* radically different from preconversion faith in God (e.g., Paul). On the other hand, Christians find numerous examples of faith during the period before the cross. The same apostle who celebrates the absolute necessity of the cross for human justification hails Abraham as one who was justified by his faith. The Epistle to the Hebrews celebrates the uniqueness of Jesus' priesthood, the sufficiency of his sacrifice, and the inadequacy of all earlier religious institutions, and yet it gives an impressive catalogue of the faithful who preceded the days of the Messiah (Heb., chs. 11; 12). There is no salvation apart from Christ; but those who before Christ lived by faith in Christ now share his Kingdom. The Messiah is the only true agent in creation; though he has been hidden from the foundation of the world, he has been secretly carrying on his saving work among those with eyes of faith.

It was noted earlier that the prophet and apocalyptist selected as pivots of previous history the moments of human rebellion and return, synchronized with the moments of judgment and mercy. And the impulse to return is provided in each case by a moment of revelation in which God utters threat and promise. Because the prophet anticipates an immediate execution of divine wrath and mercy, he discovers prototypes of judgment in earlier ages.

This grain of memory is repeated in the New Testament, but with a significant difference in accent, due to the fact that saving knowledge and power have already been mediated to the believer *through the cross*. Whereas the prophet points ahead to a covenant-restoring event, the apostle already has experienced the new covenant in the cross. In looking backward, then, he notices those events when deliverers appear in the midst of unmerited suffering, those moments when true life is mediated through apparent death. Events which earlier had appeared to represent postponement or miscarriage of justice are now seen to express divine mercy. Abel, for example, is no longer an example of injustice long unrequited, but an example of justification by faith and of life received in death (Heb. 11:4). The prophets are blessed in the very persecutions by experiencing divine power to endure and to conquer. Abraham's willingness to sacrifice Isaac illustrates his dying to the world, his confidence in God's power to give new life to the dead (Heb. 11:17).

It is possible that such reinterpretations of the past tell us more of the Christian's experience than of Abel's or Abraham's. In such a narrative as Stephen's speech (Acts, ch. 7), the historian who seeks objectivity will deal first of all with the faith of the author of Acts. Then, in a secondary way, he will try to recover Stephen's actual attitudes; only in a tertiary fashion will he be concerned with the events of Israel's past to which Stephen appeals. And in this case, it is obvious that Luke's account of those early events in the Mosaic period cannot claim to be objectively more accurate than the Old Testament narratives. Yet inferences drawn from this observation need to be guarded. The New Testament retrospect is more than free rationalization of tradition in the light of Christian experience. In the Christian's personal memory, the conflicts of faith which pervade Israel's story formed a large part of the apperceptive mass with which he responded to the story of Jesus. His response of faith was thoroughly impregnated with the inner dilemmas produced from the corporate experience of the chosen people in their relation to God's purpose. His faith in Jesus as Messiah was itself occasioned by hearing the word of the apostle concerning previous events. He did not himself create the Passion story but was transformed by it. In his case as in ours, the past, present, and future are inseparable, interacting components of a single continuum of experience. In his case, more than in ours, the axis of all history lies in the dynamic spirit of the living God. With him it was axiomatic that access to God's purpose should include access to the mystery of all creation. To him the cross becomes the key to all memories and all hopes. He views his horizons from the standpoint of the cross; the voice which is heard in the cross is the voice which has been speaking through all ages; and it is not the voice of man.

THE REVISION OF HOPE

We move then to a summary of basic changes in the Christian's attitudes toward the future. In this area too there is an intimate weaving of anticipation and realization, a spiritual correspondence between God's end and man's appropriation, and a bifocal view of the end as being at once a creative and an eschatological act. Through faith, man has become the slave of a coming Messiah who has already come — in the form of a slave. In the midst of Satan's *kairos* he has been called into God's *kairos*. Through his relationship to a Messiah, who dies through men's sin but is raised through God's power, he is himself born anew through the same death and resurrection. Henceforth, in his consciousness the antithesis between the chronological present and future is submerged by the antithesis between the dimensions of existence appropriate to the old man and the new. In Christ one can say, " In my end (my dying to this age) is my beginning (rebirth in the new age) "; he can also say, " In my beginning (rebirth in the new age) is my end (the fulfillment of the new covenant)." And in Christ these different moments of spiritual dynamics may be experienced simultaneously.[8]

The new Adam continues his struggle against the old Adam; the member of Christ is on occasion tempted to become the member of a demon or harlot; the self which has been created after the image of Christ must be nourished with milk, while the self which has been enslaved by Satan seeks repeatedly to gain the whip hand over the " babes in Christ." In the pull and push of this conflict, the future realization of Christ's Kingdom is at stake; the anticipation of that future

[8] Cf. T. S. Eliot, *The Four Quartets*, pp. 11-17. 1943.

remains one of the anchors of man's security in Christ. The future thus remains a vital matter, though man's relationship toward that future has been greatly changed by its pressure upon the present. Some of these changes are apparent on the surface:

1. The Christian is more conscious of the *nearness* of the Kingdom than was his apocalyptic predecessor. At times he expresses this by the affirmation that the Kingdom is " nearer to us than when we first believed." More frequently he expresses it by the attitude of infinite enthusiasm, of vigorous hastening toward the coming day, by a stretching forward to apprehend " the prize of the high calling of God in Christ Jesus." His mood is one of alert watchfulness and readiness. Refusing to be like Lot's wife, he leaves the dead to bury the dead. He is the virgin at midnight who keeps the lamp filled with oil. He is the householder awake to hear the cry, " The Lord comes! " He is the merchant who sells all that he possesses to buy one pearl. He sees the fig tree putting forth its buds, and knows that the summer is at hand. Like Abraham, he leaves all in search of a better country. The Kingdom comes in the very expectancy that awaits its coming; it is received by the humble disciple in the act of praying, " Thy kingdom come."

2. This electric expectancy is associated with an inner *certainty* of the Kingdom's approach. " Faith is assurance of things hoped for," or, in an alternate reading, " Faith is the giving substance to things hoped for " (Heb. 11:1, margin). Hope is the spontaneous derivative of faith. The object of hope remains unseen, but the source of hope is actually known and trusted. The future consummation thus becomes more than simply an object of desire; this future articulates the certainty of faith, assured of its own *telos*. Faith communicates a trust that enables one to abandon all anxieties, for Christ's power to shape the future is implicit in his power now to vanquish every enemy.

" There are some here of them that stand by, who shall in no wise taste of death, till they see the kingdom of God come with power " (Mark 9:1).

The creation-wide manifestation of God's power constitutes the Kingdom, and even now that power is at work, silently but irresistibly. The Christian sees Satan " fallen as lightning from heaven " and knows that " there is nothing hid " that shall not be revealed. He comes in contact with the leaven and knows that ultimately the whole dough will be leavened. He hears the word and experiences its power. Henceforth the parables of the seed articulate his confidence in the coming harvest. No matter what may be the odds against the martyr, he knows that all power has been given to the Lamb that was slain. He is convinced that the magnitude of the opposition is itself proof of the Messiah's coming victory.

"He that spared not his own Son, but delivered him up for us all, how shall he not also with him freely give us all things?" (Rom. 8:32).

3. The memories of Jesus of Nazareth and the activity of the risen Lord give to the disciple a clue to the *character of life* in the Kingdom, a clue which prophets and apocalyptists had not possessed. Although the Christian readily admits that his knowledge is still fragmentary and partial, he knows that the love of Christ is a sure index to the final situation, "when that which is perfect is come." It is this which makes his hope something more than hope, for " Christ in you " is " the hope of glory." This hope will not be illusory "because the love of God hath been shed abroad in our hearts through the Holy Spirit which was given unto us" (Rom. 5:5). The profuse gifts of this Spirit are but *first* fruits of a harvest that is to be. The Christian knows the character of the harvest by the character of the first fruits. He knows what the sovereignty of God in human affairs actually will mean: what the reign of God will mean for an elect community, the communion of saints. The Church as the Body of Christ, permeated and energized by his love, will be purified from all that corrupts and defiles. The Kingdom will be constituted by God's rule over the community of the firstborn in heaven, saints whose activity in heaven will be the singing of Hallelujah Choruses to the praise and glory of the Most High. The feasting in heaven will be a purification and extension of the Lord's Supper, now shared in this age. No longer are pictures of the coming Kingdom compensatory dreams that supply the *deficiencies* of life on earth: bread for the starving, houses for the homeless, power for the proletariat. To be sure, those factors remain, nor does one who trusts in the goodness of God need to be ashamed of their presence. But now the really compelling pictures of the coming Kingdom are drawn from the *adequacies* of life in the Messiah. " The kingdom of God is . . . righteousness and peace and joy in the Holy Spirit "; the return of the Messiah will simply mark the full and unimpeded sway of the Spirit. The New Testament overflows with testimonies to the all-absorbing

glory and wisdom and wonder and blessedness of life in the new age; and these testimonies are in part transcripts from the actual experience of Christians who have felt the Spirit moving through their wills.

4. The apostle also found in his new beginning a trustworthy clue concerning the manner of the Kingdom's approach and the means by which it comes. He knows that the initial impulse, the first act in the drama of restoration, is the death and resurrection of the Messiah. He knows that it is the word of the cross that brings the Kingdom near to men in the experience of rebirth. Knowing how the Kingdom comes, he knows all that he needs to know concerning its future coming. God

" begat us again unto a living hope by the resurrection of Jesus Christ from the dead, unto an inheritance incorruptible, and undefiled, and that fadeth not away, reserved in heaven for you, who by the power of God are guarded through faith unto a salvation ready to be revealed in the last time " (I Peter 1:3–5).

His own experience teaches the apostle that the Kingdom does not come by human efforts " to build the road from man's world to God's world." The cross effectively *blocks* such a road as Zealots, Essenes, Pharisees, or their counterparts, would construct. The apostle knows that the Kingdom does not come by speculation or by observation of external phenomena, when men say, " Look, here it is." Rather, the Kingdom touches men as a power working secretly in their midst. It comes as a gift which men receive, not by estimating the population in the coming age, but by their personal striving to enter. They do not enter by calculating the relative merits of various people or the relative values of different rewards, but only by forsaking all to follow Jesus, by losing one's life for his sake and the Gospel's. The disciple knows how narrow is the gate; but he also knows how easy is the yoke of the Messiah, once one has accepted him as the Way. He knows how inevitable are poverty and hunger and persecution and death for those along that Way, but he knows also how the joy of the martyrs actually constitutes the morale of the blessed community of the new Jerusalem. Henceforth, his own sufferings are signs of the final judgment and the final redemption.

THE MESSIAH'S RETURN

The Christian, standing in the new *kairos,* shares the first fruits of a harvest yet to come. But he also faces the certainty of being winnowed in that coming harvest. The *kairos* of sin is ended; God's *kairos* has begun; and the believer stretches forward to apprehend its completion. He experiences the end, but this end is a beginning as well. The Messiah has come, and comes again. Faith without this hope is dead; that is, it is no longer genuine faith in Jesus as the Christ. In entering the Body of Christ all other hopes may die; still the new man inherits a hope that will not be put to shame.

Like his predecessor, the apostle draws a distinction between the Kingdom that is hidden and the Kingdom that is manifested, between the period in which the Kingdom is manifested to eyes of faith and the period when it will be manifested to all creation. In its fullness, the Kingdom of God is that sovereignty of God which ends all lesser sovereignties; it is that end-time which ends all times; it is that elect community which ends all other communities.

The Christian's consciousness is suspended between two polar realities: he senses the coming of the Kingdom in his own experience; at the same moment he experiences the rejection of the Kingdom by this age. Ever and anon, the Messiah comes to his own, but his own receive him not. The recognition of the incompleteness of God's Kingdom (in sovereignty, time, and community) is clearly stated in The Epistle to the Hebrews:

" For in that he [God] subjected all things unto him [the Messiah], he left nothing that is not subject to him. But now we see not yet all things subjected to him. But we behold him who hath been made a little lower than the angels, even Jesus, because of the suffering of death crowned with glory and honor, that by the grace of God he should taste of death for every man. For it became him, for whom are all things, and through whom are all things, in bringing many sons unto glory, to make the author of their salvation perfect through sufferings " (Heb. 2:8-10).

This sense of incompleteness is expressed by faith in the Parousia of Christ, when he will put every enemy under his feet, when he will bring the present age to an end, and when he will gather together his elect from the four winds. (The dual attitude toward the end-time is perhaps indicated by the double connotation of the term " Parousia." It means both *presence* and *coming*. There is also a double connotation to the term *apousia* — the *absence* of the Messiah.) It is also expressed by the parallel faith in the parousia of Satan, the archenemy. And it is clear that Satan's resistance to Christ will be most vigorous at these three points: in the exalting of other sovereignties, in the manifestation of man's slavery to pseudo history, and in the effort of the false communities of that history to exterminate the communion of saints.

The intensification of this conflict means that, when the Messiah returns to extend God's sway over creation, he must come as Judge. The traditional pictures of the Son of Man, coming from heaven on the clouds, with legions of angels at his command, continue to have relevance to the Christian. In this expectation the use of violence is implicit: the Lamb must come as a lion. The drama of world-wide catastrophe is still visualized in gory and even grotesque fashion. Christians also continue to emphasize the corporate nature of the final assize. Individuals appear before the Judge, and are divided into two camps. A final verdict is issued covering the destiny of races and cities and nations. The historic legends concerning the fate of Sodom and Gomorrah continue to provide prototypes of the coming destruction.

One accent, however, seems to be distinctive. Whereas Jewish seers had often visualized the new age as centering in Israel's institutions, such as Jerusalem, the Temple, the law, and the Sabbath; the Christian, who had seen the enmity of those institutions demonstrated in the cross, more frequently envisaged them as casualties of the Judgment, part of the debris of destroyed idolatries. Now the Kingdom of the Crucified *is* the New Jerusalem, his " body " *is* the temple " not made with hands," his Way *is* the law, his promised " rest " *is* the Sabbath.

Another significant motif in the new anticipations of the future stems from the recognition that the Christian himself is still far from being worthy of entrance into the Kingdom. And the Church, also, is engaged in constant conflict with sin within. The Christian is reborn, but the new self, received through Christ, lives only by its vigorous battle with the powers of this age. The teacher is constantly alarmed about those who

" were once enlightened and tasted of the heavenly gift and were made partakers of the Holy Spirit, and tasted the good word of God, and the powers of the age to come, and then fell away " (Heb. 6:4-6).

He must warn these how terrible a thing it is to fall into the hands of the living God. The apostolic trust in God does not eliminate the fear of God, and the existential expression of that fear is the threat of judgment. Christians know that that judgment is contemporaneous with the sin. One who crucifies Jesus afresh dies to his Kingdom. But they also know that such punishment must have a final verification. The Last Judgment is experienced now in the end of this age; henceforth the Christian lives by reference to the end of the new age.

The continued emphasis upon this coming judgment relieves the leaders of the Christian Church from the task of judging men. "Vengeance is mine; I will repay," saith the Lord (Rom. 12:19, King James Version). The Christian has no business pronouncing judgment upon his fellows. Though he realizes that Satan is actively sowing tares in the wheat field, he knows too that only God in his final judgment can give a just verdict. This helps one to understand a paradoxical feature in the New Testament portrait of the Messiah. How is it that the meek and gentle Jesus who comes to forgive sinners is pictured as the final Messiah who causes "weeping and the gnashing of teeth"? One reason is this: Faith that final judgment belongs to Jesus alone enables the Christian to practice Jesus' commands to forgive, without obscuring the distinction between sin and righteousness, or leading sinners to rely upon lenient treatment from God. The visions of violence in Revelation do not extenuate Christian vindictiveness toward oppressors; rather, these visions express the demand of the crucified Messiah that they *refrain* from committing evil against their oppressors. The central imperative is directed against Christians who have turned lukewarm, and who are being divorced from Christ by heresy and suffering. The real threat of judgment is the possibility of their own exclusion from the coming age. In the awareness that believers are subject to heavier judgment lies the answer to the question, "Shall we continue in sin, that grace may abound?"

In all the New Testament pictures of the Judgment Day, one notes three interpenetrating motifs:

1. The final judgment is directly related to the events that are now taking place in the Christian's struggle.

2. The judgment begins with the Christian in his relation to the kingdom of Satan, to his own sin and death.

3. The judgment is wholly a prerogative of the Messiah, who alone has the right to declare men justified. The knowledge that this Messiah is Jesus prevents the Christian from usurping his authority for purposes of self-vindication.

In earlier apocalypses, the coming of the Kingdom coincides with the resurrection of the dead; because of the universal sway of sin and death, this resurrection was extended to cover all men, whether for punishment or for reward. Early Christians take for granted these basic axioms; but distinctive experience of new life in Christ produces new accents. The resurrection of Jesus signals the beginning of the general resurrection. The Kingdom comes through the Messiah. Inasmuch as the Christian shares in the life of the risen Lord, he participates already in the final and general resurrection; he enters the gateway into eternal life. The new creation is even now proceeding, and to belong to this new creation relates one directly to the new heaven and the new earth. "We all shall not sleep," writes Paul, underscoring the basic continuity between the life in Christ now and life in the Kingdom. "But we shall all be changed, . . . in the twinkling of an eye"; thus Paul affirms that the return of Christ will not require further resurrection for Christians, but simply the sloughing off of the corruptible accompaniments of existence in this age. Even for those Christians who have died, there is no need for future resurrection. They are not even dead, but only asleep. Their life is now hidden with Christ in God. When the Messiah comes, he will awaken them. He will make manifest to all creation those who are his. In his house are many mansions (John, ch. 14). His elect who are absent from the body are at home with the Lord (II Cor., ch. 5).

CENTER AND CIRCUMFERENCE OF CHRIST'S KINGDOM

All these radii of the disciples' experience point to a single center, Jesus Christ, the "pioneer and perfecter of faith." The existence of each disciple is defined by his inner relation to this center. The meaning of all the covenants is focused at this same point. The story of Christ thus constitutes the hub of all genuine history. And the story of Christ reaches from the advent of the Galilean prophet to his return as God's Messiah.

On the other hand, all these radii point to a circumference, to the inclusion of all history within the story of God's work in Christ. Man's *kairos,* man's existence, reaches from creation to redemption in this Word. All things have come into being through him, and all things are intended for subjection to him. He is the Word by which God frames the world, sustains it, and brings it to fulfillment. In establishing his Kingdom, he will therefore restore creation to its true status as creature before

God, and thus will banish sin and death. Paradise will be restored in the perfect *rapprochement* between God and men.

In this future expectation, however, there remains a distinction of some importance. The Kingdom of Christ may be distinguished from the Kingdom of God; the ultimate consummation comes when Christ has turned his Kingdom over to God, so that God will be all in all. What motifs underlie this distinction? The answer must be highly conjectural, because the question extends beyond the existential limits of man's vision. Although the apostles attributed to their crucified Messiah both pre-existence and postexistence, they were very chary about attempting any detailed analysis of his pretemporal or posttemporal relationship to God. The Messiah is revealed on the cross: this implies that his eternal relationship to God is that of an obedient servant. In his pre-existence, and in his postexistence, his sole function is that of obedience. His work is done when all creation is made obedient, when the living Word returns full, having encompassed within his journey the whole history of man, and having completed his primal task. It is as if to say, " There is one thing of which we can be sure with regard to what lies beyond the coming triumph of Christ, and that is that he will present his triumphs to God, for his only freedom lies in that service."

There is one other motif that may be involved. The distinction between the Kingdom of Christ and the Kingdom of God may articulate the realization of the possible existence of many epochs, many nations, many areas of creation outside our ken, and perhaps beyond the range of this particular history in which Jesus is the central figure. After Christ's Kingdom is established over us, God in his mercy may provide opportunity for all times and all seasons to reach their fruition in a single *telos*. In Christ the history which we see as a unit, including creation, rebellion, and return, reaches its intended goal: God's glory and man's blessedness. But from God's vantage point there may be yet other orders of creation, which he sees as a unit. Ultimately, his power will bring all the many creations to their true destiny as instruments of his glory.

A problem that may be analogous is that which Paul faced, as a Jew and as a Christian, when he realized that the Messiah has been rejected by Israel according to the flesh. Paul was sufficiently realistic not to minimize this repudiation or to dream of an early and easy reconciliation. He carried in his heart the scars of a struggle which he knew would bar most of his friends and countrymen from life in the Messiah. Paul was acquainted with the paradox which Franz Werfel has stated so succinctly in these words: " The predestined recipient of salvation is the only one who is excluded from salvation until the last day but one of world-history." [4]

Looking through eyes of faith, Paul recognized the justice and mercy of God's program of salvation, and the reason for setting forth the Messiah as an offense. But looking through the eyes of a Jew, recalling the agonies of his fathers, brooding over the promises that have been shunned, he cannot avoid the riddle of their destiny: What of their condemnation? Is it ultimate? Stubbornly, he clings to confidence in the goodness of God and looks forward without fear to " the last day but one of world-history." If Gentiles have been saved through the rejection of the Jews, will not God yet save those Jews who in their very apostasy have served to glorify God? Faith that ultimately the Kingdom of God transcends even the Kingdom of Christ may thus evince faith in the possibility of final salvation for even the enemies of Christ; this faith prevents disciples from turning Christ into an idol and his community into an exclusive sect of the saved (Rom. 11:22–36). This vision of the ultimate triumph of God preserves the revelation that came in the cross, i.e., that God here calls men as ministers of reconciliation, with a mission to that world which God so loved.

Interpreted thus, the distinction between the Kingdom of Christ and the Kingdom of God may be visualized by reference to the parable of the Prodigal Son. The return of Christ in his Kingdom is the return of the younger son. The ultimate triumph of God in *his* Kingdom is the salvation of the elder son. But the only ground within experience for hope in that ultimate consummation is the manifest power of the Son of God who came to seek and to save the lost.

Hope radiates from that center where God speaks in Christ calling the prodigal to return. The disciple never ceases to find himself standing at the point of the prodigal's decision. The rebel hears the command to repent from one who, in seeking sinners, followed the *via crucis*. The rebel sees that cross as a sign by which the command is sustained by supreme power in the form of supreme love. In Jesus' mission the Kingdom draws near to the prodigal; in his response the prodigal draws near to the Kingdom.

---

[4] *Between Heaven and Earth,* p. 195. Philosophical Library, 1944.

"Thus is the whole of the 'concrete situation' embraced by that demand and determined in its actuality before God. And further: inasmuch as all history comes forward in the 'concrete situation,' the unconditional demand, determining that situation, also embraces the whole of history, and determines it in its actuality before God. . . . As an eschatological demand it forms an arch over and above all history, from God's creation in the beginning to his new creation at the end of all things. As such, it is at once an eschatological and a creation-demand: it commands the historical man *yet,* as if he were still a pure creature and as if he were still devoted to that perfect community with God and neighbor, for which God created him. . . . And it commands man *already,* because the situation is enlivened already from that new world, when the perfect community will return, and all conflict, all painfully endured and guilty alienation from God, will be removed." [5]

[5] H. Thielicke, *Geschichte und Existenz,* p. 366. C. Bertelsmann, 1935.

EVEN NEGATION of this world and perception of the paradox of life; even submission to the judgment of God and waiting upon Him; even " brokenness"; even the behavior of the " Biblical Man " — if these proceed from the adoption of a point of view, of a method, of a system, or of a particular kind of behavior, by which men distinguish themselves from other men — are no more than the righteousness of men. And even faith, if it proceeds from anything but a void, is unbelief.

— K. Barth, *The Epistle to the Romans,* trans. by E. C. Hoskyns, pp. 56, 57. Oxford University Press, 1933.

EPILOGUE: TO SEE OR NOT TO SEE

THIS study began in the recognition of the wide contrasts between modern points of view and the world of Biblical thought. The progress of the study has sharpened and clarified differences between that history which is seen from our point of standing and that history which prophet and apostle viewed from their point of standing. In confronting us with these stubborn oppositions, the study also confronts us with an insistent question: Which of these perspectives is true to the actual story of man's life? Which of these standpoints is the true one for understanding God's purpose for us? In which direction lies our true destiny? It is the age-old question of Job: "Where is the place of understanding?"

Not only does the Bible confront us with this question; it also presents the message of men who claim to speak with authority, and not as the scribes. Their right to be heard does not rest upon superior human wisdom, philosophical acumen, historical knowledge, or moral virtue. Of those bases of human judgment they have learned to be profoundly distrustful. Rather, their authority is a God who communicates his purposes and his demands in what he says and does. And since, to them, he is the only true Lord of history, the history which he creates and guides is the only true history. And the only standpoint wherein man apprehends that history is the standpoint of faith.

In submitting the question to us, therefore, Biblical characters make it clear that we shall not arrive at an appreciation of truth by summoning their "theology" before the court of scientific investigation and submitting its claims to a jury of human authorities. No one will arrive at their position by objectively reviewing the entire panorama of human history for the purpose of selecting the most accurate recording of the destiny of men. No one will come a whit closer to faith by listing the alternate solutions to the tragic riddle of existence, and by choosing the one that best suits fancy or desires. The question, Where shall we stand? will not admit of adequate answer by any effort of the mind, no matter how great or how earnest that effort.

And there is much in current confusions which justifies such an attitude on the part of the prophets. For to us as individuals, lost in the maze of bombed cities and homeless refugees, external history becomes "an anarchy of faces." Forced to choose among the welter of movements and institutions the one which is worthy of our eternal destiny, who is not confounded by the kaleidoscopic reversals of modern life? Everywhere we see creation groaning in agony until now. It may be that to the eye of a sociologist or historian of civilization there is a pattern to the earthquakes now rending organized society. But to the eye of man as man, as he searches the rubble of securities and the debris of human hopes, the plaint of Job comes with poignant power: " Canst thou by searching find out God? " In such a world, the effort to choose a perspective on history, an angle of vision, the horizon of one's existence, is bound to lead to a striving after wind.

Perhaps we may listen to the Biblical insistence that we revise the form of the question. For it was not by asking, " Where shall I stand? " that Jeremiah, Jesus, or Paul arrived at their perspective. To them only one genuine history existed, the history that begins and ends in God. To them man could find abiding significance only in listening to what God says and does in the depths of creaturely existence, at the source of events where God has dealings with men. They did not achieve a solution by picking and choosing, but by being chosen and by being sent on a mission. The seal of authenticity of that mission was their vigorous effort to evade it and the failure of that effort. Their urge to rebel was overcome by God's call to return, mediated by parable and sign. They knew that their only true destiny lay in abiding within the *kairos* which was revealed to them by the creative word.

A modern poet, speaking of the artist's call, describes the struggle for integrity that characterizes the prophet:

" As soon as an artist has once found the living center of his activity, nothing is so important for him as to remain in it and never to go further away from it (for it is also the center of his personality, his world) than up to the inside wall of what he is quietly and steadily giving forth; his place is never, not even for an instant, alongside the observer and judge. . . . Indeed it requires an almost acrobatic skill to leap from that observation post back into the inner center again, neatly and unharmed (the distances are too great, the places themselves all too shaky for such an eminently inquisitive feat). Most artists today use up their strength in this going back and forth, and not only do they expend themselves in it, they get themselves hopelessly entangled and lose a part of their essential innocence in the sin of having surprised their work from outside, tasted of it, shared in the enjoyment of it. The grand and moving thing about Cezanne . . . is that during almost forty years he remained uninterruptedly within his work, in the innermost center of it . . . and I hope someday to show how the incredible freshness and purity of his pictures is due to this obstination . . . while most painters already stand facing their own pictures, enjoying and relishing them, violating them in the very process of their work as onlookers and recipients." [1]

Rilke's statement indicates why no objective analysis of the prophetic consciousness can succeed; it also indicates the inherent sinfulness of the method adopted in our study, in hopping back and forth from one universe of discourse to another; finally, it underscores the radical transition of perspective required of those who hear the word. In their case, the speculative question of the onlooker, " Where shall I stand? " becomes the existential question of the creature, " To see or not to see? " The issue is that of faith or sin. God lays an ambush for man, and man must choose. Which master is he to serve? The faithful man knows that his whole life is set between these two alternatives. And he knows that only with eyes of obedience does he receive the gift of God's peace. He recognizes, with W. H. Auden, that " sin fractures the vision, not the fact."

" The faithful man . . . knows that the intellectual eye of his soul is now, not indeed extinguished, but diseased, and is therefore liable to see things distorted, not because they are so, but because it has lost in part its healthy capacity of vision. Under the treatment of the Great Physician it hopes to recover perfect healthiness of vision; which recovered, it does not doubt that there will be an entire identity between what it then sees and what faith has now received and believed." [2]

Biblical witnesses further testify that the true answer is given only in faith, through faith, and by faith. They indicate, too, how such faith comes. It comes by hearing the word of God, not by studying objectively the records of the past, not even by studying the Bible. It comes by accepting a gift that contradicts man's self-chosen ends, not by weighing all the imagined options. It comes by a leap of the heart in response to God's promise, not by careful calculation of various future possibilities. It comes as a total response of the self to God's eschatological demand,

[1] Rainer Maria Rilke, *War-time Letters,* trans. by M. D. H. Norton, pp. 224, 225. W. W. Norton & Company, 1940.
[2] Augustine, quoted in R. G. Trench, *Exposition of the Sermon on the Mount,* p. 11. 1869.

not by surveying actions that seem expedient at the moment. The men of the Bible do not encourage us to identify faith with accumulative knowledge that sets us above other men, with an intellectual act that affirms certain propositions to be true, with an emotional act that cultivates moods felt to be desirable. Faith is not something self-produced, but rather a newly defined self which God creates.

"Faith is rooted in the totality of our person. It moves our personal center towards God. Faith is the revolutionary act in which God gives himself to us, person to person, and in which we have nothing to do, but everything to receive . . . not a supernatural habit, but it is a living, restless power. The right faith is a strong, powerful, active thing. . . . It makes the personality, not conversely. 'Faith creates the person, the person creates the works, not the works the person.' . . . Faith is religion itself." [3]

Faith is the continual re-enactment of the Lord's Prayer in the disciple's heart; it is the reality which leads men to pray,

"O Lord, open thou my lips;
And my mouth shall show forth thy praise."

The men of the Bible speak with accord at this point, a unanimous witness to common experience: God alone can open one's eyes; he alone can create the faith by which we see our sin and his righteousness, our helplessness and his power.

One further point requires emphasis. In the Bible it is made clear that faith is real only in the present, as an expression of full contemporaneity with God and his activity. Faith is always oriented by the memory of what God has done yesterday, and by the hope of what he will do tomorrow, but it is always a reality today, and today alone.

"Today if ye shall hear his voice,
Harden not your hearts, as in the provocation " (see Heb. 3:15; Ps. 95:7).

To rely upon yesterday's faith or to bemoan today's guilt does not reflect faith, but absence of it. The moment faith becomes a possession, a stopping place, a refuge, a source of self-assurance, that moment is it dead. Faith is the mode of existence of those whose steps are now drawn by the magnet of divine purpose, and who renounce their present home for a better country. This mode of existence is known by renunciation, patience, and expectancy, by bold confidence and ardent hope, by eager

[3] Cf. Paul Tillich, *Christendom*, Vol. VII, pp. 524 f. 1943.

enthusiasm and deep joy, maintained at the point of greatest suffering.

Charles Péguy has a probing description of honesty that suggests the extreme dangers and demands of faith:

" In the history of the world one could easily find a very great number of examples of persons who, suddenly perceiving the truth, seize it. Or, having sought and found it, deliberately break with their interests . . . their political friendships and even with their sentimental friendships. I do not believe that one finds many examples of men who, having accomplished the first sacrifice, have had the second courage to sacrifice their second interests, their second friendships. . . . They are most willing, for the sake of the truth, to fall out with half of the world — not without a little repercussion — they usually make partisans among the second half of the world; partisans who ask nothing better than to be the antagonists of the first half. But if, for the love of this same truth, they foolishly go about breaking with this second half, who will become their partisans? . . . A superbrave man would have to be found to make a second break; but of these, there are hardly any left — and yet, the life of an honest man must be an apostasy and a perpetual desertion. The honest man must be a perpetual renegade, the life of an honest man must be a perpetual infidelity. For the man who wishes to remain faithful to truth must make himself continually unfaithful to all the continual, successive, indefatigable, renascent errors. And the man who wishes to remain faithful to justice must make himself continually unfaithful to inexhaustibly triumphant injustices." [4]

To this statement of the case it seems impossible to take exception. Yet men of the Bible speak of a mode of existence infinitely more difficult. For they are not concerned alone with discovering recurrent dishonesties and deceits in *other* men. They are more deeply concerned with their own sin, and the roots of sin are daily discovered to be less eradicable. To be faithful to the God of justice and mercy is to be faithless to the self-centeredness and pride in oneself; to be perpetually faithless to the inner dishonesties and deceits, the subterfuges and escapes, the covert rebellion and inner idols. How lonely and painful to renounce all that one has, all one's world, all *one's own* history, for the sake of following the commands of God! And then to repeat this renunciation daily!

How can one have such strength? How is such faith possible? How can one surrender his freedom thus? Only through the compulsion of One who is stronger; through the mercy of One who is more righteous; through the gift of the Creator and Lord. Is it possible then? " Yes," answer prophet and apocalyptist. No matter how fully this age denies

[4] *Basic Verities,* trans. by A. and J. Green, p. 49. Pantheon Books, 1943.

the demand of God, obedience remains an open door. However faithless men may be to their created destiny, God remains faithful to his promises. His covenant is an everlasting covenant, though all his creatures may repudiate it.

The apostle also says, " Yes." For he has experienced new birth into a Kingdom where such faith is not only possible but actualized through God's grace. He experiences sufficient grace entering his life through the word of One who suffers all the enmity of the world, all temptations to unfaithfulness, and yet remains faithful. This One gives his life, not for righteous men, but for sinners. In obedience to his vocation he endures the cross. In anointing him as King, God establishes the gateway into the Kingdom. The cross becomes the " still turning point of the world," where God meets man in a final, ever-repeated act of creation, judgment, and redemption. When man responds in faith and takes up the same cross, God appoints to him a heritage in the Messiah's household. Henceforth that faith is itself a sign of God's faithfulness, a fruit of the Spirit, an earnest of coming fulfillment.

Indexes

INDEX OF TOPICS

suffering 57, 76, 112, 125 ff., 166, 212,
245 f., 250, 264, 281
Sumerian 140 f.
temple See cultus
time 22 f., 34 ff., 41, 47 f., 56, 76, 84,
97 ff., 108 ff., 141, 214 f., 222 f.,
229 f., 273 f.
future 27, 35, 52, 76, 88 ff., 102 f., 136,
190, 221 ff., 227 f., 247 ff., 278 ff.
See also hope
past 60, 84 ff., 102 f., 189, 203 ff.,
244 f., 274 ff.

See also memory
present 47 ff., 60, 84 ff., 102 f., 190,
195 f., 201 ff., 227 ff., 259 ff., 294
See also interim
transiency 119 f.
trust 49 f., 54, 112, 250, 279
vanity 52 ff., 121 ff.
vocation 32 f., 41 f., 149 f., 188 f.
word 53 ff., 89, 106, 168, 184 f.
worship 12, 39
Zealots 137, 281
Zoroastrianism 72

INDEX OF AUTHORS

INDEX OF SCRIPTURE PASSAGES